"Canada's health care system is sick, and it will only get worse as our nation reels with the fallout from COVID-19 and growing pressure from our nation's aging population. Canadians need to pay more attention to our underperforming system and the need for reform. Dr. Whatley's book is a great place to start."

Colin Craig
President of *SecondStreet.org*

"For decades, medicare has been dependent upon its unexamined historical myths and a protective anti-Americanism in order to excuse its terrible performance, and Whatley leads the charge at demolishing these myths and attitudes in order to clear the way for change."

Shane Neilson
Poet, physician, critic
MFA MA PhD CCFP FCFP
Assistant Clinical Professor (Adjunct), *McMaster University*

"In this caring and clearly-written book, Dr. Whatley performs precision surgery on Canada's failing public health care…"

Dr. William Gairdner, Author of *The Great Divide—Why Liberals and Conservatives Will Never, Ever Agree*"

"We cannot fix Canadian healthcare until we admit that it needs fixing… You need to read this book… before you or someone you love gets sick."

John Robson
Journalist

When Politics
Comes Before Patients

When Politics Comes Before Patients, Why and How Canadian Medicare is Failing
© Ottawa, 2020, Optimum Publishing International and Shawn Whatley

LIBRARY AND ARCHIVES CANADA CATALOGUING IN PUBLICATION
When Politics Comes Before Patients, How Canadian Medicare is Failing, Shawn Whatley
ISBN: 978-0-88890-311-2 Digital Version of the book is also available ISBN: 978-0-88890-312-9

When Politics Comes Before Patients. I. Title

Cover design and Illustration by Sarah Baxendale
Inside text design and layout, Mathew Flute

For information on rights or any submissions please write to: Optimum Publishing International
144 Rochester Avenue Toronto, Ontario, Canada. M42 1P1
Dean Baxendale, President

www.optimumpublishinginternational.com
Twitter @opibooks

Printed in Canada

OPTIMUM
PUBLISHING
INTERNATIONAL
MONTRÉAL | TORONTO

When Politics
Comes Before Patients

Why and How Canadian
Medicare Is Failing

Shawn Whatley, MD

Contents

Preface

THERE ARE NO experts in health politics. No one knows it all, although academics know much about their niche. The trouble is, they know so much it silences everyone else. The message is clear: if you hate feeling stupid do not get involved.

But wait a minute. Yes, the topic is big, and experts are scary. But that is precisely why you *should* dive in. Nudge academic experts near the edge of their niche and watch them panic. They will run back to safety in minutiae designed to intimidate. You will be awed by their recall. Suitably silenced, conversation ends and lectures begin. They now have a bully pulpit from which to write books for colleagues who agree and to dispatch opponents who do not exist. They can tell what is, what shall be, and what to do to get there.

This ruins healthcare. Adults learn from conversation, not lectures. The best conversations bounce opposing ideas back and forth. Each party learns and gives, listens and grows. Canada has lost its healthcare conversation. This book is my attempt to get it back. It falls second in an informal series of three books. It serves up the meat in a sandwich between practical advice in my *No More Lethal Waits: Ten Steps to Transform Canada's Emergency Departments*, published in 2016, and a third book in the planning. *No More Lethal Waits* was a short read about change disguised as a book about emergency departments. The last chapter called readers to get political. This book is meant to help them answer that call. But before new solutions (what about funding?), we need new thinking. We must think before we do; chew before we swallow. If we skip the meat offered in this book, the practical advice in book three will make us choke. Book three will be practical — a principled how-to book — but you need the meal offered here to get that book's full nutritional value.

My publisher, Dean Baxendale, has healthcare in his blood. His father published Monique Begin's *Medicare: Canada's Right to Health,* 1987. The book you hold now offers a different view, and still Dean fights for the righ to share it. You might not find a more enthusiastic, generous, and articulate conversationalist.

Don Bastian, editor extraordinaire, is ruthless, kind, and wicked smart. He needed all of it to manage this book. I cannot say how pleased I am with his work and exceptional mind.

Many people read early drafts. I cringed as they nodded through my notes, but I am grateful. Philip Whatley read multiple versions and offered invaluable notes. Matt P. dissected chapters with blunt kindness and keen insight. Matt D. smiled and palpated (hard!) some sore spots. I hope the Matts will heap abuse on me for any advice I did not take. Harley Price and Paul Conte plowed through early drafts and prodded with encouraging questions. Brian Lee Crowley gave the best advice I have ever received about structuring a large project. The whole team at the Macdonald-Laurier Institute — David, Brett, Sean, Brian, et al. — supported my distraction, though I suspect they wished I had kept my focus on an MLI project they had assigned to me. Bill Gairdner shared energy and advice on writing, publishing, and healthcare: priceless. Bruce Pardy helped with insight from his book *Ecolawgic: The Logic of Ecosystems and the Rule of Law,* 2015. Andrew Siren and Marko Duic reviewed chapters but, more importantly, endured several years at the foot of my soapbox, helping me develop concepts. Many others, too numerous to mention — for example, regular contributors to my blog, www.shawnwhatley.com — shared stories and ideas. If you find something familiar in here, I probably learned it from *you.*

Despite all the help received, know that none of it informed the errors; I came up with those all by myself. This book straddles specialties, surely a warning for fools rushing in and so on.

Finally, I could not function without my family. This is not meant to be quaint or kind. It is fact. I cannot begin and will not try to list all the ways my Mom and Dad deserve credit. My children — Lara, Kate, Jonathan, and Emma — endured Dad lost in a daydream, sometimes for hours. Accept my apology and gratitude: I love you guys. Most importantly, I must acknowledge Monica: my one, only, and eternal love.

Introduction

In the Kingdom of Ends everything has either a price or a dignity. If it has a price, something else can be put in its place as an equivalent; if it is exalted above all price and so admits of no equivalent, then it has a dignity.
—Immanuel Kant

AT SOME POINT you likely will find yourself lying in a hospital bed. There is a good chance your bed will be a firm rubber pad held between two rails and parked along a corridor in a busy emergency department. Messy hairdos will stick out from the stretchers lined up ahead of you. Moans of "nurse!" will echo all around.

But in that moment you will feel relief, not fear. Relief and a fierce, jealous attachment: at least you have a bed! You are out of a packed waiting room and finally able to lie down. Your relief, however, will be tempered by a heightened awareness of how people treat you. Does the nurse come when she promised? Does the doctor make eye contact and treat you like you matter? When you call for help to empty your bladder, does anyone answer? When someone finally comes, will she say, "You have a diaper," and walk away? Does your bed have a sheet, a blanket, a pillow?

These questions are not hypothetical. Broken promises, rushed formalities, diapers, and rubber mattresses all happen to real patients in Canada. Few complain or even mention these problems at first. When asked, they report details about diagnosis, tests, and treatment. But when they start talking about their experience, they all use the same word: *undignified.*

Patients want two things: excellent medical care and great patient service. Excellent medical care means getting attention when they need it that fixes the problem they came for. It means access to the best that medicine has to offer, given the current standard of practice. Great patient service means being treated like the most privileged patients in the system — athletes, celebrities, and the friends and family of those who work inside the system.

Everyone supports excellent care and great service, but, as this book will show, our medicare system cannot deliver these consistently. Some Canadians get outstanding medical care, but most get mediocre and, too often, poor care. Doctors and nurses try to provide more care with reduced resources. As for great care, that is an aspirational goal; something to pursue if all the other essential work has been accomplished.

Medicare in Canada is failing, and it is failing because it places politics before patients. How did this happen? It will help, at the outset, to take a quick tour of the history and structure of Canadian healthcare.

ALL THE MAJOR BITS of medicare legislation passed in Canada with nearly unanimous support. In some cases, it was unanimous. The Liberals explored socialized medicine first, in 1919. The far-left New Democratic Party promoted it after World War II. The Conservatives, for their part, launched a commission[1] to explore it in 1961, and then they supported the Medical Care Act, 1966.[2]

Medicare legislation deals with money primarily, not patient care. At the founding of Canada, the Constitution Act of 1867[3] gave control of healthcare to the provinces. However, the act also gave the federal government the power to tax and spend. So the federal government used its spending power as a catalyst to entice (bribe) provinces to build health insurance plans. Federal healthcare laws mandated conditions to control the flow of federal money.[4] If provinces meet the conditions, money flows. Ostensibly, everything is voluntary, but provinces cannot afford to offer services without federal funds. It is a bit like saying doctors voluntarily renew their medical licenses when they cannot function any other way. What may have started out as catalyst soon became control.

So, for more than fifty years, provinces have taken federal money and complained about the conditions dictated by the federal government. For example, Quebec Premier François Legault told reporters recently: "We will not be dictated to by the federal government [on healthcare]."[5] Provinces bristle at federal arrogance. But the reality is that the feds pay the piper, so they call the tune.[6]

Voters pay the taxman for healthcare: contributing to Canada's high income taxes. Each province and territory organizes and operates its own insurance plan using provincial and federal tax dollars. But taxpayers never know exactly how much of their taxes go to care. All the tax disappears into the treasury. Some provinces, such as Ontario, collect an extra health tax ("premium"), but even it goes into general revenues with no accounting for how much of it actually goes to care. (Healthcare for the unemployed is paid for by taxes on the employed.)

Taxes, however, do not cover the cost of prescriptions or of a private room in a hospital — people need private insurance for those costs.

Small provinces rely more heavily on federal money — known as health transfer payments — but even larger provinces could not offer the same services without federal help or increased provincial taxes. Again, if provinces and territories follow the federal rules, they qualify for federal funding.

Physicians bill their provincial or territorial insurance plan for the services they provide. Payment for necessary medical services flows to doctors from a single payer (for the most part). However, physicians, strictly speaking, are not government employees. Canada Revenue views physicians as independent contractors much like any other small business. Given this, many American physicians look north with dewy eyes. Just imagine private medicine with only one payer, which pays 100 percent of the time. Could it be true? Advocates of socialized medicine work hard to keep this myth alive.

Some politicians opposed socialized medicine from the start. In 1969, Ontario premier Robarts said, "Medicare is a glowing example of a Machiavellian scheme that is in my humble opinion one of the greatest political frauds that has been perpetrated on the people of this country."[7] But overall, most people saw socialization of medicine as a good idea. It simply took the popular physician-built medical insurance plans, which already covered a majority of Canadians, and rolled them into one national plan that covered everyone.

Around the same time, however, there was a movement against socialism itself, particularly in the 1950s and 60s. As Amity Shlaes has written: "In America red baiters called people 'socialist,' sliming their targets and themselves in the process." And: "The very word 'socialism' had [become] toxic."[8] Socialized medicine, as a name, got swept up in the sliming. Supporters struggled to avoid using that name and switched to a softer one: single-payer healthcare. But this is a euphemism, because single-payer healthcare is not socialized medicine, and socialized medicine is what Canada has. To say Canada just has single-payer healthcare misleads in important and meaningful ways, which we will explore.

Meanwhile, it is no longer necessary to avoid using the term "socialized medicine." Socialism is back.[9] A 2019 Harris poll found that 50 percent of voters under the age of thirty-eight would prefer living under a socialist system.[10] Today, self-described socialist politicians draw enormous support, especially among younger voters. After apparently dying in the early 1990s and sparking best-sellers with titles such as "The End of History," socialism has recovered.[11] In the process, socialized medicine seems to have recovered as well. Politicians, actors, activists, and the popular media defend it as an appealing idea, without needing to repackage it in more palatable words. As an intelligent hipster friend said to me, "Of course I'm a socialist!" Without question, people still hold strong opinions about socialism. Nevertheless, we can, once again, use "socialism" and "socialized medicine" as descriptive terms without being dismissed as crass or impolite.

Between 1968 and 1977, socialized medicine in Canada simply paid for all care, from trivial to traumatic, no questions asked. Federal health grants in the late 1940s had sparked a hospital building boom. Every community had empty hospital beds, and free medical care offered a way to fill them. Patients and doctors loved it. And politicians took credit for public gratitude. The dream lasted until the mid-1970s, when the money ran out. Since then, Canadians have lived off the glow of the initial dream as provinces close hospital beds by the thousands and ratchet up regulations on the care patients are allowed to access.

TODAY, MOST PEOPLE inside and outside healthcare agree the time is ripe for improving care in Canada. The needs are obvious, starting with ubiquitous hallway medicine and long wait times for care. It should not be that hard to change. However, when faced with big issues in healthcare, too often we select a scapegoat — doctors, bureaucrats, politicians, or patients — and blame them for all the problems. But scapegoats are not solutions, so medicare remains mired in mediocre outcomes and an endless stream of headlines about crisis and impending collapse.

If we all agree that patients need great care and we all want to improve the system, why does medicare continue to lag? Why do long waits, lack of access to necessary care, and horror stories about hallway medicine keep making headlines? The answer is twofold: first, socialized medicine puts politics before patients, and second, politicians and public opinion have decreed that Canadians cannot consider any ideas but the ones socialized medicine allows. Canada is locked into a worldview, a way of looking at healthcare, that invites panic and outrage if anyone questions it.

Normally, if the promise of change outweighs the pain of staying the same, we simply make a change. If our car keeps failing when we need it most, we take out a loan and buy a better one. We do not worry about how a new car might change our identity as car owners. But that is not what we do with medicare. We essentially say we can only change the tires and the window wipers on our car. We must never change the car itself. That would be unCanadian.[12]

All change creates pain; even happy changes such as weddings and babies. But change becomes impossible when people fuse arguments against change with fundamental notions about identity, culture, and history. We need a fearless, dispassionate assessment of how socialized medicine has delivered on our initial dreams for it. Do the core ideas give patients what they need? Or does socialized medicine lead to anti-patient policies that often strip them of care and dignity?

CANADIAN HEALTHCARE will not improve unless we first determine *why* and *how* it is failing.

The *why* part of this book, part one, examines the worldview behind our medical system — healthcare as a means of achieving social equity — and the inevitable debilitating results: inequity, less access, less efficiency, and more waste, including the waste of the motivation and talents of doctors and nurses. Part one details the way socialized medicine was built on a myth: a grand story about Tommy Douglas's leg that was not true. Douglas used childhood memories to fuel his campaign for socialized medicine, and no one thought to question him. Canadians live with the dream that patients should get the care that doctors and nurses think patients need. Experts call this the Naive Clinical view. We will look at the real political goals driving medicare, which overshadow the Naive Clinical, and how "values" are used to shut down criticism of the system.

We will also explore another inevitable result: the broken promises of *care regardless of ability to pay*, not by accident, but by design, through waits and rationing. Despite visions of equality and fairness, medicare creates privileged access for the few.

Most of the examples come from Ontario, Canada's largest province. But the concepts apply across the country, indeed to anywhere that people pursue socialism.

The *how* part, part two, shows how government control, central planning, and administrators doing the government's bidding have created a system far more inefficient, haphazard, and wasteful than advocates would have us believe. Worse, they have created a tragic misalignment between the healthcare system and its resources, on the one hand, and the intense, individual care needed by patients as would be performed by doctors and nurses if they were left unhampered, on the other. We will see that central planners do not have enough data or computing power to make better decisions than the ones doctors and patients can make at the bedside. Central planning fails because no one can know enough to plan accurately. Overreliance on experts and managers leads to managerialism. In addition, managers misunderstand what it is they hope to manage. They think medicine is more like a factory than an ecosystem. Overreliance on external controls — carrots and sticks — leaves healthcare workers frustrated and demoralized. We take a look at how regulatory failure makes things worse: governments write laws to control the system, and regulators write policies to control behaviour. The state is not a business and will never run like a business. It does not have the tools to manage health care, but this does not stop it from trying. Finally, we end the *how* part of the book with a look at structural and process reasons that make governments behave as they do and limit what they can achieve. Good government depends on government sticking to what it does well.

In the conclusion we turn our attention to the environment in which excellent patient care will grow. Care cannot flourish in a political science laboratory. Medical care needs less central control and more economic liberalism, fostered in an environment of humanism and community. We will consider how we might do this even within a fully tax-funded approach. But our discussion will, by necessity, be general, for it will take this book, and arguments similar to the ones it makes, to convince Canadians — politicians, administrators, doctors, nurses, patients, and the citizenry — that fundamental change is needed. The next book, based on this book's argument, will drill down on the specific changes medicare so needs. In summary, those changes will put undiluted attention back on patient care: the end for which medicare is supposed to exist. Patients have intrinsic value and should not be used as instruments to achieve someone's social vision outside of patient care. Great patient care cannot bloom without relationships and dignity as non-negotiable essentials. Patients need a connection that transcends episodes of service. Interacting with faceless bureaucracies or interchangeable providers of continuously changing care "teams" will not support great care. Dignity — an essential for all institutions in civil society — demands patient choice. Patient choice requires physician freedom to deliver.

THE CASE AGAINST our healthcare system will either be weak or strong. If the case is weak, then we should abandon the debate and embrace the fundamental ideas behind the system we have now. However, if the case is strong, then we must be open to change. We must be open to exploration and innovation by people who have been trying to improve care and service for patients. Resistance should stop forthwith. And even if the case falls somewhere in the middle — a mixture of good points and bad — then, at the very least, we should re-examine our rigid and unbending devotion to medicare.

The sky will not fall. Canada will not cease to be Canada. If socialized medicine is not delivering all that it promised, then there is no reason to block patient care that falls outside the rigid approach dictated by medicare. For medically necessary services, Canadians could continue to live the dream of "free" care without the nightmare of central control.

Canadians deserve better care. Doing nothing is not an option. We can either redouble efforts on socialized medicine or explore alternatives. What we cannot endure is a continuation of the piecemeal efforts of the last fifty-plus years and the growing indignity they create for Canadian patients. Fear and despair are not Canadian values. We will not improve healthcare without the character and fortitude to move beyond the pseudo-security offered by socialized medicine.

PART ONE

Why Canadian Medicare Is Failing

Chapter One
The Worldview Behind Canadian Medicare

Every man, wherever he goes, is encompassed by a cloud of comforting
convictions, which move with him like flies on a summer day.
–Bertrand Russell

Practical men, who believe themselves to be quite exempt from any
intellectual influences, are usually the slaves of some defunct economist.
–Lord Keynes

IT WAS MONDAY not long before midnight: the busiest time in emergency departments all across North America. A triage nurse approached me.

"Sorry to bother you," she said. "A woman miscarried in the waiting room toilet. Should I send the products to the lab?"

"Are you sure?" I said. "Is she okay?"

"She's stable. But you can see a small piece of white tissue the size of your thumb floating with a dark bag of clot."

Her full description removed all doubt. Our patient was tearful; shaky but stable. And still in a crowded waiting room.

"No, they won't want it," I replied. "The lab said not to bother, last time."

I did not ask about a bed or a room. If they were available, she would not have miscarried in the waiting room in the first place.

What was it like to stand in a crowded waiting room, no place to sit, cramping, bleeding, waiting in line for the bathroom, crying? Was she alone? Did she have enough supplies with her?

Vaginal bleeding is a common complaint in emergency departments, but women are all different. Many feel distressed with a threatened miscarriage; some do not. Focusing on a miscarriage, however, misses the bigger point. Canadians assume they will get care when they need it. They assume that, no matter what happens, medicare will be there for them.

It used to work this way. Patients decided when their symptoms were bad enough for them to see a doctor. Physicians and patients worked out plans to investigate, diagnose, and treat the problems. Individuals, not administrators, politicians, or anyone else, made decisions about when and where they went to get care.

"When I began practicing medicine nearly twenty years ago, the very idea of waiting for care in Ontario would have seemed far-fetched,"[13] Dr. Albert Schumacher said in 2001, when he was president of the Ontario Medical Association. "How the world has changed — waiting lists have become the norm rather than the exception." If patients did wait, it was because their doctor or nurse was busy with someone else. Patients never waited simply to save the system money.

Today, doctors and nurses apologize and blame the "flu season" or "a really busy evening." However, patients do not wait because of any situation or event. They wait because system planners design the system to make them wait. Canada rations care by cutting corners on technology, hospital beds, and professional staff. Too often doctors have to send patients home for tests in the community that used to be done in hospital.

A local family doctor wrote a letter to our emergency department when I was chief. He had instructed his patient to go to the hospital and "do not leave until you get care. Do not let them send you home without answers." But while doctors tell their patients to raise hell to get care, administrators decide which patients get treatment and which have to wait. As Dr. Charles Wright states, "Administrators maintain waiting lists on purpose, the way airlines overbook. As for urgent patients on the list who are in pain, the public system will decide when their pain requires care. These are societal decisions. The individual is not able to decide rationally."[14] Or as a former deputy minister of health of Ontario puts it, "We have waiting lists for some procedures as a means of better organizing our system."[15]

Wait times, however, are not even the core issue; they are a danger and a nuisance, but the real problem lies deeper. Waits occur because, in socialized medicine, the state believes it has the right and the responsibility to create appropriately long waits. No one ever says it that way, but the state decides which patients can and should be made to wait. Government planners with no knowledge of patients' conditions decide when patients will get care and the kind of care it will be.

Planners worry that, unless they control choices, patients might not choose care that is good for them. Richard Musgrave, an American economist, coined the term "merit wants" as what consumers ought to consume, whether or not they choose to do so on their own. As a senior Canadian health researcher has said, "I think we have to be very careful about empowering the consumer because they will make choices that are not in their own health interests."[16] Elites all over the world believe they can and should intervene to protect consumers, and especially patients, from themselves: "The consumer must be protected at times from his own indiscretion and vanity," according to Ralph Nader, the American political activist.[17] Canada's foremost health economist, Bob Evans, writes that the "rational consumer" is a "highly dubious assumption."[18]

When these ideas infect healthcare, patients suffer because bureaucrats have more impact on care than do doctors and patients in a system that, as one Chinese delegate has put it, is more restrictive and controlled than anything in Communist China.[19]

The idea that patients are not able to make decisions about their own care flows from the very nature of socialized medicine. The same arrogance once infected medicine, even into the 1980s: *doctor knows best; always do what the doctor says.* But patients resisted. They demanded to take part in decisions about their care. It became recognized and accepted that paternalism does not produce excellent patient care. Today, however, socialized medicine suffers from *bureaucratic paternalism*, based precisely on the thinking we should expect from a centrally controlled, government-rationed system.

The notion that anonymous experts know a patient's body and pain better than the patient or doctor manifests itself in different ways; for example, in their views that waiting for care is not so bad for most problems; committees can decide how long patients should wait; public servants make better decisions than individual doctors or patients about how and where to offer patient services; patients often ask for too much, or for things that are useless and even harmful.

The Assumptions Behind Socialized Medicine

SOCIALIZED MEDICINE draws on a thick syllabus of ideas and presuppositions that comprise a distinct worldview. Assumptions about patients represent only one stanza of the socialized hymn. Other assumptions include priority-setting; for example: we need to focus on population health, not individual health,[20] and patient care improves with standardization, not the individualized therapy[21] patients misguidedly seek.

Socialized medicine takes its own spin on quality; for example: rules and regulations are the best way to improve the quality of patient care and we must monitor doctors at all times lest they provide useless treatments and sham surgeries on unsuspecting patients. But patients expect doctors to do what is best for them as patients, not to blindly follow rules. Rules and regulations can never replace ethics and professionalism, so why do we place so much hope in them?

Ideas about management in socialized medicine lead to views that Canadian healthcare is basically good and fails only when we do not try hard enough and would function better if doctors and nurses would stop sabotaging it. Socialized medicine even encapsulates ideas about itself; for example: the public system is generous and compassionate; socialized medicine is efficient and fair; and all that matters is that we have altruistic intentions guided by good moral values.[22] But wanting to do the right thing is not the same as doing it. Intentions win elections but do not get patients the care they need when they need it.

Fans of socialized medicine object. Some argue that many of these ideas, and especially the more distasteful ones, are not a necessary part of state-funded, single-payer medical care. Leaving patients out of decisions could happen in any system. Blaming doctors and nurses happens all over the world. Others say socialized medicine does not have to fail patients if we could just find a way to keep the good intentions and reject the bad outcomes. Still others say that, for goodness' sake, stories about miscarriages in waiting rooms simply represent rare failures when doctors and nurses do a bad job. We should not blame every sad patient story on socialized medicine. That is not fair.

Socialized medicine has not been tried and found wanting. It has been nibbled at, sabotaged, and then found wanting through no fault of its own, *because it is what it actually intends to be.* Which is precisely the point. Socialized medicine does not struggle because we do not try hard enough. It struggles because of the ideas it necessarily supports.

The Worldview Behind Medicare

PATIENTS EXPERIENCE medicare at two levels: care and coordination of care. But healthcare goes much deeper than that. Dysfunction in socialized medicine manifests itself at four levels: not only care and coordination of care but also culture and concepts. Here are all four:

1. Care is what patients experience: long waits, hallway medicine, and bad patient outcomes. Most people focus on this level.
2. Coordination is what managers[23] do to shape care, through policy, strategic plans, and management decisions. Full-time administrators and policy people focus on this level.
3. Culture refers to the accepted behaviour inside a group or system that guides people's behaviour. Good culture grows and adapts. Bad culture ossifies; it becomes an ideology. No evidence can change minds that are transfixed by ideology. Socialized medicine exists at this level.

4.   Concepts are ideas that shape how we think about other things. For example, economists often assume that life is all about meeting material needs; that doctors, like all rational people, work to maximize their material needs and wants. Ergo, doctors only care about making more money.

If we build a case against socialized medicine by looking only at level one issues, it will read like a long list of problems about patient care. Worth discussing, but not enough.

If we build a case at level two, by examining bad policy and corrupt political decisions, it will read like a history of chaos. Some books focus on this level, either as a record of carnage or a call to a brighter future.

As for level three, while a debate around ideology rages in the United States right now, most Canadians have given up: they assume that socialized medicine has won, that it works well enough and includes more compassion than any alternative.

We need to probe one level deeper if we want to explore meaningful improvement. Level four includes our ideas and feelings about freedom, power, and the appropriate extent of state control — concepts that form our worldview.

Our worldview shapes the kinds of questions we ask and the sorts of solutions we seek. It shapes our evaluation and explanation of events. For example, healthcare experts often blame system failure on excess freedom, claiming doctors, nurses, and patients have too much autonomy. Canada's list of failings secured the country last place standing for wait times among other nations in the (infamous) Commonwealth Fund Studies.[24] "Each of these failings can be laid at the door of a system that has privileged independent private practices and institutions as part of the founding profession-state bargain."[25] In other words, Canada fails because it is not socialized enough.

"Independent," "private," and "privileged" are loaded political words that presuppose a particular view of how civil society should function. We need to uncover the ideas that lead authors and academics to use such words and politicians and administrators to ape them. Although no one holds all the same ideas at the same time and in the same way, it is possible to identify a particular worldview by piecing together the set of ideas behind it.

The example above, in which economists explain doctors' behaviour as a pursuit of money, offers a case in point. Explaining behaviour as the pursuit of material ends forms the basis of Karl Marx's "materialist" view of history. As Roger Scruton, author, philosopher, and former Cold War activist, writes, "Where others might study law, religion, art, and family life, Marxists concentrate on the 'material' realities, which means the production of food, houses, machinery, furniture and means of transport."[26] Nothing else matters, and it is mischievous to suggest otherwise. "Economic activity is the 'base' upon which the 'superstructure' of society rests."[27] By highlighting an economist's materialist assumption, we can make sense of his comments and debate them.

Socialized medicine advances a worldview that upholds some or all of the following: trust in teams; suspicion of individuals; faith in experts and elites; distrust of the average person; a benign view of government; suspicion of private enterprise; faith in planning; skepticism of innovation; trust in progress and process; distaste for tradition and prejudice; regard for managers and managerialism; disdain for independent practitioners; a desire to change the future; a distrust of the past; the belief that life is a zero-sum game; an abhorrence of profit; faith in rationalism; and an anti-capitalist bias.

This worldview does not see wealth as arising from creativity, knowledge, and the need to provide what people want. It sees wealth as unearned privilege or theft. It sees life as a battle between victims and oppressors, a view that foments envy and class warfare. The economist John Goodman has spent decades on research and writing about health policy in the United States. He notes that data and argument do not define the biggest debates in healthcare. "The most important differences stem from differences in fundamental world views."[28]

Medicine Is a Moral Enterprise

THE CASE AGAINST socialized medicine is by necessity a moral one because patient care is a moral endeavour. Whereas evidence, budgets, and benchmarks dominate discussion in healthcare, a patient stands, or at least should stand, at the heart of every decision, every discussion. "Medicine is, at its centre, a moral enterprise grounded in a covenant of trust."[29]

When medicare began in Canada in the 1960s, support for socialized-medicine-as-insurance was straightforward. The question posed was whether Canadians wanted to pay for medically necessary care as part of a national insurance scheme. Most Canadians said yes, and most still do.[30] Government can do things that citizens and businesses cannot. Otto von Bismarck, German Chancellor in the 1880s, built the first state health insurance plan. On the one hand, Bismarck said sickness insurance is just "applied Christianity."[31] However, on the other, he confessed he was using it to "bribe the labour classes."[32] To be clear, *moral* does not mean *religious*. For our purposes, *moral* simply refers to the shared assumptions within a community about what counts as good behaviour and constitutes the good life.

But socialized medicine is no longer just an insurance program. Many would argue it never was. Today, socialized medicine is more like managed care. Each province operates a mammoth health maintenance organization that uses mechanisms of the state to shape important details about care. Socialized medicine is a planned medical care economy. However, since all medical care is moral, we must use the language of morality to evaluate medicare, not just the language of economics (economism).

That does not mean we should reach for a textbook on medical ethics. No doubt were physicians to act like the state and deny care, cause harm, and offer special access to a privileged few, they would lose their licence. Then why is it right for the state to act in these ways? The so-called Georgetown Mantra defines morality in medicine as autonomy, beneficence, non-maleficence, and justice,[33] which means patients should make the final decision about their care and doctors must offer help, avoid harm, and make sure all who are sick get the care they need. As we will see, the state ignores these principles by design.[34]

Socialized medicine cannot function without rationing. This necessarily builds a culture that assumes it is good and normal for doctors, nurses, administrators, and bureaucrats to decide whether patients deserve to be seen, often without even seeing them. *We* can tell that your complaint about fatigue means you can wait for hours in the waiting room or weeks at home for an appointment. *We* know that a patient with a chief complaint of "I feel old" does not need emergency care. But when doctors finally see the patient — an actual case — the previously healthy gentleman is full of metastatic cancer. Patients will not tell us they have malaise, cachexia, or prostration. The only way for them to know if they need to see a doctor is to see a doctor.[35] And yet socialized medicine encourages a faulty logic in which it is normal and good to disparage "demanding" and "frivolous" patient complaints. There are incentives to *not* care.

Of course, patients often do make frivolous requests. But how can they know the difference? How can they know that back pain with a numb foot is nothing serious but back pain with numb buttocks could require emergency neurosurgery?

Socialized medicine fosters a culture of cynicism and sorting. "The individual is not able to decide rationally." "These are societal decisions."[36]

These ideas create a bureaucratic bulwark that requires education, intelligence, and connections on the inside for patients to penetrate and access care. Patients are often "confused, disoriented, and lost."[37] They need patient navigators, much like the *Tokachi*, or "fixers," in the Soviet era, to get access to care. Great service requires sophisticated advocacy that poor patients, especially, cannot produce.[38] Those without the means, skills, or connections do not get as good care as those with privilege and connections. The ideal of equality crumbles at the touch of reality.

Philosophers of science tell us "any theory, suitably revised, can be made consistent with any data, and any data rejected in the interests of the theory."[39] In other words, data about performance will not create the change we hope for. And the data that matter — evidence about management culture, attitudes, and norms — do not even exist. Bad outcomes just mean we must try harder. Political philosopher James Burnham says it well:

"A dispute about scientific theories can always be settled, sooner or later, by experiment and observation. A dispute between rival ideologies can never be thus settled. Arguments about ideologies can, and do, continue as long as the interests embodied by them are felt to be of any significance."[40]

Defenders of the status quo should be able to answer the question: "What specific evidence, what observations, happenings, experiments, might *conceivably* prove you wrong?"[41]

For many, the first step to improving socialized medicine is to embrace its fundamental design — its core values. To them, stories of patients dying in emergency department waiting rooms simply show we need bigger emergency departments, not that the system is failing. When a teenager dies because we cannot find a hospital bed for her treatable condition, it only shows we need more hospital beds.[42] And sad stories about routine suffering in waiting rooms, well, those stories happen in every waiting room the world over. Besides, these are just stories, bubbles in an ocean of a noble design that, on the whole, does a pretty good job for most people. Socialized medicine is basically good with plenty of bright spots amid the challenges.

This consensus is changing, however. Journalist Ian Mulgrew captured a number of comments made by Dr. Jeff Turnbull, a strong supporter of medicare, when Turnbull was president of the Canadian Medical Association, 2010-11: "We're living under the delusion of what Medicare ought to be rather than seeing it for what it really is." In another speech, Turnbull said:

> Canada now ranks below Slovenia in terms of effectiveness, and last or second last in terms of value for money ... I don't think any of us would have thought that we would be practicing in a system where five million Canadians do not have access to a family doctor, or (where) one in 10 Canadians cannot afford their medications. Where getting a knee-joint replacement for severe and disabling pain within one year is considered to be an ideal target for quality care — incidentally, a target we don't achieve very often.[43]

Canadian healthcare was once great. In the 1970s, Canada had more hospital beds than other countries and too few sick people to fill them. However, a comment by leading healthcare journalist Andre Picard of the *Globe and Mail*, on US Senator Bernie Sanders' congratulatory tour of Canadian healthcare in 2017, is telling. *Contra* Sanders, Picard tweeted, "On health reform, Canada needs a kick in the ass, not a pat on the back."[44]

No one in the world copies Canada's restrictive system anymore. How can Canada hope for change if ideological soulmates among American politicians tell Canadians to *"be a little bit louder!"* about their system?[45]

Stoking the Myth

IN SEPTEMBER OF 2018 comedian Jim Carey spoke about Canadian health care on *Real Time with Bill Maher*.

> I grew up in Canada, OK? We have socialized medicine. I'm here to tell you this bulls**t line you get on all the political shows from people is that it's a failure … in Canada.
>
> It is *not* a failure in Canada.
>
> I have never waited for anything in my life. I chose my own doctors. My mother never paid for prescriptions. It was fantastic. And I just got back from Vancouver and I keep hearing this: "Canadians are so nice. Canadians are so nice." They can be nice because they have healthcare …" [wild applause] "… Because they have a government that cares about them! That doesn't say, "Sink or f**king swim, pal, or you live in a box!" There are certain people in our society that need to be taken care of. There are people without as many opportunities that need to be helped toward those opportunities. There are people who are sick; you shouldn't have to lose your home because your mother got sick.[46]

Patients call in to radio shows and say much the same thing. They talk about the great care they received. Then they attack anyone who dares to criticize medicare. They are frustrated with people who complain. *It could be much worse.* Complaining suggests selfish motives or a lack of support for Canadian exceptionalism. Those who complain should be a little more grateful and a lot more quiet.

This insouciance toward other patients who are suffering would seem remarkable if it were not so common. It is as if Mr. Carey and company had survived the crash of the *Titanic* and, while being paddled to shore, scolded anyone who pointed out passengers who were drowning.

Perhaps Mr. Carey meant something deeper when he said, "It is *not* a failure in Canada."[47] Maybe he meant it, as author Brian Lee Crowley explains, more as "a statement about morals, beliefs and desires ... [which] transcends any assessment of quality."[48]

Those who scold follow up their rebuke with a well-worn threat: "You don't want an American system, do you?" It makes no sense for Canadians to assume the only alternative to a Canadian system is an American one. Nor does it make sense to dismiss, wholesale, another country's approach. Fear-mongering somehow justifies suffering. A bit of patient suffering is worth the price of avoiding an American system. It is a small "sacrifice welcomed as a personal contribution to the price of collective redemption."[49] An almost jingoistic fervour infuses Canadians on this one issue. Perhaps it is the only thing that proves we are not American.

Carey and company might reply that patients dying in waiting rooms or languishing in hallways are nothing like passengers freezing in Arctic water. They might say the analogy shows insensitivity to the *Titanic*'s survivors. A huge number of that ship's passengers died, whereas only 4 percent of Canadians experience acute care in any given year. Most patients access non-acute care. Although patients sit and wait, they eventually get in front of a doctor.

Canadians have placed healthcare behind debate-proof glass;[50] it is a holy icon, a social religion protected from rational discussion. Medicare has acquired its own identity.[51] We cannot imagine life without it. No amount of bad patient outcomes can justify change to such a noble vision.[52]

Chapter Two
Socialized Medicine's False Premise

*The first function of the founders of nations, after founding itself, is to
devise a set of true falsehoods about origins — a mythology — that will make it
desirable for nationals to live under a common authority, and,
indeed make it impossible to entertain contrary thoughts.*
–Forrest McDonald

*The outstanding trait of the men of our period may seem in retrospect to
have been the facility with which they put forth untried conceits as "ideals."*
–Irving Babbitt

SIR WILFRID LAURIER, Canada's first Liberal prime minister, once
said, "Canada is free and freedom is its nationality." One hundred years later,
Canadians think, "Canada is free healthcare and medicare is its nationality."[53]

Free care for all is Canada's grand narrative. To the rest of the world,
free care embodies the spirit of Canada: "The fact that anybody who needs
healthcare can get it, without payment, satisfies the basic collectivist spirit of
the nation."[54] Grand narratives include a defining myth or myths: a story to
capture the essence of a bigger vision. In the case of Canada, the epic tale is
Tommy's leg. Like all epic tales, it starts with history and goes on to become a
legend, which then becomes myth.

Tommy Douglas was six years old when he fell and scraped his knee,
in Falkirk Scotland, in 1910. His knee became infected. Infection invaded
the bone. After multiple surgeries, and narrowly avoiding an amputation,
he recovered with the help of a famous surgeon in Winnipeg, who offered
to work for free as long as his students could watch. Master Douglas grew

up, entered politics, and became premier of Saskatchewan and the father of medicare. As leader of the Canadian Commonwealth Federation (CCF), he formed North America's first socialist government, in his province in 1944.[55] He did not waste any time: "A month after the CCF victory, Douglas had sent a telegram to Dr. Henry E. Sigerist, professor of the history of medicine at Johns Hopkins University, inviting him to survey the health needs of the province and make recommendations." Sigerist was "a recognized expert on the Soviet system of socialized medicine."[56]

Canadians picked Douglas as the Greatest Canadian, in 2004, for his lifelong quest to create socialized medicine.[57]

Douglas often pointed to his leg infection, and his "great debt of gratitude" for his surgeon, as what sparked his conviction and belief. He loved to tell voters his old, old story, in a way that only a politician and Baptist preacher could.[58] He said, "I think it was out of this experience … I came to believe that health services ought not to have a price-tag on them."[59]

Douglas moved Canadians. His story still moves us today, and many a reference about medicare mentions Tommy's leg.[60] All major books on the history of medicare in Canada point to it. It is without question the epic tale that informs the grand narrative of socialized medicine in Canada. No other story comes close.[61] It has everything: conflict, suffering, victims and villains, scandal and rescue. But the cruel system Douglas described did not exist. His story was not about a little boy who almost lost his leg save for a charitable surgeon. Douglas made a scurrilous accusation about the medical profession. Packaged as an appeal to compassion, his story indicts a profession as so cruel and corrupt we should marvel that it could have exited in a democratic country. More so, Douglas indicts a whole country for allowing it to happen in the first place. How could Canada allow kids to lose their legs because they were poor?

Douglas gave a set of interviews in 1958 that later were collected in a single volume, *The Making of a Socialist: The Recollections of T.C. Douglas.* The book gives us his own description of his experience. "Just before coming to Canada," he said, "and while living in Falkirk, I injured my knee by a fall, with the result that osteomyelitis set in."[62] This led to three operations in Scotland, "in which the femur was scraped," to clear the infection.

> After three of these operations, it was hoped that I had been cured. Later on in Winnipeg, the osteomyelitis recurred, and I went through a long period of hospitalization. The doctors attending me told my parents that the leg would have to be amputated and they were given some time to decide whether or not to agree to the amputation. During that period in the Children's Hospital in Winnipeg, about 1913 or 1914, Dr. R.J. Smith, a very famous orthopaedic surgeon, was going through the wards with a group of students and became interested in my case. He interviewed my parents and told them that he was prepared to take over, providing that they would allow the students to observe. As a result of several operations, he saved my leg.
>
> I always felt a great debt of gratitude to him; but it left me with this feeling that if I hadn't been so fortunate as to have this doctor offer me his services gratis, I would probably have lost my leg. My parents were having quite a difficult time during the depression, money was very scarce, and they couldn't possibly have hired a man of Dr. Smith's standing. I felt that no boy should have to depend either for his leg or his life upon the ability of his parents to raise enough money to bring a first-class surgeon to his bedside. And I think it was out of this experience, not at the moment consciously, but through the years, I came to believe that health services ought not to have a price-tag on them, and that people should be able to get whatever health services they required irrespective of their individual capacity to pay.[63]

Douglas, a masterful politician, preacher, and polemicist, packs a powerful narrative into two paragraphs. We need not doubt the details of his personal experience. His story is just the hook to make a bigger point. We need to watch what happens after Douglas sets his hook. He makes at least five harsh accusations but packages them as an appeal to compassion: (1) doctors let poor children lose their leg or their life if they could not pay;

(2) some doctors would actually amputate the leg of a child knowing the leg could be saved; (3) doctors offered treatment only in return for some form of payment, in this case, the opportunity to teach medical students; (4) he would have received better care if he was rich; and (5) he finally got the standard of care from the charity of a passing surgeon. These accusations overlap, but each point carries its own bite and enhances the myth.

But perhaps this is just political theatre from an expert politician. Maybe Douglas just made points in theory, to get support in principle, for his vision of free care for all. Douglas might have been saying, "No boy should depend for his leg or his life," in the same way that a politician says, "No boy should ever fear for his life while riding a bike."

But a politician would never make such a comment unless it referred to something real. It makes no sense to appeal to the audience, even to support a theoretical position, unless the appeal is based on something that either actually, or potentially, could exist. Douglas gains agreement from his audience by implying that some boys *could* lose a leg or their life. People make the connection and assume that, therefore, some boys *do* lose a leg or life.[64]

We must take Douglas's words as points of fact, not political theatre. He is not just making a rhetorical point, in an attempt to win political support. He levelled a set of serious accusations at doctors. They deserve deeper analysis.

Tommy's Accusations

1. Doctors let poor children lose their leg or their life if they could not pay.

First, Douglas says if you had money, you could keep your leg. If you could not pay, you might lose it. "I felt that no boy should have to depend either for his leg or his life upon the ability of his parents to raise enough money to bring a first-class surgeon to his bedside."[65] A non-medical reader might not catch what this means to medicine. Douglas's phrase, "his leg or his life," strikes at medicine's moral code, for the very existence of medicine is to preserve *life and limb*. Nothing matters more. *Life and limb* is the priceless value doctors vow to protect.[66]

No court will excuse negligence in protecting life and limb. *Life and limb* is repeated over and over in advanced life-saving skills courses, such as Advanced Cardiac Life Support and Advanced Trauma Life Support.

On top of that, Douglas inverts the doctor-patient relationship. He reverses the exchange at the heart of medical care. For three thousand years, medicine has survived by treating people first and accepting payment later. Medicine exists primarily to provide patient care, not to receive payment for care.

Douglas sets up a fundamental conflict: Medicine either helps sick people, as an end in itself, or it focuses on money and lets a poor patient lose "his leg or his life." His accusation seems to presuppose the materialist economics of the socialized worldview we discussed earlier: doctors always aim to maximize their rational self-interest and make more money.

If it was true that doctors did not treat without payment, then there should have been large groups of people, whole neighbourhoods, who lived with deformity and disease in a modern Dickensian landscape. Remember, Douglas made these accusations throughout the 1950s and 60s. So I interviewed a number of older physicians who practiced during that time, before socialized medicine, asking: "Did patients who could not pay go without care in the days before medicare? Were people left to suffer and endure amputations, or even death, because they could not pay for necessary care?" Each physician said, with passion and dignified outrage, that every single patient got "great care" regardless of ability to pay. Modern standards of practice applied. These doctors added that, in fact, far more physicians refuse care *today*, under socialized medicine, because they feel they cannot work any harder, or they have too many patients already, or the state does not provide the resources for care.

The stats support what the doctors said. Medicare did not usher in a marked shift in life expectancy,[67] neonatal mortality,[68] or maternal mortality.[69] Death from heart disease has decreased steadily from the 1970s, but this is more likely due to advances in therapy, not advances in how to pay for therapy. The biggest change pre- and post-medicare came in more than double the number of services delivered to patients.[70]

Before medicare, doctors competed for patients.[71] Aside from the change in medical treatment options, the only major difference in practice before medicare was that doctors often worked for free. One doctor I interviewed recalled collecting only 67 percent of billings. Other physicians recalled similar collection rates, with some sources reporting as low as 50 percent. But each doctor cared for every single patient who came to the clinic, emergency department, and the hospital, including those who required surgery.[72] We cannot blame poor access to care, in the days before medicare, on doctors refusing to treat without payment.

Even today, many patients still show up without medical coverage, in the emergency department. The government has invalidated their provincial insurance card (an ongoing irritation, because of an address change, for instance), or they are travelling, or they live in a province that often refuses to pay for out-of-province care (Quebec). Doctors care for them all. After almost thirty years in training and practice, I have never seen any doctor turn patients away for medically necessary care when they cannot pay. No doctor would ever tell a patient who could not pay for care today, "I am sorry. The standard of care for your problem is x. But since you cannot afford it, I will give you less-than-x instead." If x is the standard of care, then that is what doctors must give, regardless of whether a patient can pay for it. This is not a new. And it is not due to medicare or modern moral superiority. If patients need medically necessary care, they get what they need based on the accepted standard of modern medical care. In fact, medically necessary care is mandated legally, which leads to Tommy's next accusation.

2. Some doctors would actually amputate the leg of a child knowing the leg could be saved.

Whereas his first accusation took aim at what doctors would *not* do — provide appropriate care — the second took aim at what doctors would do instead, which is an attack on the morality of doctors. According to Douglas, his fear for his leg was not due to a lack of surgical resources, medical technology, knowledge, or skill in the community; only money separated him from proper care.

But if a surgeon knew a child could keep his leg if he got the right care, which was available in Winnipeg, would he cut off a leg to "treat" the child's infection? Or worse, would medical care at the time allow a child to die because the child's parents could not pay? How can we make sense of a surgeon, bound by sacred oath, advising amputation when a better option existed?

If doctors provided two standards of care — one for the rich, another for the poor — it follows that they provided substandard care to poor people. Substandard care is, by definition, harm. The courts call it negligence. Doctors have never been free to follow whatever practice happens to pay the bills. Douglas's own doctors were licensed by the College of Physicians and Surgeons of Manitoba. The college was established in 1871 as the Provincial Medical Board of Manitoba, for "maintaining medical standards of practice in the province."[73] Doctors could not simply choose to offer substandard care to poor children and their parents and hope to keep their licences. Especially when life or limb were at risk, doctors had to provide whatever care was deemed best at the time, based on available resources in that community. And if a patient needed care beyond that available in a particular community, they were transferred to where they could get what they needed.

Winnipeg was not a remote, logging settlement or other isolated place in the early twentieth century. It was a booming town. It supported a solid medical community, with an approved medical school. Douglas was in the Winnipeg Children's Hospital, four years after the Flexner Report, 1910.[74] Flexner had reviewed medical education in the United States and Canada and had levelled scathing reviews of many schools, to weed out low performers and decrease the number of schools overall. But he found only one Canadian school inadequate (University of Western Ontario). The University of Manitoba's Max Rady College of Medicine was founded in 1883 and had passed Flexner's review. It was in its fourth decade by the time Douglas was in Winnipeg Children's Hospital. Suggestions that his surgeons were second-rate, out of date, or working in a backwards medical community do not fit the evidence.

3. Doctors offered treatment only in return for some form of payment, in this case the opportunity to teach medical students.

The third accusation is more subtle but equally pernicious. Douglas said Dr. Smith "interviewed my parents and told them that he was prepared to take over, providing that they would allow the students to observe."

Even though Douglas mentions later that the surgeon offered to provide the service "gratis," many writers imply that having the students watch served in place of payment. I could find no evidence that Dr. Smith would have demanded payment, or refused treatment, had Tommy's parents refused Smith's students. Smith's offer was simply to provide care for no fee, and his students got to watch.

Too often those who promote socialized medicine try to paint a picture of care before medicare as including an explicit exchange of some sort. It promotes the idea that the purpose of doctoring is payment not patient care. It turns patients into the means for doctors to make money, distorting medicine's traditional focus of patient care as an end in itself.

4. Douglas would have received better care if he was rich.

The fourth accusation implies that Tommy faced amputation because he was poor as opposed to proper care if he had been rich. Only the charity of a passing surgeon — someone his parents could have never afforded — let him keep his leg.

However, all of Tommy's surgeries at Winnipeg Children's, and even the surgeries performed by Dr. Smith, would not have cost as much as an eighteen-month stay in the specialty hospital. Not even close. Even if the hospital stay was offered free, all the doctors' and surgeons' fees, over those months in hospital, would have added to a much larger sum than even the fees of the one "very famous" surgeon.

It is very possible that the whole duration of his specialty medical and surgical care, all the hospital fees, and the more than half a dozen surgeries were all given free of charge. Douglas's story actually provides evidence of a system that provided an inordinate amount of truly free care, before Canada had any kind of health insurance at all. We might ask how all that free, donated care compares with the current approach of rationing, regulation, and control.

5. Douglas finally got the standard of care from the charity of a passing surgeon.

This makes no sense. If Dr. Smith offered nothing more than the standard of care when he "became interested" in Tommy's case, Tommy's doctors would have already offered it themselves. Or Tommy's doctors would have already referred Tommy to Dr. Smith as the local expert on Tommy's condition.

Referral to an expert is standard of practice. If one surgeon does not have the skill or ability to provide the standard of care, he refers his patient to one who does. It is a stretch to suggest Douglas's original surgeons not only failed to provide the standard of care for Tommy but also failed to even consider referring him to the one surgeon who could. It seems far more likely Dr. Smith was offering an innovative or experimental technique. This fits with the fact he was an academic surgeon who worked and taught at Winnipeg Children's Hospital and the Manitoba medical school. Perhaps Douglas's physicians mentioned their difficult case to Dr. Smith or asked him for advice. Maybe Smith had seen a similar case or had heard of a new approach. He thought it worth a try to prevent the amputation.

In other words, *contra* all five of Douglas's accusations, it seems unlikely his experience and outcome had anything to do with ability to pay.

Tommy's Dream Actually Destroys Access

DOUGLAS USED his childhood memories from the turn of the twentieth century to describe medical practice in the 1950s and 60s. His claims demand evidence to support them. Was and is medicine the sort of profession that supports the unnecessary amputation of a child's leg? How could the public trust such a profession?

Many people offer stories of being unable to access medical care during that same time in Canada.[75] Medical services for necessary medical care often did not exist — more often because of geographical, not financial, barriers. People suffered in remote communities, or even just rural ones, unable to travel to town to see a doctor.

Many towns in Canada still have no doctor today. Hospitals were rare, before the 1940s hospital building boom. Tough Canadian pioneers found creative ways to manage many of their own illnesses and injuries. Most families can recall at least one relative who did not have necessary care: there were no doctors for them to see, or they were too proud to ask for help they could not pay for. My mother remembers her father, a carpenter, draining a large abscess in her toe, at the kitchen table, in rural northern Ontario.

But lack of access to care is a very different problem from the one Douglas painted with his story. Hardy pioneers did not pursue home remedies because doctors refused to see them. Canada was not full of disfigured people suffering from untreated disease because doctors refused to save life or limb. Simon Laplace, a nineteenth-century scientist, is said to have stated: "The weight of evidence for an extraordinary claim must be proportioned to its strangeness." Or, as Carl Sagan, the famous American author, has popularized it: "Extraordinary claims require extraordinary evidence." Lack of access to care remains a serious issue for many of Canada's most vulnerable patients. It is a problem medicare has not fixed.

Tommy's dream created a system where a "very famous orthopedic surgeon" cannot exist, at least not in the same way the famous surgeon existed when he was a child. Socialized medicine makes every surgeon the same and puts every patient on the same wait-list. Even if we grant the possibility that the surgeons who work in academic hospitals qualify as "very famous" surgeons in socialized medicine, Canadians cannot access them the way they could before medicare. Now, the only way to access "famous" surgeons is to get a referral and wait on a wait-list with everyone else, or travel outside Canada. So Tommy's dream of giving every little boy the chance to see a very famous surgeon when care was needed has not come true. Now such a boy gets to see whichever surgeon the state system can provide, whenever the state decides the boy needs care.

Douglas received an extraordinary amount of care, which included multiple surgeries, for up to two years (if we include his care in Scotland), before Dr. Smith tried a novel approach. Heroic surgeons who craft creative surgical solutions, based on a hunch, exist only in Hollywood. Today those heroic academic surgeons cannot offer valiant attempts on lost causes as opportunities to teach students. Surgeons need approval from research ethics boards, hospital medical advisory committees, finance, and bed allocation departments. Academic surgeons continue to take on the toughest cases. But they see them on the state-rationed wait-list. No one can access them the way Douglas had promised. As Sally Pipes, CEO of Pacific Research Institute, puts it: "While recovering in the hospital, little Tommy Douglas did not conclude that it was a good thing that the private economy produced enough wealth to make such generous charity possible. Rather, he concluded that governments ought to make such charity unnecessary by funding universal health care."[76]

Misplaced Pride?

TOMMY DOUGLAS used his leg as only a politician could. And it worked. The Association for Canadian Studies conducted a survey from June 28 to July 1, 2019 and found that universal health care made the top of a list of very important sources of personal or collective Canadian pride.[77] Some 73 percent of Canadians found personal or collective pride in universal health care, 70 percent in the Canadian passport, 67 percent in the Canadian flag, and 65 percent in the Canadian Charter of Rights and Freedoms. The national anthem and the Armed Forces also won more than 50 percent support.

Strong pride in medicare is explainable partly by the fact that only 4 percent of Canadians need an acute care hospital bed in any given year. Most people never experience health care beyond twisted ankles and prescription refills. Vulnerable patients, who wait two years, or longer, with pain and disability, represent a much smaller cohort. They are often older, with less to lose financially through waiting. The "majority support" that advocates hurry to highlight rests on voters who have never needed anything major and older/sicker patients who will be grateful for any care they can get. Thus, majority support tells us more about the nature of the majority than about the system itself.

It is true that medicare in the 1970s gave Canadians a legitimate reason to be proud. We had far more hospital beds than we needed and fewer sick people who needed them. Government poured money into medicare between 1968 and 1976 to make the program stick. But in 1977, the first Prime Minister Trudeau produced the Established Programs Financing Act (1977), which stopped the federal blank cheques that used to cover 50 percent of whatever the provinces spent on healthcare.[78] The Feds' switch to block grants meant provincial politicians had to pay for their own election promises and could no longer rely on the federal government to pick up half the bill.

Having run out of other people's money (as socialism always does), the provinces cut services, closed beds, and cut payments to doctors and nurses. The dreams and heady period of spending and expansion came screeching to a halt.

Every single promise, full or in part, has been broken or ignored over the fifty-plus years of medicare. And the public is catching on. The Canadian Medical Association surveyed Canadians in 2019 and found that 61 percent have a negative outlook for the future, and 65 percent cite healthcare as a major source of worry.[79]

What Socialized Medicine Really Is

SOCIALIZED MEDICINE means different things to different people. For some, it simply means compassion for all. It fosters images of a kind and efficient Canada compared with a fearful, competitive, and wasteful US.

What many people call socialized medicine is neither socialized nor medicine. They use it to describe everything that happens relating to health in Canada. Spreading the definition as wide as possible helps give the impression that medicare has variety and nuance, that it clearly is not a state-controlled system that outlaws patient choice. But socialized medicine is just one part of healthcare. It is a big part but only one piece of the larger healthcare industry, which includes drugs, medical supplies, eyecare, dental care, public health, and non-medical care, such as physiotherapy and home care. We confuse people if we give the impression that everything related to healthcare is the same as socialized medicine. For some, this is an honest mistake. But for many others, the equivocation fuels a political agenda. The confusion gives them the opportunity to point out that 30 percent of "healthcare" spending in Canada is not socialized but comes from private sources. That is, taxes only cover 70 percent of the larger bucket they have defined ahead of time as healthcare.[80] Framing the definition this way allows defenders to give the impression that medicare is a blended industry, like delivery services. The post office handles most mail; courier services like UPS and FedEx handle the rest. Medicare covers doctors and hospitals; private insurance covers the rest. Patients have options. Government allows choice. See, socialized medicine is open and diverse.

But it is not true. If we use the words precisely, socialized medicine is state control of medical care. But even this is confusing. Doctors will jump in to tell you they are not employed by government; government does not control their every action. There are no civil servants hovering in clinics watching every move doctors make. As Danielle Martin, founder of Canadian Doctors for Medicare, puts it: "Aside from public health departments, we have almost no public delivery in Canada. In fact, we have a highly private health care delivery system. That hasn't changed much since the pre-medicare days."[81] This builds on the narrative popularized in the book *Private Practice, Public Payment*, by Dr. C. David Naylor. However, Naylor's depiction of a perfect blend of innovative free enterprise matched with unquestioning state support (payment) disappeared in the 1990s, shortly after he laid down his pen.

The Promise of Care Regardless of Ability to Pay

AND SO we must turn now to socialized medicine's core promise of care regardless of ability to pay. This slogan represents the aspirational heart of medicare. Sometimes stated as care based on need, not one one's ability to pay, it presents more of a vision than a program or system of care.

Canadian doctors never tell patients how much medically necessary care will cost. In fact, most doctors have no idea what care costs. Care regardless of ability to pay means patients carry provincial health insurance cards instead of cash to get care. It includes the promise that no Canadian should ever go bankrupt from medical bills. For the most part, doctors submit one bill to their provincial ministry of health each month, and the ministry pays.

At the start, Canadians believed the promise of *care regardless of ability to pay* because they believed in government. World War II had convinced them of the power of collective action. Canada had just helped win victory against impossible odds. Trust in government was at nearly 60 percent.[82] Politicians took this trust and used it to build socialized medicine: the biggest plank of Canada's welfare state.

Leveraging the success of WWII, using military metaphors, Liberal prime minister Mackenzie King said in 1945: "The enemies we shall have to overcome will be on our own Canadian soil. They will make their presence known in the guise of sickness, unemployment and want. It is to plan for a unified campaign in Canada against these enemies of progress and human well-being that we have come together at this time."[83]

King echoed feelings felt around the free world. In the British welfare state, after which Canadian medicare was initially modelled, citizens expected the state to take care of everything citizens might depend on: the economy, education, poverty relief, labour, settlement, employment, and more.[84] This ethos fit perfectly with Tommy Douglas's campaign to build socialized medicine. He could leverage the myth about his leg to create his vision of a state that fixed social problems and took care of everyone.[85]

Initially, the Liberal party embraced sickness insurance as a vehicle to promote freedom. A sick person is not free to do as he pleases. We needed to free Canadians from their sickness. Furthermore, many Canadians were ineligible to fight in WWII because they were deemed medically unfit for duty. Canadians had suffered through the 1930s in a way no one wanted to repeat. So politicians promised a solution starting with hospital insurance in the 1950s followed by medical insurance in the following decade. As a basic promise to pay for care, no one could argue against it. Given the political entanglement of the whole process, it is impossible to unravel the motivation between caring for sick people and the motivation to win political power.

The public did not ask for socialized medicine, according to Carolyn Tuohy,[86] professor emeritus of health policy at University of Toronto. Tuohy calls it an elite project,[87] dreamt up by experts, politicians. Public leaders believed government offered a better bet for quality care, at a lower cost, than anything private businesses could offer. As Steven Lewis, healthcare consultant, has said, "Medicare is the crowning achievement of post war optimism."[88]

Today, politicians, authors, and pundits point to medicare and *care regardless of ability to pay* as precisely what we would expect from a people who value fairness and equity. "Universal care is part of a society that values fairness."[89] A fair society will have universal care, where everyone can get care, and having universal care makes a society fair. The tautology is politically persuasive: Canada has universal care, so Canada is a fair society. Although it is hard to know whether a Canadian values fairness more than a Norwegian or Nigerian, flattery has always worked in politics: it is a staple tactic politicians use towards their greater purpose.

But even though *care regardless of ability to pay* has become the defining slogan of medicare, it still does not fully explain the purpose of medicare.

Chapter Three
Socialized Medicine's Concealed Purpose

The best interest of the patient is the only interest to consider.
–William J. Mayo, MD

LET US RETURN to where we left you at the beginning of this book, lying on a rubber mattress in a hospital hallway. What do you want your doctors and nurses to focus on when they come to see you? On finding out what is wrong and fixing it. On you, nothing else. Of course, doctors hold many things in mind at the same time that may or may not impact a particular patient's care: thoughts about the disease; worry about the last three patients; concern over workflow, liability, risk, and reputation. Some distraction is inevitable. But patient care is still the ultimate end. As Claude Bernard, a French physiologist and the first to suggest blinded experiments, said in the nineteenth century: "A physician is by no means a physician to living beings in general, not even physician to the human race, but rather, a physician to a human individual and still more physician to an individual in certain morbid conditions peculiar to himself and forming what is called his idiosyncrasy."[90]

Why Does Medicare Exist?

PATIENTS RANKLE at the thought of doctors being used to do anything else besides helping individual patients. Medicine exists to provide care for patients. It does not even occur to them that care has anything to with a concealed purpose comprising the system's rationing of care, redistribution of services, and creation of a fair and just society.

Indeed, experts see things differently. For them, the whole system of socialized medicine does not exist to improve care but to achieve political goals.[91]

This sets up another fundamental debate, between political objective and patient care. We can sneak up on it by using the local grocery store as an example. Why does the store exist? What purpose does it serve the people in the community? An economics student might tell us it exists to provide an income for the owner. Without the desire for income, no grocery store. Adam Smith famously said, "It is not from the benevolence of the butcher, the brewer, or the baker that we expect our dinner, but from their regard to their own interest." However, might not the brewer brew primarily for the love of beer? Perhaps self-interest cannot be reduced to the desire to make money. Despite economists reducing the world to rational self-interest, most students enter medicine or nursing because they want to help, not just to make money.

But why does the store exist *in the eyes of the customer*? Why do customers want a grocery store to exist in their community? Customers who need groceries want a grocery store to provide fresh groceries. Nothing else. The store might lead to many other good things, for instance, employment, support for local farmers, or an increase in the tax base for the municipality. But the store exists, first and foremost, to provide groceries to hungry customers.

What seems obvious for grocery stores remains a big debate in healthcare. The fact is, patient care is only one of many competing reasons why medicare exists, and it may rank near the bottom. Those who question why or suggest otherwise are suspected by supporters as not truly understanding the ethos of medicare.

Health journalist André Picard starts one of his books[92] by asking why Canada has medicare. Is it only to provide care, or is it to redistribute wealth? Is it to create a national identity, or is it to enlarge the size and control of the state? Or is it to win elections? The answers are not clear, he says

The experts seem to agree on some or all of the following. Medicare exists to redistribute income, maintain a national identity, support the vision of a welfare state, achieve administrative and operational efficiencies, protect citizens from medically related financial loss, build or maintain political support, provide an attractive environment for businesses to relocate, undermine federalism and build a unitary state, enforce national standards, increase the size of provincial budgets ... Patient care just happens to be the *service* medicare provides. Care is only one reason medicare exists, and a not very important one at that.

Whereas medicine exists to *provide* care, socialized medicine exists to *distribute* and *regulate* patient care, according to criteria and rules the state defines, controls, and oversees. Is it any wonder patients often feel they do not matter? If medicine is used as a means to achieve ends other than care, we should not be surprised when care is sacrificed to achieve the other ends when need arises.

The Naive Clinical View of Medicine

MOST CLINICIANS have never heard of this debate. Like most Canadians, people working in healthcare believe socialized medicine exists to provide care for patients. Experts call this the Naive Clinical view, which Bob Evans describes thus: "People should get the care they need, as judged by a qualified clinical practitioner, regardless of the cost ... This ethical norm is so deeply embedded in clinical practice that it is probably no longer recognized as a particular ethical position, among other possibilities. It is simply what you do."[93] Evans is a big supporter of socialized medicine, and socialized medicine does not support the Naive Clinical. Instead, it aims to benefit the greatest number of people without privileging any single person. It aims for an equal distribution of care.

This makes a world of difference. Doctors provide care; they do not distribute it. Physicians give patients what they need, when they need it (assuming government has not rationed the supply of care). Provision of care puts patient care as an end in itself; distribution of care uses patient care to achieve the greater good. Distribution of care promises the biggest benefit to the most people. It uses patient care as a means to achieve a utilitarian vision. Distributing care equally for all citizens might mean no care for some. A perfect distribution of care might mean that many individuals will have to wait, or might, in some cases, even die without care.

A conflict of visions, between provision and distribution, lies at the heart of socialized medicine. It creates internal conflict for clinicians. They devote their careers to patient care as the primary end. They swim upriver to provide care in a system determined to distribute it. Tending to patients whom the system has deemed do not deserve care causes "moral injury" to caregivers, akin to the moral trauma experienced by soldiers.[94]

This conflict seems insurmountable. But advocates of socialized medicine have found a way around it.

Using Values to Shut Down Debate

POLITICIANS LOVE to talk about values in socialized medicine. But they avoid talking about patient care. US senator Bernie Sanders offers a case in point. After his aforementioned presidential campaign tour of Canadian healthcare, he said, "When you talk about health care, you're not just talking about health care … You're talking about values, because how a society deals with health care is more than medicine. It's more than technology. It is about the values that those societies hold dear."[95] Writer and academic Katherine Fierlbeck puts it this way: "It is important to keep in mind that discussions over health care funding are not simply about the allocation of money and the regulation of services, but rather about the interplay of human relations, the resolution of political struggles, and the kinds of values that democratic societies reflect through their public policies."[96]

Faced with the conflict between providing care and distributing care, advocates of the latter seek refuge in values. They start the debate with a short list of values, preselected to support the outcome they want to achieve. For example, Ginette Petitpas Taylor, federal minister of health, offered opening remarks in her Canada Health Act (CHA) Report, 2018.

She emphasized how the fundamental objectives of social work, "human rights and social justice," are closely linked to the values upon which the CHA rests,[97] namely, "equity, fairness and solidarity." But the CHA report offers no mention of patient dignity, compassion, excellence, service, innovation, and individualized care.[98] Aside from justice, the CHA values do not even reflect the core values of medical ethics. Equity is a state of affairs, not a value statement.[99] The CHA short list reflects a particular worldview aimed to achieve a political end.

Advocates attempt to win the debate before it has begun. They start with values so they can take the high moral ground. There they stake a claim to compassion, fairness, and equality. If you disagree with their policies, you appear to lack compassion, to be unfair or elitist. It makes people suspicious of your Canadianism.[100] This is an ingenious gambit. First, it rules out a discussion of any option or solution, which the values-prophets have deemed offensive to the values they profess.[101] Second, it shifts focus from performance to intention,[102] even though intention without action is dead. Edmund Burke addressed this issue in planners and politicians several hundred years ago: "In the manifest failure of their abilities, they take credit for their intentions."

No one argues with the need for moral values. The debate over healthcare is not between people who have values vs. unsociable miscreants. Nor is the debate about *you* having a particular value, or a claim to a particular value, which *I* do not have or cannot claim for my own. Everyone values compassion, fairness, and equality.

Starting with values is a political tactic. Getting opponents to concede the moral high ground means there can be no discussion of medical performance. Machiavellians preach about values but then do whatever they must to get what they want. Hypocrisy infects all human action, but this is more. No amount of evidence about patient suffering, waste, or system chaos can change the debate. If people remain convinced that socialized medicine is morally pure and righteous, or as the CHA report said, based on "equity, fairness, and solidarity," nothing will change.

Conflating Compassion and Equity

THE POLITICAL TRICKERY gets worse. Advocates appeal to compassion but only to emphasize equity: equal care for all regardless of ability to pay.[103] Defenders of medicare would rather everyone in the community had worse care than allow the risk that some might get different care. Different might be better, but better would be bad. The pursuit of equity may mean we cannot care for everyone. Some may have to go without care to benefit the vision of equal care for all. We must oppose any solution that appears to undermine equity, even if the proposed solution would improve everyone's care in the long run. Equity trumps compassion. Political vision requires sacrifice.

However, rigid visions based on ideology actually *create* inequity as people seek privilege and special access. Patients will do everything in their power to find ways around the rigid, so-called equal system, and far too often the defenders of medicare themselves help to make it happen (as we will see in chapter five).

The essence of medicine is to go to extremes to help the sick, injured, or dying. Doctors do everything to save one life. They put priority on attending to the sickest patients.[104] It is why doctors and nurses exist. Clinicians are driven to provide extravagant excess for the sick. All that matters is solving patients' problems. It never crosses a clinician's mind, at the bedside, to deny care because it might be different from the care provided to the patient in the next bed. Clinicians simply focus on getting the best possible care to each patient they see. To accept a lower standard of care simply because it is equal goes against everything the vast majority of healthcare workers hold dear.

Equity and compassion are two different kinds of things. Equity, a state of affairs, is impossible to describe or measure in any practical way. Compassion is an emotion. It is a category mistake to conflate them.

Doctors combine the desire to alleviate suffering with a passion for discovery. They seek solutions for individuals. Physicians have little patience for worry about offending someone's political vision of equity. Equity, for physicians, means giving all they can to everyone who needs it. Doctors want whatever works for their patients, not what wins elections.

Treating sick people creates massive inequality. Doctors and nurses employ extravagant excess to help the sick, who may only benefit a little. Medicine drives doctors to excess. It means exorbitant expenditure for those in need. This is what patients want and expect. Medicine aims for the opposite of socialized medicine's population-based, utilitarian distribution of care that will benefit the most people.

If you will, medicine is animated by prioritarianism, while socialized medicine is animated by what I call equalitarianism: yet another fundamental tension between medicine and the state. Medicare hijacks medicine's values. Politicians, knowing that voters support medical values — dignity, compassion, service, discovery, and excellence — disguise their vision of equity and control as a call to compassion and fairness.

Medicare as a Means of Redistribution

AS ALREADY STATED, medicine seeks to provide care whereas medicare seeks to distribute and regulate it. Distribution of care, when you hear it from a politician or economist, means distribution of money. They are not talking about doctors and nurses running between beds. They are talking about dollars moving from one person's pocket to someone else's, "from the healthy and wealthy to the sick and poor."[105]

In Canada, tax dollars flow from living and unborn taxpayers to three groups: patients (payment for care), healthcare workers (incomes), and needy provinces (program support). Money flows into patient care through payment to doctors, nurses, and everyone who works in the system; and from wealthy provinces to poor ones via the approximately $34 billion in Canada Health Transfer payments.[106]

Wealth redistribution, not patient care, represents the most important political motivation driving many advocates' support for medicare. And as is often seen in people possessed by an idea, they assume their opponents also care, foremost, about redistribution. They assume the main reason anyone would oppose medicare is that "they oppose having money taken from their pockets for those less fortunate."[107] But perhaps opponents of redistribution-by-stealth are most concerned about means, not ends. We could choose to redistribute by giving people money directly.[108] Concealing redistribution behind medicare is in the best interest of a political vision. Most people I speak to who share a frustration with the dysfunction in socialized medicine are not even aware of the massive role medicare plays in redistribution.[109]

Some economists insist anything other than a single-payer, first-dollar coverage, tax-funded system would "redistribute wealth from the lower- to the higher-income individuals."[110] This makes sense only if one shares the assumption that wealth is not earned; it is a societal resource to be distributed by Wise Men. Once we realize that earned income is not considered earned at all, we can see that — *voila!* — letting people keep more of what they earned is really stealing from the poor.

There are many ways to redistribute wealth without disguising it as patient care. And it is possible to have a huge welfare state without using socialized medicine to build it. The fact that socialized medicine is primarily a redistribution mechanism was concealed from voters at the start and is rarely, if ever, mentioned today. Early advocates of socialized medicine especially went out of their way to focus on messages voters could support. But they launched something designed to achieve entirely different goals.

Private Practice, Public Payment

WHICH BRINGS US back to the debate introduced in the previous chapter casting medicare as a blend of private practice and public payment. Medicare was supposed to offer the dream of state payment for the best that private practice could offer. In fact, many Canadian doctors would insist that, because they own their own clinics, they are not socialized. Socialization means ownership and control, they say. They add that hospitals are run by private boards of directors, and that doctors and hospitals each take out loans, hire employees, purchase equipment, and do all sorts of other things private businesses do.[111] As quoted earlier: "We have almost no public delivery in Canada."[112] Or as another author writes: "Health care in Canada is government-funded but almost exclusively privately provided." Medicare advocates insist doctors are paid with taxes but deliver private care. Doctors do not work for government. As one doctor writes, "The minister of health is not my boss ... I'm not a government employee. If they want me to practice medicine differently, policy makers in the Ministry of Health could entice me to do so by paying a premium for any patient seen after five p.m., or conversely, by cutting the rates for daytime consultation."[113]

Enticing behaviour with premiums and discouraging it "by cutting rates" sounds like an impressive degree of control. Furthermore, there are over seven thousand different fees (in Ontario) for government to tweak — hundreds apply to each specialty — to entice or discourage tiny changes in behaviour. If paying premiums and cutting rates is a way to change physician behaviour, can you think of any other business that attempts this kind of minute behavioural control over employees? Regular businesses can cajole and threaten, but they cannot entice or cut as a way to micro-manage behaviour in the same way a ministry of health can with physicians. Indeed, it is hard to imagine any system that might offer any greater form of micro-management, aside from a supervisor hovering over an employee's every move.

The author goes on to explain how hospitals are fully private as well. Administrators remain "acutely aware of what the government wants from us, but our hospitals are not owned or operated directly by that government ..."[114] What does it mean to be "acutely aware" but not owned and operated? Consider three examples.

The quality of toast in hospitals became a major focus of an election campaign in Manitoba a few years ago.[115] Candidates promised to fix the toast hospitals served to patients, if elected. No one doubted whether they could.

In Nova Scotia, a hospital CEO was trying to stay within budget in a tough labour negotiation. He had been given strict instructions not to run a deficit. Then the phone rang. The premier told the hospital CEO to end negotiations and settle.[116]

Around 2004, I identified our hospital in a very short letter about emergency wait times to the editor of our neighbourhood newspaper. Our ED was small at the time, one of almost two hundred departments in Ontario. The minister of health called our CEO demanding to know what was going on. Did he need to come down and fix the wait times himself?

Any hospital administrator could add further examples. But they would never go on record. No one will publish a study on the rate, extent, or impact of government intervention in hospital management. It would embarrass the minister of health, who could retaliate with anything from appointing a new board to closing the hospital. We will return to this when we discuss hospital funding letters (chapter seven).

When discussing government control, advocates bristle at any mention of "government monopoly," which they insist is the wrong terminology. People who use it, they say, are really just objecting to the fact Canadians cannot buy their way to the front.[117]

True, "monopoly" is not the precise word. Socialized medicine is best understood as a "totality" or a "totalization" of medical services under the rubric of the state.[118] A monopoly is bad for everyone except itself. No one designs a monopoly to improve service and quality. Advocates know this, hence their tendency to bristle. So instead, they remind us it is all just health insurance.[119] No monopoly. Just freedom and equality.

Outside Venezuela, modern socialization no longer means ownership of the means of production. Early socialists pushed for state ownership of those means. They soon found this did not work well and was not necessary. In fact, socialists have not pushed for ownership of the means of production for decades.[120] Heavy regulation of businesses can achieve the same outcome with less hassle. Modern socialists push for state control and use Leviathan to get it.[121] The only time they mention ownership of the means of production is when they use this archaic definition of socialism to prove a particular example is not, in fact, socialism. Thus, based on this definition, Canada does not have socialized medicine, because doctors still own their clinics and do not receive a publicly funded salary.

But ownership is meaningless without control. A private enterprise must have control over labour, wages, and production if it is private in any nontrivial sense. As independent contractors, professionals should control when, where, and how hard they work. They should decide whom to hire, how much to pay them, and the work they do. They should be able to decide to whom, when, and where they will offer their services. Only they should control access to their office, outside someone with a warrant, if they are truly a private enterprise.[122]

Not so in Canada, where the state determines, or exerts major influence over, all the most significant details about how medical clinics operate as well as where, when, and what types of care, testing, and medical and hospital services patients can access. The state dictates who can enter a clinic; whom doctors must see; who must be referred; what kinds of care must be offered; what notes must be taken; what notes must *never* be taken; data to report; and how to report the data. Granted, this applies most to generalist physicians who work in the community. Specialists seem able to decline any non-urgent referral with no reason given. Regardless, the state currently imposes itself on prices, access to care, service contracts, documentation, records management, reporting, technology, resources, education, retraining, and pretty much everything else involved with medical care for both generalists and specialists. We will touch on this again when we focus on regulation (chapter nine).

Socialized medicine forces doctors to be socialized with respect to bills, fees, services, reporting, and much more. It allows doctors to remain part of the broader market economy with respect to leases, staff wages, insurance, clinic upgrades, etc. Normal businesses can make changes to service, fees, and quality based on cost pressures. But in medicare, government determines revenue; it regularly increases costs but cares nothing for the changes in costs borne by the physicians and felt by patients.

A system that maintains private property in name and law, as part of a planned economy, is still a socialist system.[123] Even when we find the purest possible examples of socialism in politics, medicare advocates will point to impurities that undermine the case in question.[124] David Levine, hospital CEO and former civil servant, thinks medical care in Canada is public in the full sense of the word. Calling it private risks prejudice against funding it properly.[125]

Perhaps Canadians cannot tell the difference anymore between a socialized industry and free enterprise. Maybe the state has imposed itself on so much of Canadian industry we have become blind to the distinction between public and private.[126]

The day-to-day experience of practice and care under socialized medicine lies between the two extremes of the state deciding care vs. patients deciding in consultation with their medical team. The balance changes slightly from one election cycle to the next. But for the most part, Canadian medicare is fitted out heavily on the side of a planned economy and continues to sail in that direction.

One final point about private practice and public payment. The only way to make doctors more socialized would be to make them salaried civil servants. Many physicians would love it. The state has taken away most of the benefits of being an independent contractor while leaving doctors with all the responsibilities of running a practice. A salary would offer a pension, benefits, and no responsibility to manage the risks of running an office. However, as Stephen H. Lewis, former leader of the Ontario NDP, once said when asked about putting all doctors on salary, "We could never afford it."[127]

Advocates of socialized medicine may have concealed many things, but one thing they did not conceal was the fact they were calling for "socialized medicine." Most people find this point non-controversial. What the advocates concealed was their mission to take control.

Why Control Medicine?

IN POLICY CIRCLES, planners and politicians speak openly about the movement towards greater control of medicine by the state. If the state pays, then it gets the chance (has the right?) to oversee and control spending. Most people find this as incontrovertible as it was obvious to the original planners.[128] One expert lectured recently that, in order to improve healthcare, we need to figure out "how to develop sophisticated purchasing systems [which] is a more gentle way of saying, 'How do we control the power of providers in health care?' "[129]

Starting in the 1990s, provincial governments pursued their interest in regionalizing care, moving control from the province's ministry of health out into smaller, regional offices. Katherine Fierlbeck noted that decreasing physician influence was one of the implicit goals of regionalization: "A political objective that was rarely articulated but usually implicit was the limitation of the ability of the medical profession directly to influence the way in which health services were provided, both at an individual and at a systemwide level."[130] In Ontario, the Ministry of Health explicitly excluded physicians from holding any positions on the boards of the Local Health Integration Networks.

All governments, regardless of political flavour, "are actively seeking ways of gaining increased control over those elements of professional autonomy ... that contribute to the high cost of medical care."[131] This includes fees, facilities, services, and innovation in delivery of care. "It is apparent that 'the politics of medical care is the politics of cost control.' "[132]

The politics of cost control meshed with a move away from the traditional focus on diagnosis and treatment. "The 1970s had witnessed an ideological shift — from unqualified faith in the value of acute-care services to rediscovery of prevention and health promotion ..."[133] The shift was part of a plan to move away from medical care, even though the public was told that care was the only reason we had medicare in the first place. "These developments crowned social engineering as the leitmotif of health policy-making in Canada and de-emphasized reliance on medical and hospital care in health promotion."[134]

This cannot continue. Not only have their ends diverged, but medicine and medicare face an unsustainable future together. This path damages medicine, but it will not kill it. Medicine will continue to serve individual patients as long as individuals continue to need care. And surely voters will eventually realize what has been concealed from the start, that medicare does not exist primarily to provide care for them.

Chapter Four
Broken Promises

Waiting times under the Medicare system are "real and intentional" ...
Inevitably, where patients have life-threatening conditions, some will die
because of undue delay in awaiting surgery. Access to a waiting list is
not access to health care.
–Chief Justice Beverly McLachlan, Supreme Court of Canada

CRISES DO NOT just happen. Most times, someone causes them. A patient spends thirteen days in a hospital bathroom.[135] A man has his heart surgery cancelled four times.[136] A fifteen-year-old hockey player, crippled in pain, waits ten months for hip surgery.[137] An eighteen-year-old dies after waiting months for a hospital bed.[138] Someone cut hospital beds in Ontario from 33,400 down to 18,500 between 1992 and 2017, while the province grew by 36 percent over the same period.[139] Someone keeps operating rooms closed while patients in Strathroy, Ontario, wait an *average* of 671 days for a knee replacement.[140] Someone makes patients wait, while the surgeons who replace knees go unemployed.[141] Numerous specialists are "closed" to taking any new patients — they fax referral requests back to family doctors stamped "Not Accepting New Referrals."

Whereas Tommy Douglas, in the bad old medical days, got eighteen months of care in a specialty hospital, multiple surgeries, consultations from numerous pediatric specialists, including treatment by an eminent surgeon, and all without any wait times, Canadians now have "free" care for all.

Famous for Waits

CANADA IS WORLD famous for wait times. Medicare struggles to distribute care so that everyone gets exactly what he needs at exactly the right time. It is the Achilles heel of all socialization efforts. In 2018, 1,082,541 patients were waiting for treatment.[142] "Canada's long wait times for medically necessary treatments cost Canadians $2.1 billion—or $1,924 per patient—in lost wages last year," if we only consider regular, daytime working hours.[143] As Chief Justice Beverly McLachlan of the Supreme Court of Canada wrote,[144] "Access to a waiting list is not access to health care."

On average, Canadians wait for necessary care longer than in any other country, except perhaps in the British National Health System. However, Britain allows a parallel private option; Canada does not. So, overall, Canada remains the world leader in achieving long wait times.

And we have become experts at studying them, too. Consider hip replacement surgery. The average wait time in all of Canada, for new hips, is just over three months (105 days, 2018). Three months sounds pretty good, for system planners, payers, and experts. Many patients agree. It takes some time to arrange time off work, find help at home, and juggle other responsibilities. Many people who need new hips are retired, so they have less to lose from waiting, other than pain and disability. But a three-month average wait for hip replacement is not the whole story.

The Canadian Institute for Health Information (CIHI) was founded in 1994 to study medicare. It got serious about publishing wait times[145] in the early 2000s.[146] CIHI's seven hundred employees collect data from over two dozen separate databases from across Canada. Analysts then attempt to create a report on how long patients wait in different regions.

Experts decide how long patients should wait, then CIHI checks to see how Canada performs. Experts decide patients should get their hips replaced within 182 days, exactly half of a year. This means it should take no more than 182 days from the date the procedure was booked to the date of the surgery. CIHI then reports how well each province does at achieving the target.

In 2018, three out of four patients received their new hip within six months across Canada. But only 49 percent met the benchmark in Manitoba, New Brunswick, and Prince Edward Island. The rest of the story? Wait times do not include the time between referral to the surgeon and the surgeon's first visit with the patient. And they do not include the time between the first visit with the surgeon and the time the surgeon finally books the procedure. The reported wait times also miss the months before the family doctor referred the patient to the surgeon in the first place. Most patients discuss their hip pain with their family doctor for months, or even years, before surgery. Patients go for x-rays and try physiotherapy. They eventually go for a CT scan of their hip.

Most patients do not want surgery the first time they mention an achy hip. But many patients are forced to run (or limp through) a gauntlet of repeat x-rays, more physiotherapy, or a trial of medications long after they would have seen the surgeon and had their hip replaced, if they lived in a different country.

Many patients have figured this out. They know it could take two years or longer from family doctor to surgery. So they ask for referral early to get in the queue and hope their pain will still be tolerable by the time they get to the front of the line.

The whole process has become such a game of refer early and often that the state, in many areas, has created central intake systems for joint replacement assessment. Approved teams with specially trained physiotherapists will see, sort, and identify only those patients who really need surgery; they determine access, not diagnosis. When patients ask their family doctor whether the surgeon they have been referred to is any good, he will have no idea. Patients just get assigned to the surgeon with the shortest wait-list.

Lawyer and healthcare expert Colleen Flood is a big supporter of socialized medicine. However, even she notes concerns remain about the "timeliness in delivery of care, inflexibility, and bureaucratization" often found with public and central management of care.[147] The cost of waiting is borne by the individual, not the state.[148] Government is simply not responsive to patient concerns. For many things, such as hip surgery, patients wait because government restricts operating room time. "For [other] medical services, particularly house calls and emergency care, the quantity demanded at the going price is greater than the quantity supplied."[149]

The Fraser Institute, an economic think tank, has tracked wait times in Canada since 1993. At the start, Canadians waited on average 9.3 weeks to see a specialist. As of 2018, they waited almost 20 weeks.

This raises a pernicious point about averages. Average wait times make administrators feel good. Average, for bureaucrats, means 50 percent waited a much shorter time than the average. But average for patients means something different. Average harms patients who fall on the long tail of the curve, just like the statistician who drowned walking across a river with an average depth of only 1 inch.

Just Stories …

FOR MOST Canadians, stories mean something. Patient stories about long waits or terrible outcomes indicate something is wrong. Stories mean almost nothing to academics. For them, they are anecdotal by definition, distractions at best.

The media also get tired of stories about waiting. They publish only a fraction of the content they could. Stories about patient suffering in socialized medicine have become like snowfalls in January. Snow in September makes the news, but not in January, unless something unusual accompanies; consider the impressive headline, for example, "When Toronto declared war on snow and called in the army."[150]

Stories about dysfunction grow too numerous to capture. Even a brief scan focused on wait times and overcrowding turns up a long list.

Stressed emergency departments (EDs) are unable to deliver the best care.[151] One patient reported they felt they were in a Third World country while visiting the ED at Christmastime.[152] One Brampton woman, bleeding internally and "screaming in pain," spent five days in a hospital hallway.[153] The City of Brampton even declared a state of emergency due to hospital overcrowding, in early 2020, the week before COVID-19 hit the news.[154]

A patient waited sixteen months for cardiac ablation for an irregular heartbeat, ended up in the ED where they waited eleven hours for cardioversion, which then resulted in a major stroke due to the lengthy wait.[155] One elderly patient had to wait sixty hours in a Winnipeg ED for a hospital bed.[156] One doctor in Fredericton called it cruelty and not good medicine to leave patients huddled in corners of the ED.[157]

The number of level zero events (no ambulances available because they are all full and waiting to offload at the hospital) continues to rise in Ottawa hospitals.[158] Paramedics report a 7.5-hour off-load delay with no one free to transport patients.[159] A London hospital closes 49 beds to deal with budget deficits.[160] New Brunswick loses its only pediatric ophthalmologist in the whole province.[161] Wait-lists for surgery in BC grow larger than the population of some cities.[162]

One woman's video plea for help went viral on social media after she waited two years for a cancer diagnosis in Nova Scotia.[163] Andre Picard, the health journalist mentioned earlier, started a hashtag on Twitter called #CanadaWaits. Readers can scroll through hundreds of tweets about real patient stories that never get reported: for example, a two-year wait for a knee MRI.[164] CBC News reported an eight-year wait for bariatric surgery in Nova Scotia.[165]

A study from the East Coast reported thirty-nine patients died while waiting for GI consultations, with the average time from referral to death being 348 days.[166] One woman finally headed to court after waiting four years for hip surgery in New Brunswick.[167] That same year, CIHI reported that Canadians were indeed waiting longer for hip and knee replacements as well as cataract surgery:[168] 30 percent of patients did not receive their surgeries within benchmark wait times.[169]

In Newfoundland and Labrador, patients face long waits for genetics, ophthalmology, rheumatology, with one patient still waiting two years to see a back specialist after already having waited two years in pain.[170] The headlines go on and on:

Daily Bed Census May Not Capture Full Extent
of Hallway Health Care –*CBC News* [171]

Tis the Season for Hospital Overcrowding —
but the Flu Isn't to Blame –*Globe and Mail*[172]

Ottawa Woman with MS Back Home Today After PSW Shortage
Keeps Her in Hospital for More Than a Year –*CTV News*[173]

A few years ago, I spoke to a senior health reporter at one of Canada's largest newspapers. I reported how patients at our local hospital who were waiting for long-term care were being housed in the auditorium and gymnasium, for over a year. Giant rooms filled with elderly patients, many in various stages of dementia and serious decay. Just curtains around each stretcher. No bathroom. The reporter said the story was interesting but needed a new angle. S/he would need to get inside the hospital and interview someone on a stretcher. Get a personal angle. Tell a story. Then, maybe his/her editor would agree to publish.

How Much Do Patients Really Suffer?

WAITING DOES NOT kill most patients. So Dr. Michael Rachlis, writer and public health researcher, asks, "How much do patients really suffer because of these delays?"[174] While Rachlis admits those waiting for hip and knee replacement "experience considerable pain and disability," it "doesn't affect their vital status to wait an extra few months." In other words, pain is a nuisance, but you are not going to die from it. However, Rachlis acknowledges waiting for heart surgery is bad and might even shorten one's life. For heart bypass surgery, CIHI reported that 90 percent of patients received bypass within 55 days, with an average time to bypass of 6 days, in 2019 (no benchmark for bypass surgery).[175] Rachlis continues: "Despite the talk about droves of deaths on heart-surgery waiting lists, only one in two hundred Ontario heart-surgery waiting list patients dies before having surgery" (0.5 percent). Then he adds that the death rate on the wait-list is actually lower than for those who are not waiting for surgery. Rachlis discusses "slow-growing cancers like breast, colon, and prostate." He admits that each day waiting adds risk but says "a few weeks' wait has negligible risk."[176]

It is one thing to risk your own life. Maybe a 0.5 percent risk of death over two months means nothing to you. It is something quite different to make the decision for others, to tell them they should not worry, and to give them no way out if they disagree with you. The arrogance of telling patients how long they should tolerate even a small lethal risk is matched only by the delusion that patients get care if they *really* need it. Denis Furlong, former provincial minister of health in New Brunswick and a rural family doctor for thirty years, naively or misleadingly says, "In a social health care system, those who can wait do wait and those who cannot wait do not wait."[177] Ditto two professors from Ottawa who say, "Canadians do not wait for care that is required immediately."[178] Stalwart defenders of this subterfuge of course never define "*really* needs" except, perhaps, to refer to times when a doctor gets *really* worried about a patient. Really worried *patients* do not matter.

> The good thing about our wait-times problem is that it isn't a prob-
> lem when needs are critical. In my experience as a Canadian fam-
> ily doctor, in both rural communities and big cities, if I pick up
> the phone to get something for a patient who really needs it, the
> system nearly always moves. If it's an emergency or highly urgent,
> my patient is not going to wait. Sometimes she may need me to ad-
> vocate and navigate the system for her, which is what family physi-
> cians are supposed to do. But in those critical moments, Canadians
> get the care they need, and the care they get is usually very good.[179]

I happened to read this when our local emergency department had 41 admitted patients filling all the available stretcher locations, including all the empty wall spaces where we could park additional stretchers. "Admitted" means patients need care inside the hospital. Technically, our ED only has 18 official stretchers (or "rooms") to see patients, so we were holding 23 extra admitted patients on top of all the admitted patients filling every available room. Our local ED cares for over 340 new patients each day and admits well over 40 of them into a hospital ward. The 41 admitted patients, who had no bed to go to inside the hospital, were not getting the care they needed. Doctors had already tried to "pick up the phone to get something for [their] patient who really needs it." They got a bed in a hallway. Furthermore, all the new emergencies that day were not getting care either. Commenting that Canadians get care when they *really* need it is incorrigible nonsense.

Hundreds of articles demonstrate the damage done to patients with waiting for definitive care.[180] "Care" in an emergency department hallway is still considered waiting. This waiting causes increased morbidity and mortality; patients suffer and die. Even one hour of waiting for proper acute care causes a measurable decrease in the likelihood of an elderly person going home to live independently. And, no, doctors in Canada no longer can just pick up the phone and get care. Even for "highly urgent" emergencies, such as intracranial hemorrhage, I have waited all night to transfer patients for "immediate" neurosurgery and have even had to medivac them to Buffalo, New York, for surgery.

T.R. Reid travelled the world exploring health systems. He used his "bum shoulder" as a presenting complaint in each country. He wrote rosy descriptions about how Canadians access care, which we will address later. However, when it comes to waiting, he admits that "Canada was the only country on my global quest where the waiting list was so long that I never had a chance even to meet an orthopedist or physical therapist."[181] Reid writes that Canadians do not mind waiting, as long as everyone waits the same.[182]

Thousands die from waiting each year in Canada. The Fraser Institute studied the rate of death due to waiting in Canada between 1993 and 2009. In their sample, data for female patients showed the strongest association between death and wait times. The study's authors estimated that "increases in wait times for medically necessary elective treatment may be associated with 44,273 additional female deaths" during the sixteen-year study period. They noted that many studies have established the association between waiting for care and death in other countries, but it had not been assessed in Canada. They estimated that "between 25,456 and 63,090 (with a middle value of 44,273) additional deaths among females" occurred due to waiting. If we use the middle figure, 2,767 female patients died each year due to waiting. By comparison, almost 2,911 people died in the Twin Tower bombing in 9/11.[183] If we could capture the total number of avoidable deaths of all female and male patients, it would approach, if not exceed, 100,000 patients over sixteen years: the size of a small city.[184]

The Fraser study seems outrageous. How could the authors identify, with certainty, who was going to be saved with earlier treatment? Maybe most of those women were bound to die even if they all got treatment within hours? Who determines when the clock really starts — is it when the patient notes symptoms, when they get referred, or when they get booked for surgery?

While important, these questions miss the point. Waiting can cause serious harm. No one argues that when their loved ones are waiting for treatment. And Canada has world-famous wait times for care. No one argues that either. We should be asking what a patient on the wait-list wants. No doubt this would invite attack as a crass appeal to "consumer sovereignty." And Rachlis would say waiting a few weeks "has negligible risk." But this is not about sovereignty or risk; it is about dignity. It is about understanding what it is like for the patient who is forced to wait.

Pontification about sovereignty and risk evaporates when experts get sick. They demand the best and expect it immediately. One such person attended our emergency department after hurting his/her foot. The emergency doctor suggested a plain x-ray at most. The expert demanded a CT and got it.[185] Some limbs are more equal than others.

Blaming Doctors for Waits

AFTER EXPLAINING waits as a "negligible risk" and denying that waits exist "when needs are critical," the experts blame waits on doctors.

In British Columbia, seven plaintiffs and a private surgical clinic have sued the BC government under the Charter of Rights and Freedoms.[186] The patient plaintiffs argue they had all suffered harm. One teenager had waited twenty-seven months for spine surgery and was left paralyzed. The lawyers for the province of British Columbia argued that the patients' "pain or suffering was not caused by [the state healthcare monopoly], but by decisions made by, and actions taken or not taken by, their treating physicians."[187]

The Crown argued that, if the "treating physicians, or some of them, had exercised their professional judgement appropriately, and taken advantage of options that are and were available to them within the public health care system, the unnecessary or unreasonable pain and suffering of which the Patient Plaintiffs complain could have been treated appropriately in the public system."

A piece in the *New York Times* reinforced the same narrative.[188] The writer said we cannot blame the system. Canadian doctors have a "high degree of autonomy" and do not support efforts to decrease waits and often block those who can. Other authors have even accused doctors of causing artificial waits as a way to blackmail the government to increase funding.[189]

Socialized medicine cannot continue when government fights to defend long wait times or blames wait times on doctors. Patients did not wait in the 1970s. Doctors never had to seek approval from hospital bed allocating departments before accepting a patient transfer from another hospital in the 1980s or throughout the early 1990s. When a patient needed care, there always was an open bed. The more that government has exerted control in an attempt to cut costs, the longer wait times have grown.

Access Granted … When It Makes Politicians Look Good

DESPITE WORLD-FAMOUS waiting, Canada offers great access for a few regular patients. While hospitals are filled with hallway patients and stuffed to over 100 percent capacity, the maternity wards always have room. No politician could survive if a mother in labour arrived at a hospital to find no beds available. It would be intolerable. Canadians would be outraged. Furthermore, moms with babies represent the most powerful voting bloc. No politician can keep her job by going to war with mothers carrying infants. So every hospital maintains maternity wards at close to 80 percent capacity (or less) — the ideal for flow. If a ward gets even slightly crowded, administrators decant labour and delivery first.

Canada also offers reasonable access to acute, life-threatening care. If you are in a serious car crash near a major city in Canada, you stand a good chance of being scooped up by an air ambulance and whisked into a trauma centre, the standard of care in developed countries. Your outcomes will (without surprise) match those of the other OECD countries and in some cases offer better results. Recovery, however, bumps you back onto the "elective" or non-urgent care lists with all the attendant wait times. But at least you survived.

The same thing applies to tertiary care. If you need an organ transplant or cancer therapy, once you finally get to the front of the queue and if you have not suffered irreversible harm in the process, survival rates are almost as good as those in the US.[190] Where clear standards exist, for example, cancer treatment for a particular cancer, Canada cannot avoid providing the standard of care. But most patient concerns defy standardization. So medicare makes patients endure whatever they will tolerate short of causing political turmoil.

The most vulnerable patients, those suffering from chronic or age-related conditions, wait longest and endure the worst conditions. More than a thousand patients get treated in hallways each day in Ontario, often for days at a time: no rest, no toilet, no privacy. Wait times for a long-term care bed run over 1 year and more than 2.5 years in some areas. Patients who are too sick to wait at home wait in an acute care hospital bed: we call them Alternative Level of Care (ALC) patients. In Ontario, hospitals have up to 30 percent of their acute care beds filled with ALC patients at any time. As mentioned earlier, our local hospital filled the auditorium and gymnasium with ALC patients separated by portable curtains. After several years of waiting for relief, we gave up and renovated the auditorium into a new patient-care ward.

The old and chronically sick do not vote. Their families complain but also do not want to become known as a problem family. They do not want to lose the care they have. In many cases they act with gratitude for the little bit of service they get. Everyone knows someone who got even less.

Hospital Beds vs. Bureaucrats

GOVERNMENT SPENDING is a zero-sum game. If government spends more in one place, it must spend less somewhere else, or raise taxes. Between 2003 and 2018 in Ontario, the number of health-related civil servants increased from 6,000 to 13,000.[191] So it should not surprise us that Ontario closed 17,000 hospital beds between 1990 and 2013.[192] There could be dozens of good reasons to close beds. Canada has been closing them since the mid-1970s, after the hospital building boom created a glut. But cuts to beds have come when there are already too few beds in the country.

In Ontario, there are 1.4 acute hospital beds per 1000 people, or half the average for other OECD countries.[193] Health consultant and administrator Matthew Lister has shared research showing there are 32,000 healthcare bureaucrats in Canada.[194] That equals 0.9 healthcare bureaucrats per 1000 population. For comparison: Sweden has 0.4 health bureaucrats per 1000 population; Australia has 0.255; Japan has 0.23; and Germany has only 0.06. Looking at it differently, Japan has 30,000 health-care bureaucrats for 130 million people. Canada has 32,000 bureaucrats for 35 million. Having a robust civil service to run healthcare, in a zero-sum game, impacts patient care.[195]

Steve Paikin of TVO's *The Agenda* asked whether too much of the $50 billion for healthcare went to bureaucracy and not enough to healthcare in Ontario.[196] Many others have raised similar concerns.[197] Dr. Donald Savoie, professor of public administration at University of Moncton, offered an extensive and in-depth review of the federal government that points to reasons why bureaucracy might also grow at the provincial level. Most healthcare civil servants work at the provincial level. Even so, Savoie's comments on bureaucracy remain germane. "Bureaucracy has an inherent tendency to expand, even when there is no good reason to do so."[198] Government has no trouble building new bureaucracies, but it cannot close the old ones.[199] Of approximately 210,000 federal employees, only 75 lose their jobs each year for "incompetence or incapacity."[200] "Governments per-sist in calculating the immeasurable, happily keeping many public servants turning cranks not attached to anything."[201] Civil servants are not bad people; they are good people caught in a bad system. This leads into a much larger discussion on the theory of government failure, which we will tackle later (chapter eleven).

A zero-sum game means a fixed budget to spend on care each year. We cannot care for more patients than the budget allows. That would cost more. As Quebec Health Minister, Gaetan Barrette, said in 2016: "Hospitals have fixed budgets and must not run over them...You can't just keep on accepting patients and treating them once the money has run out. It won't be tolerated."[202]

Rationing

RATIONING REMAINS a foreign term in Canada. The public expects necessary medical care without limit, free at the point of delivery. People expect *care regardless of ability to pay*. Almost no one in Canada writes white papers on the best way to ration care. We pretend it does not exist. No politician dares admit that *care regardless of ability to pay* is actually *all the care government can afford to offer*. Politicians twist their words (and often their faces) to avoid letting the r-word breach their lips. They continually promise to provide all the care patients need. Voters have heard it for five decades.

We come close to honesty about rationing when we call family physicians gatekeepers.[203] Other countries allow direct access to specialty care. Canadians do not seem to mind gatekeeping.[204] Most people see family doctors as gate openers, not keepers. Gatekeeping only works if doctors feel free to say no, without fear of complaint or reprisal. But even so, persistent patients always get through the gate. Some use anger. Others bring gifts. Like paupers, they work to win favour and access to a rationed system.

Rationing calls into question whether the original promise of medicare was true. Canada must ration care; not just here and there but every day and all the time. If not, medicare will collapse. Other countries ration by price. Canada rations by making people wait, by placing arbitrary limits on everything: beds, nurses, doctors, and technology. Many people talk about how Canada rations with wait times, but almost no one in authority admits it. So "rationing with wait times" becomes a complaint, not a real policy problem to fix.[205]

Even doctors and nurses do not interpret wait times as rationing. People working inside the system think wait times exist due to a shortage of nurses, a patient surge, or some other unexpected event that has led to their not being able to access care. Rationing, for the most part, goes unacknowledged and thus goes unseen.

Britain's National Health Service faced the same issue in the early 1960s. Enoch Powell, minister of health for the NHS at the time, said:

> The public are encouraged to believe that rationing in medical care was banished by the National Health Service, and that the very idea of rationing being applied to medical care is immoral and repugnant. Consequently when they, and the medical profession too, come face to face in practice with the various forms of rationing to which the National Health Service must resort, the usual result is bewilderment, frustration and irritation.[206]

Planners do not like to discuss rationing. It is more ruthless, in many ways, than what socialized medicine came to replace.[207] It undermines the moral vision of socialized medicine. There is no one to beg from, just a faceless bureaucracy. Advocates justify rationing on the ground that universal care must have limits. In other words, the *end* of universal care justifies the *means* of rationing. In a collectivist ethic, the end justifies the means, which, for an individual, is the denial of all morals.[208]

Economists teach us that free products and services create infinite demand. More accurately, demand for a free service will increase consumption to a point at which the marginal benefit approaches zero. With even a tiny benefit, patients will continue to consume if the service is free.

Government tries to limit supply to control costs. Notice, the supply is patient care, and the cost is patient demand for care. Demand for care creates a cost for government. Patients demand care. Patients create costs. In a socialized system, patients are seen as costs for governments.[209] This is the opposite of what should happen.

The idea that patients are costs reverberates right down to the front lines of care. Canada is one of the only countries that still funds its hospitals with block funding. Hospitals work to stretch out a fixed budget for a full year. Each patient represents a cost to the hospital. The hospital would be much better off, financially, if patients stayed away. Hospitals must limit care. They close operating rooms over holidays and for extended March breaks. They turn off MRI machines after business hours. They lay off staff. How can patients expect great service if the place where they seek care sees them as a cost, something it would be better off without?

Governments cringe at accusations of rationing. So they add other non-payment costs to the free things they offer to discourage demand. They make people fill out forms or force doctors to look up limited use codes. Or experts design behavioural hoops patients must leap through to qualify for a free service, for example, quitting smoking before surgery. While quitting smoking is always a good idea and it can make the difference between success and failure at surgery, too often we need to wonder whether such behavioural changes are set up as just one more hurdle to make services more difficult to access. We demand ideal pre-surgical conditions, which limits demand with less obvious rationing.

When government rations care by cutting physicians' fees, it leads physicians to shorten visits. Clinics post signs: "One problem per visit."[210] This frustrates patients, and physicians take the brunt of it. Patients never realize that cutting funding for any service leads either to lower quantity or quality of the service in question.

Fixed budgets make rationing inevitable. But governments never acknowledge this is an essential feature of socialized medicine. This renders rationing invisible. Is it any wonder an inevitable, unacknowledged, and unseen process often fails?[211]

Rationing occasionally makes the news in different words. Canadians hear about "denied funding." This implies that a particular bureaucracy or civil servant simply refused to pay for care. For example, a Grimsby teen had endured a life of pain while the provincial health insurance plan denied funding for treatment of a rare syndrome.[212] A family in Timmins had to crowd-fund support for care.[213] A government website lists court cases where government denied coverage for patients.[214]

Media often report shortages of medications, cancer drugs, and even flu shots.[215] These are business as usual in socialized medicine. They rarely register as part of an intentional push by government to ration care.

Some rationing cannot be hidden. Canada has unemployed medical specialists plus world-famous long wait times.[216] This is truly maddening: for the patients waiting for the care the unemployed specialists could provide, and for the frustrated referring physicians, who are trying to get care for their patients. Kelly Grant, health reporter with the *Globe and Mail*, has written that "neurosurgeons, radiation oncologists and orthopedic surgeons [are] the likeliest to be unemployed." They cannot work without access to hospital beds and operating rooms.[217]

As we noted earlier, 30 percent of patients do not get their hip surgery within the generous six-month benchmark. Dr. Glazebrook, the incoming president of the Canadian Orthopaedic Association (COA) in 2019, said, "We have unemployed orthopedic surgeons who are dying to meet this need" but "the government can't afford it."[218] Britain does not hide rationing anymore. People talk and write about it regularly.[219] Debate has ended about whether the UK should ration. Now Brits wrestle about who gets to decide and what process should be used.[220]

Healthcare Finance Before Patient Interests

MANY DOCTORS worry that medicare will run out of money. Conscientious health providers age prematurely trying to balance patient interests and healthcare sustainability.[221] As the point of access for many patients, emergency and community physicians feel particularly pressured to manage system costs and make up for inefficiencies elsewhere, by putting costs before patient interests. Those who congratulate parsimony, and push to choose wisely, disappear when a doctor gets sued for not ordering enough tests, for not providing enough care, or for making patients wait.[222] After a medical disaster, doctors get no official support to explain how overcrowding created an environment for bad outcomes.

Clinicians experience heart-wrenching cases: mothers dying shortly after childbirth, toddlers who choke to death, kids clipped in traffic walking to school. Sick patients create bad outcomes. Sick patients require split-second decisions that are naked to dissection from the armchair of retrospect.

Emergency departments get "helped" with hours of meetings and external reviews from one bad outcome, but no one wants to discuss overcrowding and waits that often play *the major role* in catastrophes. Rationing causes the problem, but once the problem has occurred, no one is there to discuss it. If planners want decreased emergency department use, they need to offer something that attracts patients to seek care elsewhere. Clinicians should not bear the responsibility of rationing care for the whole system.[223]

We should follow the advice of one physician educator who said, "So many times I've given this speech to medical students and residents when they present a patient who needs a test, which they want to deny the patient because that's what they've been taught to do." Once disaster happens, the advocates of parsimony put on "retro-spectroscopes and argue that in *this* case ... the test of course was necessary. But regardless of [the advocates of parsimony], our most important, and only, duty is to the patients ... We never signed up to compromise the interests of our patient with the interests of politicians, taxpayers, or hospitals — or indeed, our own interests."[224]

Given the rate of advance and growth in medical technology and treatment options, the standard of care has outgrown any reasonable attempt by any state, anywhere in the world, to promise all citizens medically necessary *care regardless of ability to pay*. It simply cannot be done as originally promised. Welfare states attempt to "allocate" scarce resources in equitable ways.[225] "Perhaps instead of buying the latest medical equipment we should insist on better driver training, add fibre to foods or invest more in job training."[226]

Rationing presupposes that someone other than the patient can, and must, define medical need.[227] But the people who make the decisions about spending (allocation) do not know what patients need. And those who provide the care do not know how much it costs. The traditional supply and demand equation becomes supply and need, with ignorance on both sides of the equation.[228]

Canada Has Changed, Medicare Not So Much

IN 1965, when medicare began, Canada looked more like a college crowd. The average age was 25. Only 7 percent of Canadians qualified for an old age pension. Being poor meant wearing hand-me-downs, skipping meals, and using sneakers long after toes poked through ragged holes. Almost 60 percent of those young, healthy, and often poor Canadians trusted government leadership, in 1968.[229] Doctors gave patients morphine and oxygen for a heart attack and put them to bed. Citizens were more often passive, obedient recipients — pawns, essentially — of whatever help the government offered.[230]

The late 1960s brought revolt against personal responsibility, Victorian morality, and public institutions. The hyper-individualism of the nineteenth century had created an overemphasis on the ability of individuals to make decisions and control their environment. Matched with Victorian moral standards, it created a world that tied social outcomes to morality. Poverty meant you were slothful or intemperate. Sickness showed you did not take care of yourself. This led to "means testing" to identify the "deserving poor" who qualified for welfare programs. It amounted to a system of Victorian inquisitions. Society pushed back. People rejected the social judgment that came with personal responsibility and accountability. The 1960s rejected moralizing and doubled down on individualism. Young people embraced individualism and ignored demands on personal behaviour. Means testing was out. Universal, first-dollar coverage was in. Everyone qualified for every social good regardless of behaviour. You had rights.

This gave us "free" medicare. It fit the 60s zeitgeist — an overcorrection to moralistic, nineteenth-century hyper-individualism. Patients became passive victims of a social environment. The poor became "at risk" for certain behaviours, never the ones who chose to act those ways.

They "experience" crime and illegitimacy, they do not commit them.[231] Poor health had little to do with individual responsibility.

Today, the average Canadian is in their 40s.[232] Over 15 percent of voters can get senior discounts. Many of the people considered to be poor have cell phones, microwaves, two or more TVs, education, and a car in the driveway. Today, only 28 percent of voters trust government to lead. Politicians are the least trusted professionals in repeated polling.[233] Canada got old, rich, and skeptical of government.

Medicine changed also. Today, a heart attack feels almost as routine as delivering a baby, as long as the resources and technology are in place.[234] A patient gets crushing chest pain. Paramedics send an electronic copy of the cardiogram to the hospital and alert the heart team that someone's coming in with signs of an acute MI. Minutes after the paramedics scoop up the patient, cardiologists inflate a tiny balloon to open blocked arteries.[235] They leave a drug-eluting stent in place like a scaffold to prop the artery open. Patients go home a few days later. They start an exercise program: cardiac rehab. No more bed rest; it could kill them.

In 1960, medicine offered very little, and most Canadians did not need what medicine offered. We were too young and healthy. Today, medicine offers all kinds of miracles, and many more people need them. Patients are more educated; they know what they want and how to get it.[236] Despite this, medicare remains the same. It promises everything that offers the slightest benefit for health, the slimmest hope for survival, and every popular fad in between.

First-dollar coverage means patients do not pay anything, ever, for medically necessary services from doctors and hospitals. They never need to consider cost. Doctors never need think about a balance between financial costs and medical benefits. There is no balance. All that matters for doctors and patients is that patients get every possible medical service that might remotely help them.

It should not surprise that first-dollar coverage increases medical services. If everything is "free," people will try to get as much as possible. Industry scrambles to invent wonderful new drugs and treatments, no matter how slim their benefits over older medicine. And taxpayers foot the bill.

Chapter Five
Privileged Patients

*Liberties appear when liberty is lacking: they are the special privileges and exemptions
that groups and individuals may acquire while the rest are more or less unfree.*
–Friedrich Hayek

*In a country where the sole employer is the State, opposition means death
by slow starvation.*
–Leon Trotsky

EVERY SOCIALIST effort in history soon enough creates a *de facto* class system. Soviet leaders shuttle between drab Moscow offices and lavish country *dachas*. Members at the top of the Chinese Communist Party send their children to prestigious universities in the West. The dictator Kim Jung-un maintains his sleek proportions on a non-North Korean diet. And privileged patients skip to the front of the line in Canadian medicare.

The list of people with privileged access includes those with connections, celebrities, hospital donors, injured workers, and politicians. "Three or four times a week, sometimes, I would arrange preferred access to medical care," Dr. Arnold Aberman, former dean of the University of Toronto medical school, said in an interview. "I wasn't proud of it, to tell you the truth, because by helping someone I knew, I was hurting someone I didn't know. It's a zero-sum game."

Who asks for special access? Most people imagine it is wealthy businesspeople who are out to undermine the system. Not so. "Many of those who asked Dr. Aberman to pull strings were staunch advocates of preserving medicare as we know it."[237] Danielle Martin writes:

> Some people occasionally leverage social networks to get faster and "better" care ... I sometimes see this in my practice, when patients call or email me to say that they've arranged an appointment for themselves next week with a specialist who's a friend of a friend (and who has a six-month waiting list). Would I mind faxing over a referral?
>
> I do mind, of course, because it feels so unfair when that person's problem isn't urgent, but yes, I've done it anyway, when I didn't know how else to preserve my relationship with my patient. Most of us know someone who was able to get quick access to something they didn't need urgently, because their aunt is a secretary in the hospital or they have a friend who's a surgeon.[238]

This is not new. In 1998, a study of almost 800 physicians and hospital executives found over 80 percent of physicians and over 50 percent of hospital executives "had been personally involved with managing a patient who had received preferential access on the basis of factors other than medical need."[239]

This led the Ontario government to pass a bill, The Commitment to the Future of Medicare Act, 2004, designed to outlaw queue jumping.[240] The act "also prohibits patients from paying an amount or some other benefit in order to receive preferred access to insured services." The act makes it mandatory to report queue-jumping. "Failure to report can result in a fine as set out in the Act." But no one has been fined. Preferred access for insured services comes from relationships, popularity, or political influence, not cash.

Voters expect to see privilege at work in society. Plane crashes or skiing accidents that involve public figures always involve more spending than they might have otherwise.[241] But voters have been promised privilege does not (will not!) exist inside medicare.

Mark Cuban, television star and owner of the Dallas Mavericks basketball team, shared his story about passing his kidney stone in a crowded Toronto emergency department. Someone recognized Cuban and bumped him to the front of the queue. He got a bed, a room, and prompt treatment for his concern, because he was famous. Everyone else waited. This then led Cuban into a Twitter battle about special access for wealthy donors to hospital foundations: "When wealthy patients donate to hospitals, they don't just mail a check. They meet the top folks at the Hospital and get their [phone numbers]. They call ahead. They get their standard issue gown sooner and with more attention."[242]

Foundations at large hospitals in Toronto, Vancouver, and Montreal have larger fundraising budgets than the total operating cost for hospitals in smaller centres. Big donors let their foundation know whenever they themselves or one of their relatives goes to the hospital. Staff members at the foundation call administrative leaders in whatever department the donor needs care.

As Medical Program Director for a large emergency department, I answered calls regularly from administrators about wealthy donors or their family members. The correct response was to call the charge nurse and make certain Mrs. Smith had been put into a room and has been seen by the doctor on duty.

Defenders of medicare jumped to dismiss Cuban's tweets as just stories and rumours — anecdotes at best — that prove nothing.[243] Hospital executives lined up to deny that anything like this ever happens at their hospital. Any administrator working inside the system speaking up to confirm Cuban's story would have been looking for work outside the system.[244]

Hospitals need happy donors. On the one hand, socialized medicine could never function without massive donations from generous donors. Therefore, donors do not wait in the waiting room, at least if you ever hope to get another donation from them. On the other, generous donors also undermine the central slogan of equal access regardless of need.

Injured workers do not wait for care either. Waiting workers cost the Ontario government so much money it built a private, special, rapid-access path that is only available to injured workers. It saves the government money. While everyone else waits ten months to see an orthopedic surgeon for knee pain, disabled workers see a surgeon in ten days.[245] If a worker injures her right knee playing soccer, she waits ten months. If she injures her left knee at work, she waits ten days. In addition to lost wages, patients bear major, unfunded, and often hidden costs associated with medical care (pharmaceuticals, appliances, dressings, home modifications, travel). Waiting for care costs patients themselves over $5.2 billion each year.[246]

Finally, politicians do not wait for care. Prime Minister Jean Chretien,[247] Premier Danny Williams, Belinda Stronach, Jack Layton, Quebec premier Robert Bourassa and many others have opted for care outside the Canadian system.[159] Chretien even used the PM's private jet on separate visits for himself and his daughter to the Mayo clinic south of the border.[248] When powerful decision makers can opt out when they need care, what motivation remains for them to improve the system for the rest of us? Healthcare is known as the third rail of politics: touch it at your peril. Dr. Brian Day, former president of the Canadian Medical Association, writes:

> Politicians and trade union leaders often bypass wait lists, turning to the private sector when they or their families need care. They enjoy private insurance for themselves [for non-medically necessary care], which covers ambulances, prescription drugs, prosthetic limbs, braces, dentistry and physiotherapy. Thirty percent of Canadians lack this insurance and have inferior coverage. In Canada the lowest socioeconomic groups suffer from the poorest access and have the worst outcomes. An Italian health law expert recently characterized Canada as being hostile to the poor and underprivileged, describing our Medicare as "tailor made for very rich people who can get medical care abroad."[249]

Given all this, Canadians routinely leave Canada for care. As mentioned earlier, Statistics Canada keeps data regarding Canadians' travels abroad for "medical or health reasons." It shows that hundreds of thousands seek care[250] in other countries. Canadians have been leaving their country for care for over thirty years. Whole surgical centres, such as North American Specialty Hospital,[251] advertise outside care.[252] The Cayman Islands, Turks and Caicos, Mexico, and the United States offer attractive locations to receive care; "Statistics Canada estimates Canadians spent $1.9 million per day on health-care trips to other countries in 2017. That's up from $1.2 million per day in 2013."[253]

Canadians looking for care outside Canada can buy Janet Barrister's book *Medical Tourism—Surgery for Sale! How to Have Surgery Abroad Without It Costing Your Life*, published in 2016.[254] Back in 1995, when asked about patients on wait-lists in BC seeking treatment in the USA, that province's associate deputy minister of health is reported to have said, "If we could stop them at the border, we would."[255] Medical tourism is embarrassing for socialized medicine; it would not exist if medicare worked as promised.

Responding to decades of reports about desperate Canadians travelling abroad for care, Bob Evans, mentioned earlier, worked as senior writer on a study in 2002 to find out, once and for all, whether any of these allegations were true. The ardent and outspoken defender of socialized medicine wrote that Canadians travelling south for care were just "Phantoms in the Snow."[256] Advocates often quote Evans's study, the only one of its kind. As such, we need to spend a moment on it. Funded by the Canadian Institutes of Health Research (formerly the Medical Research Council of Canada), the authors contacted 136 facilities around Buffalo, NY, Detroit, MI, and Seattle, WA. They also looked at hospital discharges in the three states and determined that 80 percent of the Canadians who visited did so for emergency or urgent care. They also surveyed the twenty "best" hospitals in America, and they reviewed the National Population Health Survey data from Canada.

The Evans team concluded that, despite all the stories, actual Canadians travelling south for care are just "phantoms." They add the spectre of "powerful interests," which probably/allegedly/might support (fund) the opposing viewpoint. Never mind that Evans was funded by the Canadian government. The article concludes that leaving Canada for care is just another healthcare zombie — an idea that infects the mind and refuses to die no matter how hard you try to kill it.[257]

Name-calling proves nothing and works both ways. We expect it from adolescents, not academics. The US has over 7,200 acute care hospitals,[258] 10,680 diagnostic facilities,[259] and over a million physicians.[260] The Phantoms study seems rather small by comparison. Is it reasonable to rely on one limited survey to nullify all the other reports by dedicated research teams about Canadians leaving Canada?

Payment Without Money

SOCIALIZED MEDICINE cannot eliminate human nature. Just because patients do not exchange money in the clinic for medically necessary care does not mean there is no exchange and no market for care. Relationship exists on the possibility of voluntary exchange. Without reciprocity, there is no relationship. This is a feature of all human interaction, not unique to any service or profession. I do something for you. You do something for me in return. Money simplifies the process. Without exchange, interactions become servitude or slavery. People feel entitled to a service that has been paid for already. People served by a slave feel no need to pay the slave, and the slave feels no need to offer extra effort beyond a minimum to avoid punishment. Servitude and slavery lead to the lowest common denominator of exchange. We think we are getting a bargain, but we get far less than if we actually paid for the service in the first place.

The tragedy lies in the fact most Canadians have no idea what they are missing. They believe medicare is better than all the options. Some suspect they might be the victim of rationing. They sit with skeptical expressions when told their knee pain does not warrant another MRI scan. They wonder whether their gatekeeper is just trying to keep the gate closed. We experience the same social interactions when we visit a provincial ministry of transportation. The civil servant's paycheque is paid by our tax dollars. We have all met delightful people at a government service kiosk. But as far as they are concerned, they do not work for us. They provide a service. We accept that service. They define quality. If we have a problem with it, we can write a letter.

Direct payment, even a few dollars per service, creates a completely different attitude on the part of the person providing the service. Patients know an interaction without reciprocity will never carry the same service as a relationship built on mutual exchange. So, as mentioned above, patients bring gifts to their doctors, without demand or prompting. They donate to hospital foundations. Or they go out of their way to build relationships based on friendship and civility; most people do this because they are simply kind, generous people, but they are aware of the need for exchange in all relationships. We are not robots. *Care regardless of ability to pay* becomes service like you get at the government service centre.

Can't Find a Doctor

CANADA PROMISES a doctor for every citizen. It is one of the key selling features of socialized medicine. In his section on Canadian health-care, T.R. Reid struggled to contain his breathless enthusiasm for what he saw in a family doctor's office, in Saskatoon, Saskatchewan: "For an American observer sitting in the corner of the office, the striking thing about Steven Goluboff's practice was the broad socioeconomic range of his patients ... middle-class ... well-dressed businesspeople ... But there were also unwashed, ragged patients ...But they had no problem seeing a doctor in Canada when they needed it."[261]

Reid tells a moving story about a young patient needing an appendectomy. The physician allegedly said, "We're going to fix you up — probably remove your appendix, which you don't need anyway. And of course, we're not going to charge you for it."[262] Dr. Golubuff had to see fifty or more patients per day.[263] Reid never mentions the need for super short visits in order to see so many. "[Canadians] can choose any doctor anywhere, and insurance will pay the bill."[264] Except that this is not true. Fifteen percent of Canadians cannot even find a family doctor who will take them.[265] Even if you find a doctor, it can still be hard to find care. Books such as *Navigating Canada's Health Care: A User Guide to Getting the Care You Need* can help.[266] Patients often find the "complex, almost cryptic health care system" overwhelming.[267] In other countries, patients need books that teach how to *choose* a doctor. "Many Canadians have no choice at all. And, where there is a good doctor (family or specialist), they are typically so booked up that a successful appointment is one conducted in sound bites."[268]

Rural patients find it especially hard to access care. One study compared spending on patients in two areas of Canada and found an almost threefold difference between those living in a large vs. a small urban area.[269] Residents of Vancouver received an average of $609.50 of specialty services per year, whereas residents of Peace River received only $231.60. If we turn this around and look instead at the total cost per citizen to provide care in different regions, we find that spending varies even more widely. Patients in remote communities generally cost more and *still* receive less care. Patients in Nunavut (the most northern part of Canada) cost $19,061 per person each year, and the average patient in all of BC only $6,548. Roughly 18 percent of Canadians live in rural and remote areas.[270] They pay the same in income taxes but get a fraction of the care.

It gets worse. Small towns often raise their own money to attract doctors. Officials offer hundreds of thousands of dollars, including free clinic space and even subsidized housing, for physicians to come and live in their communities. These costs are not tracked. (Would they be considered a medicare administrative expense?) The money usually comes from municipal taxes or local fundraising efforts. As already mentioned, it is illegal to pay physicians for necessary medical care — prices are fixed; no market exists. But a booming market exists to attract physicians to work in rural and isolated places. The same high costs apply to any other business setting up in an isolated area. It only seems perverse in the case of medicine given the nature of socialized medicine. Various governments have tried to force doctors to work in rural areas by using restricted licences and other tactics.[271] It does not work well for doctors or patients.[272]

I grew up in rural northern Ontario. The closest city, Thunder Bay, has just over 100,000 people, with 50,000 more in the surrounding district. My parents still live in the same house, and I have physician friends who work in town. Two plastic surgeons cover the 104,000 square kilometres of the district. The city lost its only dermatologist and has been recruiting for replacements without success for over one year, last time I checked.

I currently live just outside Newmarket, a town of similar size in southern Ontario. We have six plastic surgeons and an equal number of dermatologists. On top of that, I can send my patients to a number of family doctors who have taken dermatology fellowships, and a number of others who focus on removing "lumps and bumps." Even with all these resources, my patients still often wait far too long. Geography creates insurmountable inequity in socialized medicine, but we are not allowed to try to fix it with anything beyond our socialized approach.

PART TWO

How Canadian Medicare Is Failing

Chapter Six
Inefficiency and Chaos

Just think how likely it is that Henry Ford would have been allowed to introduce the
assembly line if his proposed reform had to be negotiated with all the existing car
companies and factory workers, all of whom were at the table to protect their interests.
–Brian Lee Crowley

IN LOOKING at *why* Canadian medicare is failing, we have examined the
socialist worldview on which it is based and surveyed its medical discontents: the inevitable inequities in medical care that result from its concealed
political mission to achieve a political vision of equity. We now turn to
consider *how* medicare is failing: problems that flow from medicare's faulty
worldview — inefficiencies caused by organizational mismanagement; the
failure of central planning; medicare's misplaced faith in rational technique;
the mismatch of laws and regulations and the profession they are imposed
on; and the arrogance of *government knows best*.

A Flappable Moment

"HOSPITALS CAN'T run because you can't make a f***ing decision," said
the chief of staff, a senior executive at a large hospital. "Everything has to go
through a committee. No one can take a good idea and just make a decision."

He started to attract attention. Cocktails had just arrived after a rowdy
afternoon conference about healthcare improvement at a swanky Toronto hotel
in mid-August. There are many words to describe long discussions in warm,

dark conference rooms; rowdy is not normally one of them. This conference was different. The last speaker, an American, had told doctors to "change or become obsolete."

Canadian doctors are responsible for things they did not build and cannot change. Many already feel victims of an unresponsive system. The speaker was asking the impossible and threatening the inevitable. It filled the room with commotion, like gasoline on a grass fire.

"When I have a good idea," the chief went on, "I have to take it to a committee. Then I have to bring it to the board. Then I have to bring it to a subcommittee of the board. Then I have to engage a stakeholder group."

He was almost shouting now. "Then I have to do public outreach, get a legislative review, lobby for new legislation, nurture it though policy development, do a beta group assessment. We have to convince hundreds, even thousands of people, before we can make one f***ing decision!"[273]

To be clear, most physician leaders are unflappable. They spend their days listening to patients, families, and staff members flap at them. It takes some effort to draw one out and make him flap. But given the right topic, and a bit of liquid encouragement, they will give you a speech.

CEOs will, too. Dave Williams is a writer, former astronaut and leader at NASA, serial CEO, and recipient of the Order of Ontario. "It's not clear to me who runs the hospital," Dave said, soon after he started as CEO of Southlake Regional in Newmarket, Ontario. Dave never complained. He saw everything as an opportunity: another challenge, like a spacewalk at zero gravity and minus-127 degrees Celsius. "Compared to what I'm used to, it's challenging to get things done."

Bragging Rights

AT ONE TIME, Canadian politicians and pundits enjoyed saying how little Canada spent on care.[274] Today, it sounds silly. *Cost containment* used to be one of the most attractive features of socialized medicine, especially for governments.[275] Between 1960 and 1998, spending on healthcare in Canada grew at only 0.8 percent annually, whereas at other OECD countries it grew at 2.3 to

2.7 percent.[276] Cost containment remains one of the central aims in planning and health policy.[277] But as Canada grew famous for wait times and rationing, enthusiasm about how little we spent started to fade. Spending less on essentials makes sense only if you actually get the essentials you need. The Canadian approach of spending less, and getting less, makes no sense at all. Most people can see through it, like someone bragging about his Lada. "Cheap is not the same as efficient."[278]

Furthermore, advocates of socialized medicine never want to spend less. They want to spend more and socialize as much as possible the drugs, medical appliances, and other healthcare needs not currently covered by medicare. They only ever stop spending when money runs out.

Canada spends more on healthcare than most other countries.[279] Even if we look only at wealthy countries, Canada ranks within a few hundred dollars of the top, aside from the US. Most people have stopped using cost containment as a major benefit of socialized medicine, outside of comparisons to what the US spends. Instead, advocates have now made the subtle shift to efficiency: socialized medicine is great because it is so administratively efficient. It is the second-best reason to support medicare, after equity. Less of what we spend goes to wasteful things, such as advertising or corporate profits. More money goes to patients, even if we do spend less. "Canada's elegantly simple single-payer system spends less than 2 percent on insurance overhead," Dr. Danielle Martin writes in her book *Better Now*.[280] This figure is ten times lower than highly rated charitable organizations in Canada; only a few small, volunteer-run charities report overhead in the 1-5 percent range.[281] In *Healing of America*, T.R. Reid offers similar praise: he says Canada spends only 6 percent on administration.[282] We find a third percentage in a study based on 2017 data. The authors compared administrative costs between Canada and the US and reported the latter spent 34 percent on administration, whereas Canada only spent 17 percent.[283] If we ignore the exact number, the message seems clear: Canadians enjoy outstanding efficiency from socialized medicine. Even the 100 top-rated charities in Canada could only achieve an average 20 percent overhead, in 2019.[284] A recent piece in left-leaning *Prospect* magazine notes Canadian doctors do their billing "in one hour on a Sunday evening at the computer,"[285] while American doctors hire "more billing staff than medical staff." No matter what patients experience when they finally receive care, they can be sure very little of it went to paperwork, marketing, claims submissions, and so on, far better than the leanest charitable organizations.

Except it is not true. The Auditor General of Ontario, in a 2015 review of home care, found as little as 61 cents out of every dollar went to patient care.[286] Between 19 and 39 percent went to administrative costs in Ontario's Community Care Access Centres (CCACs), comparable to the 34 percent quoted above for the US. These centres are just one government agency among dozens, each with their own budgets. Furthermore, the CCAC budgets do not include the cost of raising capital. Nor do they collect, track, and report all the other costs that private businesses (including US medical clinics) would track.

Accounting expectations in publicly funded agencies are nothing like those found outside the state. As Michael Decter, former Ontario deputy minister of health, writes, "One of the unintended consequences of single payer, government insurance of hospital services and global budgets was the elimination of detailed accounting in hospitals in the 1950s and 1960s."[287] Why spend hospital money on accounting for something when you can just ask for more in next year's budget?

American healthcare businesses have had to respond at length to these allegations that the US Medicare program is efficient but US private healthcare businesses are wasteful and greedy. But we in Canada cannot even start to compare the reported costs in government vs. business, because government so rarely knows the costs of much of what they do.[288] No public agency tracks the costs of raising money (tax collecting). Public agencies often use outside agencies to perform administrative work that is not reported as administration.[289] Taxes and licensing fees on private businesses are included in administrative costs, whereas governments do not impose the same costs on their own agencies.[290] Since administrative costs are relative to the cost of care, institutions that care for sicker patients will appear to spend a lower percentage on admin costs.

Taking all this into consideration, the Heritage Foundation reported in 2009 that administrative costs for the US Medicare program were not lower than those found in the private healthcare sector.[291] Some suggest that many US Medicare services could be delivered at 88 percent of the cost of the public system.[292]

But even if we ignore all this and grant the claim to efficiency for socialized medicine, we can still ask: Does it work? Does socialized medicine tend to create industry-leading business practices and operational efficiency? How many ways has socialized medicine — not medicine itself — actually increased the quality and quantity of medical care an individual doctor can provide (aside from simplifying billing)? Unfortunately, the data do not exist. As Decter mentioned above, hospitals got rid of big accounting departments. We now catch sight of snippets. For example, a hospital lost $260,000 running its Tim Hortons coffee shop,[293] one of Canada's most profitable franchises, with unionized hospital staff pouring coffee at $28 per hour.[294]

For another example, when I sat on a regional committee that looked at emergency and home-care issues, one of our CCAC partners raised an awkward problem. As year end approached, they had too much money left in their budget, well over $1 million. If they did not spend it, they would have their budget cut the following year.[295] They had been considering a computerized referral system but had not started work on it. Such a system seemed to offer a quick way to use up the cash. The CCAC had no time to consult frontline staff or end users. But the new system dealt with the unspent money and got rid of the old paper-based referral system. However, the new system turned a 30-second paper-based referral process into a 5- to 20-minute job to enter all the additional information CCAC requested. It required the IT departments in each hospital covered by the CCAC to invest hours setting it up (with new passwords for providers, of course). Hospitals tried to force doctors to do the work of entering all the new data. Doctors argued that would pull them away from patient care. So hospitals had to hire more nursing staff to enter home-care instructions into the new computer system. The ongoing operational cost dwarfed the money CCAC would have "lost" if it had not developed its new computer system in the first place. This happens year after year. Hundreds of agencies scramble to spend at year end and add a layer of bureaucracy to the fifty years' worth below.

Costs Hidden in Physician Billings

FORCING DOCTORS to perform non-medical, administrative tasks achieves two things. First, it slows doctors down, which decreases the amount of care they can provide. This serves to limit utilization (it saves money) and allows the state to ration care overall, as we discussed earlier. But, second, it also buries the costs of administration inside doctors' billing. Since doctors perform the work without submitting a separate fee for it, the administrative work looks like it did not cost anything. Patients do not realize their care has not only been rationed but also diluted.

Canadian hospitals strive to make doctors do as much non-medical work as they can, short of embarrassment, in the name of clinical safety and other important things, of course. Since physicians bill the government for their services, hospitals do not worry about physician efficiency. It saves hospitals money to force doctors to do clerical work, instead of hiring more clerks.

When I was chief of emergency medicine, our department set about purchasing radio-frequency identification (RFID) equipment to improve efficiency in our emergency department (ED). The provincial government, at the time, had allocated money to be spent on improving ED wait times. But they did not want it spent on anything that had been tried before. It had to be new, innovative. The Ministry of Health will only approve "something new and sexy," our VP said.

RFID seemed to fit the criteria. It involved special (expensive) electronic badges, which allowed us to track the movements of anything the badge was attached to. An American company gave us a lengthy presentation. RFID could tell us how much time each physician spent on each activity, down to the second. For example, the system could track time spent charting, attending at a patient's bedside, walking for coffee, and so on. I tried to explain we wanted RFID to track the patients, equipment, and nurses, but not the doctors. The company reps could not understand. How do patients, equipment, and nurses drive costs for hospitals in Canada? Doctors drive costs, don't they?

No, I said. We do not care about what the doctors do. The hospital does not pay for the doctors. As hospital administrators, we only care about nurses, patients, and equipment.[296]

Hospitals can stretch their budgets by off-loading administrative duties onto doctors: for example, logging into computers, printing day sheets and labs, calling consultants, and a thousand other duties doctors do not need to perform. In the past, hospital administrators invested in things that made doctors' work more efficient. It increased the number of patients doctors could treat. Today, it makes good business sense for hospitals to remove supports and load non-medical clerical work onto doctors. Good for the hospitals but not for the system.

Given the lack of support from the hospital to increase physician efficiency, we developed a model in our ED in which doctors can hire a "physician navigator" to help on their shift. PNs handle all the non-clinical tasks, which at one time were handled by clerks, porters, and even nurses and other allied health staff.[297] PNs improve MD efficiency by 25 percent in some cases.[298] One of our most efficient PNs started while still in high school. That is correct: medicare makes physicians perform clerical tasks that can be done equally well by bright, motivated high-school students.

If hospitals invested anywhere close to the amount of support required to keep doctors and nurses — medicare's most expensive professionals — maximally productive, we might conservatively estimate a 25 percent increase in reported clerical (administrative) costs, just for hospitals.

Bureaucracy steals from patients by forcing doctors to fill in detailed forms; respond to lengthy surveys;[299] review and respond to threats by government; digest complex tentative physician service agreements; adhere to reporting requirements; and spend time on reappointments, licence renewals, data capture, and on and on. All of which steals time from patient care, at a cost that goes almost entirely unreported.

A multi-stakeholder, province-wide Administrative Burden Committee tackled this issue between 1997 and 2003. Physicians on the committee drafted twenty recommendations to consider. The committee ignored them all. The other stakeholders benefitted from the forms doctors had to fill out.

They outvoted the doctors and demanded that physicians should provide the "service." Around the same time, the Ontario Medical Association (OMA) lobbied government successfully to create a bilateral Forms Committee to challenge the explosion of forms doctors were being asked to complete. For the most part, bureaucratic forms do not contain medication orders. They usually ask for signatures confirming medical conditions (which are already documented in the chart), explanations about clinical features, and regurgitated treatments that have all been recorded elsewhere. These forms get designed in cubicles to serve bureaucratic ends. The Forms Committee now reviews and approves every new form thrown at physicians. This does not protect physicians from useless forms, but at least it offers a formal process to slow bureaucratic bloat.

Note also that all the bilateral committees are usually funded jointly by government and medical associations. The cost of paying physicians to sit on dozens of these committees represents yet another administrative cost that is not tracked, since it usually comes from the association dues paid by the larger group of physician members.

We could go on and on. Ben Franklin once told a young tradesman, "Time is money." In an age of distraction, everything takes time. Economists call it opportunity cost. Successful businesses know new work costs money. Either old tasks go undone, or staff have to be hired to tackle new projects. Corporations go broke if they do not pay close attention to how workers spend time on the job. Medicare's managers do not seem to know this. Patients experience the hidden costs in the form of shorter visits with an increasingly rushed physician, while advocates continue to brag about medicare's efficiency.

Cost Control vs. Efficiency

CANADA SPENDS more on healthcare each year. As we saw earlier, Canada in 2019 spent $264 billion on healthcare, or 11.6 percent of GDP, $7068 per person.[300] A typical Canadian family consisting of two parents and two children (with an average household income of $140,049) will pay $13,311 in taxes for public healthcare in 2019.[301] After adjusting for inflation, that is an increase of 65.8 percent since 1997. "The cost of public health care insurance for the average Canadian family increased 3.2 times as fast as the cost of food, 2.1 times as fast as the cost of clothing, 1.8 times as fast as the cost of shelter, and 1.7 times faster than average income."

As others have said, we could find useful ways to keep spending more on care until we get to the point of investing our whole GDP into medical services and things related to health in general.[302] Reflecting on spending growth in healthcare, Dalton McGuinty, former premier of Ontario, said, "At these rates, there will come a time when the Ministry of Health is the only ministry we can afford to have, and we still won't be able to afford the Ministry of Health."[303]

In 2015, the Canadian Health Policy Institute reported the average provincial spending on healthcare, as a percentage of total revenue, was 43 percent.[304] But many provinces do not raise all the money they spend. The federal government transfers money from productive provinces to unproductive ones. When we look at only provincial-source revenue, healthcare consumed 59 percent of what provinces could raise on their own and up to 75 percent in Newfoundland and Labrador. Without massive transfer payments, medicare would almost bankrupt many provinces.

On the one hand, care costs more because we can do more. Governments recognized this in the 1970s. Demand outstripped our ability to pay for all the care voters wanted.[305] On the other, many observers complain the growth did not come from giving more care to patients, but from more money to doctors and nurses. Economists call it Baumol's cost disease: "wage growth eclipses productivity improvements in the public sector."[306]

Every free service creates moral hazard, the tendency for people to pursue riskier behaviour if they do not have to bear the consequences. When we apply this to free care, we find people tend to use up a free service to the full extent, even for a tiny benefit, since it costs them nothing. Patients will continue to consume free care until the time and bother of getting to the clinic surpasses the perceived value of the visit. For people who place little value on time and find the clinical experience enjoyable, medicare offers no easy brake on consumption.

Every opportunity for government to provide a free service creates a moral hazard for government, too. Free stuff generates a brokerage fee for government off every tax dollar collected to pay for the handout, without personal risk for the politician or bureaucrat. Politicians promise projects voters do not really need. Physicians offer tests to avoid complaints and lawsuits. Patients request MRIs they could live without. Moral hazard makes us all do things we might not otherwise.[307]

Given that "nobody knows what anything costs" inside medicare, the whole program starts to look like a giant millstone on the public treasury.[308] The pay-as-you-go funding model means we pay more as we go. Researchers at the University of Calgary argue this is unsustainable and, by definition, a Ponzi scheme.[309] They call for more "cost-efficient" ways of managing medicine.

So far, provinces have not found them. Instead, they continue to cut beds and shorten hospital stays. A recent article held up Ontario hospitals as the model of efficiency with the "fewest, shortest, [and] cheapest" stays.[310] It did not mention patients' experience at being turfed to recover at home.

Input Up, Output Down:
Gammon's Law in Medicare

CANADIAN MEDICARE also offers no obvious brake on spending, aside from arbitrary caps and cuts. Medicare obeys Gammon's law, or the theory of bureaucratic displacement: as we spend more, we get less — "increase in expenditure will be matched by a fall in production."[311] It comes from Gammon's study of Britain's NHS between 1965 and 1973. Hospital staff increased by 28 percent and administrative staff by 51 percent. But the average number of occupied beds declined by 11 percent.

Usually, progress and volume decrease cost. Only in healthcare do we find that improved technology and performance increase costs. Governments work to a different bottom line than private businesses. Despite this, we still hear experts like Stephen Birch, professor of health economics as McMaster University, blame an oversupply of providers for driving up costs.[312] Birch says patients do not demand healthcare. Costs go up because doctors give care that no one asked for. Health economists show less interest in examining system efficiency, the impact of unions on wage and benefit costs, or why Gammon's law is a law at all.

Others point to government itself as a major cost driver. After WWII, Britain wanted to extend its victory to social issues, so Aneurin Bevan, left-wing Labour party leader, launched a campaign to create state medicine. The British Medical Association resisted. It did not want bureaucrats controlling medicine. Opposition threatened to ruin Bevan's plan. So he "stuffed their mouths with gold," he said.[313] This was not about negotiations of fees for services. It was about control, not funding, and most definitely not about efficiency. Bevan simply poured money into his plan, making it irresistible to anyone who disagreed. We see the same approach in medicare. Even unattractive programs become palatable when washed down with enough funding. Milton Friedman, Nobel Prize-winning economist, states it this way:

> When the government is taking over any activity, there is money available. But what typically happens is once the government has taken it over, the situation changes. There are no votes to be gotten by taking it over some more. You have to move on to new areas and take over new fields in order to get some new votes. And the result of that is those areas already taken over get stormed. And instead of there being more resources available there are fewer.[314]

Entitlements win votes only once. "Once the bulk of costs have been taken over by government ... the political entrepreneur has no additional groups to attract, and attention turns to holding down costs."[315] Efficient indeed.

A Medicare Trilemma: Care vs. Cost vs. Technology

CANADA IS STUCK in a medicare trilemma: a situation with three options but that allows for only two at any one time. For example, consider this trilemma from the Soviet era: You can be honest; you can be smart; and you can be communist. Pick two. If you are honest and a communist, you cannot be smart. If you are smart and a communist, you cannot be honest. And if you are honest and smart, you cannot be a communist. Patients want individualized care, which involves an element of choice and involvement in decision making. Patients also want access to the best medicine and technology (given current standards of care). And we want to control the cost of care. Hence this medicare trilemma:

- If we want individualized care and the best technology, we cannot have low costs.

- If we want individualized care and low costs, we cannot offer the best technology.

- If we want low costs and the best technology, we cannot offer individualized care.

Socialized medicine solves the trilemma by debating the definition of *best technology* and *patient need*. Doctors talk about offering the standard of care, as being the best. But what, exactly, *is* the standard of care? Could we not redefine the standard of care as a middle ground that seems more affordable and still offers decent care? Besides, does medical care really offer all that much benefit to citizens?

This path of reasoning has no end. We are caught in epistemic skepticism. We do not know anything for sure about needs, care, or patient wishes. So why not just start with a clean slate and offer what we can and forget the whole trilemma?

Canadian Chaos: Medicare's Misaligned Incentives

PATIENTS CRINGE at the chaos they see while waiting in a Canadian emergency department. They feel the same chaos when their family members get admitted to a hospital hallway, instead of a room, or wait for hours in a crowded clinic. Patients experience chaos in Canadian hospitals because hospitals are designed to function that way. Their function fulfills the purpose of socialized medicine. Form follows function and function follows purpose.[316]

- In Canadian hospitals, nurses get paid for *hours of work*. Physicians get paid for *work accomplished*.

- Nurses get paid from the hospital budget. The province pays physicians directly.

- Nurses' contracts specify duties, hours of work, benefits, and grievance processes. Physicians' contracts specify billable services.

- Hospitals *spend* money to help more patients. Physicians *earn* money to help more patients.

- Hospitals *save* money by seeing fewer patients. Physicians *lose* money by seeing fewer patients.

In Canadian hospitals, everyone pulls in opposite directions. Players seek to serve the one who pays them, which may or may not include a focus on their own productivity.[317] This chaos applies to clinics, labs, and most other places patients attend for care.

When I started in the ED, many of the nurses worked part-time. They were full-time farmers, who needed to earn extra income. Even though they were unionized, they could never adopt a time-wage mentality. The clock meant nothing. Only the work mattered. Farmers make hay when the sun shines. They work hard now because they might not get the chance to do the same job later. Full-time unionized workers have no incentive to work any harder than absolutely necessary as defined in their contract. It is irrational to do otherwise. Workers who choose to work harder than average inevitably invite the ire of their colleagues. The unionized environment necessarily brings everyone down to whatever level of performance the contract allows.

Journalist Julia Belluz, in an article for *Maclean's* in 2012, tackled whether how we pay health-care workers affects how they treat us.[318] She focused on how staff are paid, not how hospitals are funded. She found that surgeons often complain about "slow turnovers between procedures in their operating rooms." "They've had to send anxious patients home who were scheduled for surgeries," that had to be cancelled due to cleaners and nurses moving too slowly. "The reason for the slowness? Money — or so they believed. While [surgeons] are paid on a fee-for-service basis, the cleaners and nurses who prepped the OR are salaried ... The doctors felt the salaried hospital workers had little incentive to move quickly, while [surgeons] did."

Belluz asked Steven Lewis, well-known health consultant, whether this idea that incentives influence behaviour had any merit. Lewis got "right to the heart of the issue" by saying, "That's hugely disrespectful to nurses and housekeepers to make the assumption that the only thing that would motivate them to work efficiently and effectively is to be on the same the fee-for-service treadmill as those physicians." Disrespect applies to politeness, not performance. Whether the idea is "disrespectful" should not matter as much as whether it is true. The article seems to indicate that Lewis could not answer the question.

Belluz asked Rick Glazier, of the Institute for Clinical Evaluative Sciences, the same question. Glazier noted that every model has pros and cons: fee-for-service risks factory medicine and unnecessary care; capitation (paying a flat rate per patient per year) risks cherry-picking and shirking; and salary risks staff slowing down and shirking responsibility.

Lewis rarely misses an opportunity to criticize fee-for-service medicine. In one example, "Deal with Doctors," an article published in *Policy Options*, June 3, 2013, he offers a long critique of fee-for-service.[319] He does not hesitate to ascribe and explain physicians' behavioural motivations. He even makes the (hugely disrespectful) implication that age, gender, and whether one works in a city impacts a physician's attitude about system efficiency. Lewis pontificates about how financial incentives impact physician behaviour, but he finds it "hugely disrespectful" to apply the same logic to salaried workers.

James C. Robinson, health economist at Berkeley, has studied and written extensively on payment models. He put it this way:

> There are many mechanisms for paying physicians; some are good and some are bad. The three worst are fee-for-service, capitation, and salary.
>
> Fee-for-service rewards the provision of inappropriate services, the fraudulent upcoding of visits and procedures, and the churning of "ping-pong" referrals among specialists. Capitation rewards the denial of appropriate services, the dumping of the chronically ill, and a narrow scope of practice that refers out every time-consuming patient. Salary undermines productivity, condones on-the-job leisure, and fosters a bureaucratic mentality in which every procedure is someone else's problem.[320]

Robinson's tongue-in-cheek analysis applies to all professionals, not just physicians. We can even apply his thinking to hospitals, if we think of block funding as a hospital on salary. Robinson suggests a blended approach. Helping patients should be the only objective that matters in healthcare.[321] Incentives should be aligned towards that goal. All providers should be rewarded for helping patients and by how much patients benefit from the care provided.[322]

But medicare advocates dislike incentives. They disparage models of care that promote entrepreneurial behaviour. They would rather pretend that incentives do not exist, that they do not change behaviour. Purists believe patient service has nothing to do with how people are paid.

Susan Fitzpatrick, then Ontario deputy minister of finance, gave a lecture about physician payment. She offered a long and nuanced argument on the need for performance incentives for physicians. Doctors need to know some of their income is at risk if they do not perform in specific ways. After her speech, I went up to congratulate her. I then asked, given her argument around performance-based pay, whether she had considered including performance pay as part of the multi-billion-dollar nursing contract she had just negotiated. "That's a good idea," she said. "I hadn't thought of that."

Everyone working inside the system knows misaligned incentives do not work out well for patients. But most are too scared to say anything.

Chapter Seven
Planning's Inevitable Failure

There are so many plans, so many schemes, and so many reasons
why there should be neither plans nor schemes.
–Benjamin Disraeli

WE NOW return to the politician Tommy Douglas, this time in 1979. Medicare was in turmoil; crisis after crisis had become the normal state. Health costs had ballooned. The federal government no longer paid for 50 percent of provincial health spending, as it had originally promised. Provinces increased hospital user fees,[323] and physicians extra billed.[324]

A large crowd of the concerned faithful met at the SOS Medicare Conference in Ottawa. Douglas took the keynote.[325]

> Those of us who talked about medicare back in the 1940s and 50s and 60s, kept reminding the public that there were two phases for medicare. The first was to remove the financial barrier between those who provide health services and those who needed them. We pointed out repeatedly that that phase was the *easiest* of the problems we would confront. In governmental terms, of course, it means finding revenues; it means setting up organizations; it means exercising controls over costs. But in the long term it was the easiest problem.
>
> The phase number two [sic] would be the much more difficult one. That was to alter our delivery system. So as to reduce costs and so as to place the emphasis on preventive medicine. The thing that we have to apply ourselves to now is that we have not yet grappled seriously with the second phase ...

Only in that way are we going to be able to keep the cost
from becoming so excessive that the public will decide that medicare is not in the best interests of the people of this country.

The faithful needed to refocus. They had wandered. Paying for care was "the
easiest of the problems we would confront." Trying to "alter our delivery
system" was always the main goal. It was never just about payment for care.
The goal was complete system redesign.[326]

Execution and Denial

IN A SOCIALIZED atmosphere, every government takes a turn at central
planning. In the early 1990s, for example, the Ontario NDP introduced legislation that would give the government power to reduce or deny payment
for services.[327] Civil servants wrote[328] at the time about managing demand
and supply-side re-engineering. Jim Wilson, minister of health in Ontario
and long-time member of the Progressive Conservatives, said in 1996, "We
will go from being simply a passive player to an active manager."[329]

Planners typically woo voters by offering a plan to build something
good. Then they justify planning as a way to reduce costs.[330] True, a few
politicians win support with plans to cut costs, but they usually drop their
plans long before the next election.

With government paying for patient care, "The state has indirectly
entered [into] the 'practice of medicine.'"[331] But by the 1990s, governments
grew tired of paying; they wanted to manage. Governments acted unilaterally. They used legislation to insert themselves into medicine and drive
change directly.[332] Despite the shift to management and making bold moves
such as closing "tens of thousands of hospital beds," governments did so
with little sense of the impact of their decisions.[333]

Today, the state makes all the major decisions about healthcare, including funding, limits on care, and what kinds of facilities are available.
Strong public approval apparently justifies government intervention.[334] If
it is popular, it must be right. Medical leaders tell us, "Your local practice
shouldn't have a choice about whether or not its doors are open to you."[335]

Of course, your local medical practice, at least on paper, is supposed to be a privately owned and operated small business. But no matter. Public need trumps private choice, so physicians should play along. Again, these opinions pop up in all political parties in Canada. Socialism has all-party support when it comes to medicare. For example, a Toronto-based, politically conservative health consultant said, "We should pass a law against solo practice."[336] Planning would work if only we could get people to cooperate.

Building on our discussion about government monopoly in chapter three, we find again that many people refuse to admit central planning even exists. Planners themselves are often blind to their own planning, or they want to hide it.

Mikhail Gorbachev once told Margaret Thatcher that communism was superior to capitalism.

"Don't be silly, Mr. Gorbachev. You can barely feed your own citizens."

"To the contrary, Mrs. Thatcher! Our people live *joyfully.*"

"Oh, do they? Then why do so many of them want to leave? And why do you prevent them from leaving?"

"They can leave if they want to!"

"That's not what I hear. And by the way, we're not happy about the money you're sending to Arthur Scargill" [a British trade unionist].

"We have nothing to do with that."

"Who do you think you're kidding? You and I both know that your economy is centrally controlled. Not a kopeck leaves without the Politburo's knowledge."

"*Nyet, nyet,* you misunderstand. It's not centrally controlled."

"Oh, no? How does a Russian factory decide how much to produce?"

"We tell them."[337]

Why Plan?

EVERYONE PLANS, even if they plan to make no plans. Socialized medicine operates on the conviction that planning is a social virtue,[338] and that
planners, not individual voters, should be the ones to impose their plans
on everyone else.[339] "Intellectuals are naturally attracted by the idea of a
planned society, in the belief that they will be in charge of it."[340]

Recall Prime Minister Mackenzie King speaking at the end of
WWII, calling for a "plan for a unified campaign in Canada against these
enemies of progress and human well-being."[341] He believed Canada could
achieve, through planning, not just freedom from sickness, but freedom
from "want." King's comments fit a shared nostalgia of post-war optimism, albeit sounding grandiose, even slightly demented.[209] [342] Classical
liberalism had created social prosperity. Limited governments maximized
freedom, and prosperity had followed. But politicians grew impatient.
Planners tired of waiting for the "common progress" to improve people's
lives.[343] They argued that people needed immediate relief from unbearable
and unnecessary suffering and planners could provide it. The free enterprise approach favoured by liberalism seemed chaotic and slow.[344]

At the same time, progressives all over the free world shared a
suspicion of private activity.[345] They viewed solutions outside the state as
unpatriotic.[346] John Maynard Keynes, the British economist from the
Depression era, argued that, if governments managed the economy, citizens
would experience less chaos from the natural changes that occur when
markets are allowed to cycle on their own. His approach is called Keynesianism. All parties loved it. Even Republican president Richard Nixon
famously said, "We are all Keynesians now."

Keynesianism gave governments licence to plan. It assumed that
government — wise, beneficent, and all-knowing — would seek the public interest and not its own.[347] No one questioned the uncritical faith in
the civil service.[348] Keynesianism remained in fashion around the birth
and early development of socialized medicine. As former Canadian prime
minister Stephen Harper writes, "The term 'bastardized Keynesianism'

was coined in the early 1960s to describe how Keynes's ideas had come to justify any or all government interventions in the economy."[349]

Keynesianism crashes against the Naive Clinical. Recall that most clinicians and most Canadians assume people "should get the care they need, as judged by a qualified clinical practitioner, regardless of the cost."[350] Experts think this unwise, that perhaps they should reconsider and find a better approach: something that fits better with the worldview of socialized medicine.

Medical educators attempt to imprint new physicians with the notion they should put priority on society's needs as a whole. But practice corrupts new doctors. Outside academia, new grads find themselves in a stubborn medical culture that prioritizes individual patients.[351] Even more concerning for some, many doctors still assume a "high" and "striking degree" of physician autonomy is a necessary prerequisite for quality care.[352] Autonomy creates variation, and variation, to a system planner, highlights the existence of waste and poor care. Experts remind us that many doctors do not give evidence-based care, and they have "sophisticated batteries of fact and argument" to prove it. Physicians seem to practice highly variable care, without a sense of responsibility to society as a whole, and without regard to any sort of recognizable standard.[353]

When one clinic tests patients ten times more than another, we *should* pay attention. In most cases, incentives and restraints drive doctors' behaviour. We might examine each case and find the cause. However, planners do not want to examine. They already know. Variability comes from a lack of control over the kind and amount of care patients receive. Variability would not exist if we were better Keynesians. Planners frame it as a fight about physician autonomy and freedom, but it is actually a fight to plan, ration, and regulate. Painting doctors as unruly libertarians helps win the argument.

The need to control appears pragmatic. How else can government manage medicare? Socialized medicine cannot function without control. Control cannot happen if we allow naive faith in doctors. Perhaps variability itself is simply repugnant for certain people. Planners have always "despised gothic irregularity and variety; [and] yearned after the utilitarian squares and boulevards of social planning."[354] Regardless of their motivation — pragmatism, power lust, repugnance, or truth — planners remain focused on upending the Naive Clinical in medicine.

In developing his alternative, Evans first offers the extreme opposite of the Naive Clinical. He wants to be clear about what his vision is not. He calls this the "Mainstream Economic." It is a cold, rational, and unfeeling paradigm based on money and consumer choice. If you want care and have money to pay for it, you should get as much care and attention as you want, no matter how healthy or sick you may be. The Mainstream Economic paradigm rests "... on the alternative normative basis, 'consumer sovereignty,' that could hardly be more different. People *should* get whatever care they are willing and able to pay for, at prices reflecting the resource cost, the real opportunity cost, of producing that care. The impact of that care on their health status is irrelevant."[355]

In this model, Evans finds the sort of thinking that he applies to most other problems too restrictive for his vision of patient care. While the economic materialist position is normative and useful for explaining other people's behaviour, he finds it unworkable for patient care. Somehow rational self-interest maximization on the part of patients suddenly does not, and should not, apply. In this case, greater goals are at play, more noble things to achieve. Notice that by mentioning that "impact on their health is irrelevant," he impugns choice. He seems to imply that choice — "willing and able" — may lead to extravagance or irrelevant care. But why else would anyone choose to pay for healthcare unless to actually impact health?

Economists undermine choice by explaining that consumers are too scared, uninformed (stupid), or susceptible to wily physicians who might force their ways on patients. We can grant that in some cases all these gloomy things might align, in the same way unscrupulous merchants sometimes prey on fear and ignorance in any other industry. But this does not mean predation happens all the time or that it even works most of the time when charlatans prowl. Furthermore, it does not mean that choice is bad, *per se,* that we should eliminate choice, or that giving choice to wise central planners guarantees better outcomes. If "mainstream" economists artificially separate choice from the thing being chosen, then perhaps mainstream economic thinking should not apply to healthcare at the patient level at all.

Evans's dichotomy between the "Naive Clinical" and the "Mainstream" sets the scene to present his third way, the "Eclectic Structuralist," which now appears more attractive than it might have otherwise. "In general, its practitioners share the clinical position that people should get the care they need ..." but the Eclectic Structuralist paradigm does not carry the same "categorical imperative" as the Naive Clinical.

> The Eclectic Structuralist perspective ... includes essentially the same normative position as the clinical; people *should* get the care they need, the care that improves their health, more or less independently of their ability to pay. But it takes dead aim at the central *positive* presumption of the Naive Clinical perspective, i.e., that, under appropriate professional direction, they do. Holders of this perspective have assembled increasingly large and sophisticated batteries of fact and argument to show that the care patients actually receive depends upon much more than evidence of potential capacity to benefit.[356]

In other words, patients should get care the care they need, but doctors and nurses do not know how to give it. Someone else must decide. Evans points to Roemer's Law (1961) that "a built bed is a filled bed."[357] Because doctors are so irrational, we need central planners to direct care, place boundaries on what care the state can offer, and stop doctors from proving Roemer's Law. Evans shifts the "categorical imperative" from doctors providing patients what they need to planners deciding what patients need. Planners need control.

"Crashingly Stupid"

THE FAILURE of planning presents the biggest danger to medicare, not creeping privatization, underfunding, a lack of federal leadership, or any other threats, which so often seem designed to keep the public focused on protecting medicare instead of improving it. Government mismanagement, not private MRI clinics, will lead to the collapse of medicare.[358]

Planning a medical economy requires large, complex bureaucracies to design, build, and oversee medicare. Dozens of agencies keep thousands of administrators busy creating layers of plans and programs, each with a dedicated process piled on top of all the ones that came before. Planning creates its own complexity.[359] It creates the need to pursue even more planning to solve planning-induced complexity.[360]

We cannot plan away problems caused by planning.[361] Peter H. Schuck recalls that Friedrich Hayek "famously depicted this cycle of centralized control, failure and frustration, redoubled efforts at centralized control, then further failure and frustration as 'the road to serfdom.' "[362] James C. Scott, professor of political science at Yale, summarized his extended study of state planning with this: "If I were asked to condense the reasons behind these failures into a single sentence, I would say that the progenitors of such plans regarded themselves as far smarter and farseeing than they really were and, at the same time, regarded their subjects as far more stupid and incompetent than *they* were."[363]

Canada will always have some form of "free" universal care, as part of a safety net. But Canadians did not ask government to take control of the whole medical economy and plan it all for us. Many economists (mostly outside Canada) have raised this issue. We do not expect government to control other vital parts of the economy, so why medicine? Evans writes that it is "crashingly stupid that [these questions are] being asked at all suggests a deliberate act of intellectual sabotage."[364] In other words, the truth is so obvious that people who ask these questions must be either stupid or malicious. When people offer stupidity and malice as explanations, ideology is likely lurking nearby.[365]

"Mises was right": Planning Fails

THE ECONOMIST, best-selling writer, and lifelong socialist Robert L. Heilbroner wrote an article in 1990 that describes the fall of communism, a description that offers a parallel to Canadian socialized medicine: "The system deteriorated to a point far beyond the worst economic crisis ever experienced by capitalism, and ... the villain in this deterioration was the central planning system itself."[366] Although he pivoted slightly later in life, Heilbroner remained committed to high taxes, a robust welfare system, and a large state to manage it all. Like many who support socialized medicine, he believed in "socialistic capitalism." It is worth considering what this well-known socialist thought were the worst features of central planning to see if socialized medicine shares similarities.

Heilbroner starts with a look at price fixing,[367] a cornerstone concept in socialized medicine. He tells how bureaucrats tried to manage prices. If they raised the price of moleskins in Russia, distribution centres filled with rotting pelts. If they lowered them, supplies ran out. Civil servants were too busy to set prices: there were 24 million other prices to set, and no way to determine how to adjust them.[368]

Canadian planners simply set the prices of medical services, then they keep cutting them until doctors cannot afford to offer a service any longer. For example, venipuncture — drawing blood for a blood test — has been cut to $3.54 in Ontario.[369] The staff and supplies required to offer the test cost more than the fee. So doctors stopped doing them in their offices, which forces patients, especially in rural areas, to spend far more in getting to a lab.

As mentioned earlier, Ontario has over seven thousand fees for physician services. And each of the other provinces also has its own list of fees. Provinces and territories set fees separately, for the most part.[370] Technically, doctors and governments negotiate fees. But governments can enforce, cancel, or reopen contracts at any time. So, essentially, fees are controlled by government and cut if the need arises to fund some other program.

Heilbroner notes that, like a military campaign, central planning works only to the extent that the cost of every "nut, bolt, hinge, beam, tractor, and hydro-electric turbine [has] been previously determined."[371] Hospital funding letters offer an example of this in Ontario. Hospitals prepare detailed budgets each year, right down to what they plan to spend on specific medications. The ministry of health reviews the budgets and then sends back detailed funding letters based on the budgets, with adjustments, as the ministry sees fit. This is set a year in advance and fixed, regardless of population growth or any other change in patient demand in the community. This creates continual frustration. Civil servants resist proposals that do not align with their own ideas.[372]

Planned economies, Heilbroner notes, need to be "carved up into millions of individual pieces, like a jigsaw puzzle … and the whole thing finally reassembled in such a way as to fit." Very hard to do, even if things remained the same from year to year.

Provincial governments go through this same process every spring. They disaggregate all the different programs in a long list of entitlements. Then they try to figure out how much to allocate to each program: education, infrastructure, medical services, and so on. Then they delve more deeply: how much to hospitals, doctors, laboratory services, technology, medical education, ambulances, home care, nurses, and a million other things, each with its own bureaucracy. This process continues until they drill down to tiny programs for special drugs in selected hospitals. Pulling all this together, civil servants try to fit the jigsaw puzzle together. And then patients wonder why the "system" does not work when they raise a concern no one considered before.

Success becomes whatever the central planner decides to measure, usually in physical terms.[373] Heilbroner gives examples of yards of cloth and tons of nails. When planners dictated output based on yards of cloth, factories created giant swaths, each yard woven as loosely as possible to use the least amount of thread. If targets were based on weight — pounds of nails, for example — then factories created heavier nails, which led to the famous cartoon of a factory making one gigantic spike. Hospitals in Ontario struggle with this.[374] In 2012 the Ontario Ministry of Health announced a shift to patient-based funding.[375] It promised shorter wait times and better access to care in their communities; more services, where needed; and better-quality care with less variation between hospitals. The Canadian Health Services Research Foundation notes: "Global budgets provide[d] little incentive for hospitals to focus on efficiency, innovation, improving access, coordinating care across facilities and sectors or improving quality."[376] Government promised to increase services based on patient need.[377]

But rather than a revolutionary funding mechanism, Ontario hospitals got Quality Based Procedures (QBPs): "standardized clinical pathways based on best clinical evidence."[378] The QBPs become Ontario's version of the yards of cloth or tons of nails: detailed checklists and hurdles to guarantee 'quality' but no increased access to care. Hospitals deliver what they are paid to produce.

The same thing happens with doctors and nurses. Nurses are paid by the hour, with no productivity incentives. Performance is measured by how well nurses perform their nursing care, not how much care they offer. So nurses work hard to achieve excellence in documentation and patient education, all of which pulls them away from attending to the next patient waiting for care. The next patient presents new and added risk. But the system does not reward added risk. So nurses focus on what the system does reward, and they work to deliver as much of it as possible. One giant spike. "One minute to give Mrs. Smith a bedpan and one minute to empty the contents. Mindlessly, however, it then takes ten to fifteen minutes for the nurse to write about the episode ... time, color, shape, volume, texture, etc."[379] Without performance incentives, salaried physicians do exactly the same thing.

Heilbroner notes that "the planning process always depended on the intervention of *Tokachi* — "fixers" — who found ways of getting supplies to enterprises ..." Large companies "created their own little repair shops, construction outfits, and other service establishments," so they did not have to depend on government repair men. In Canada, we call *Tokachi* "patient navigators." Many patients cannot survive without them.

If planning has failed to deliver shoes and shampoo, wherever it has been tried around the world, why do we trust planners with heart surgery and hip replacements? Examples of planning failure could fill libraries. And every example of failure attracts a small army of planners who rally to defend the failure as due to lack of funding; outdated IT; subterfuge by unengaged staff; or hospitals and physicians having too much autonomy. Nevertheless, here are just a few examples:

- Governments encourage computerization, but local systems cannot communicate with each other. Canada spent $1,880 per person on hospitals in 2019, or approximately $70.669 billion total.[380] A large portion of this is used in hospitals, which typically spend between 3 to 4 percent of their budgets on information technology each year (7 to 8 percent, or more, in the US), or approximately $3 billion.[381] Individual hospitals spend multiple millions on IT each year. If hospitals were private businesses that relied on information transfer with other vendors, being able to communicate with outside clinics, labs, diagnostic facilities, and doctors' offices would be a priority. In medicare, it is an afterthought. Community doctors get (almost useless) summaries that their patient was in the emergency department. When the hospital changes computer systems, even that notice disappears. It takes years to create a new work-around just to get one notification that a patient was in the emergency department. Never mind the emergency physician's record and test results. Hospitals do their best, but they need not worry much about anything that happens outside their walls.
- Diagnostic images (x-rays) appear immediately using digital technology. Radiologists interpret them, often within minutes (it used to take days for them to review). But the reports are still not available to community physicians for

days and sometimes weeks. Many reports still come by fax. Too often, physicians have to send patients to the emergency department to access prompt diagnostics. The patient is not necessarily that sick, but their symptoms are too urgent to wait for a week to get results back.

- X-ray archiving systems for digital images are not shared with clinics and other hospitals. Small groups of hospitals will often create their own image sharing system. But even that does not communicate with the community clinics. This leaves physicians ordering repeat scans and tests just to complete a consultation.

- Family doctors make referrals only to find out weeks later that particular specialist cannot accept any more referrals for months. Other provinces track referrals to consultants so patients and primary care providers can follow referrals along in the process. Providers know which specialists are accepting new referrals. A common solution has been to create central referral systems, so referring doctors cannot choose the surgeon they refer to. When patients ask, "Is the surgeon any good?" we have to say, "They are all good." Ideally, we should know the reputation of the local surgeons and be able to refer patients that match the interests and expertise of the surgeon or consultant. That would work out best for the patients and the surgeon.

- Specialty services have long wait-lists or are unavailable in many communities. For example, pediatric psychiatry, neurology, and neurosurgery services are notoriously difficult to consult.

- Government slashed enrolment to medical schools in 1992, in Ontario (Barer-Stoddart report, 1991). Economists said we had too many doctors. By 2000, over 1.4 million citizens could not find a family doc. So government ramped up enrolment and increased funding. By 2012, government felt it was spending too much for physician services. Massive cuts led to unemployed physicians despite multi-year waits to see a doctor, for many specialties in many places. Feast or famine.

- Access bonuses for family doctors, if their patients do not see outside clinics, end up causing increased emergency department visits. Doctors instruct patients to go the ED to avoid penalties, when a walk-in or after-hours clinic could provide the services just as easily.

Where Planning Can Work, Sort Of

DESPITE ALL the evidence for planning failure, some things do lend themselves to planning. State medicine works reasonably well for price inelastic services — services that are immune to moral hazard — with predictable demand. Funerals and broken hips are price inelastic. Demand for funerals does not change when funerals go on sale. Aside from stealing bookings from another funeral home, price does not change demand. Broken hips are inelastic, too. Demand arises from factors outside individual preference or decisions about cost. Pathology, not preference, determines demand.

Trauma care and transplants can function under a centrally controlled system. These services still suffer from all the reasons governments fail (see chapter eleven on government's failure of medicine), but simply removing the issue of variable demand based on patient decisions about cost (price elasticity) simplifies the scenario for central planners.

Aside from disaster or some strange virus that causes hearts to fail, trauma and transplants have predictable rates. Every year, planners can expect a certain number of people to need trauma care. People who design, plan, and fund transplant programs can predict how many hearts or kidneys they will need. Even when the demand changes, planners usually have warning. Patients' organs tend to fail over years. And patients do not seek out a transplant unless they really need one. They can survive on wait-lists for a long time, which gives central planners time to secure funding and infrastructure to meet demand without disaster.

This does not guarantee planners will not cut things too close or will not raid the transplant program to fund cancer screening. There is no guarantee politicians will not make maternal care or autism a focus and start undermining support for transplants by blaming patients for the cause of their failing organs in the first place. And, of course, concerns about privilege and patronage remain relevant.

All things being equal, price-inelastic services are driven by objective needs. Planners can model and manage these concrete needs without necessarily compromising access, efficiency, or quality, if they have the political support to do so. But even for the most straightforward, objective needs, planning often fails. Political will changes. What is worse, the theoretical possibility of planning clear, objective needs makes planners think they can plan all the rest.

Managerialized Medicine

AFTER thirty years working in long-term care homes, an exasperated nurse fumed about nursing directors who have never nursed a day in their lives. She had to withstand criticism for not following guidelines that were written by experts who had never provided care.

Years ago, costly education meant fewer people had credentials. Workers earned merit through experience and skill, not credentialism. The best nurses became managers. Managers were clinicians first, managers second. Today, managers have taken over medicine, not just in Canada but around the world. A better name for socialized medicine would be managerialized medicine.

Business schools pump out managers who have been trained to lead and manage any industry. Managers manage operations, the specific nature of the business is secondary. It matters most whether managers can apply the principles of modern management to squeeze out every drop of efficiency.[382]

This movement towards managers and management has been called many things: bureaucratization, managerial liberalism, and managerialism, to name a few. Journalist and political philosopher George Will describes three liberalisms: classical, middle, and managerial. Classical liberalism celebrated the individual, free enterprise, and a limited government.[383] Middle liberalism exchanged political rights for economic rights and celebrated welfare, a managed economy, and a large government, best seen in the welfare policies of the New Deal in America and much like Pierre Trudeau's Just Society in Canada.[384] Managerial liberalism, however, started in the 1960s and describes our current society: a world run by experts, who focus on outcomes guided by the "science" of public administration.[385] Also known as New Public Management, the modern managerial approach really gained popularity in the 1980s. The state had grown too big, unresponsive, and expensive.[386] New Public Management aimed to decrease costs and increase efficiency, guided by evidence that only experts understand.[387]

The political philosopher James Burnham introduced the term "managerialism" in his 1941 surprise best-seller *The Managerial Revolution: What Is Happening in the World*.[388] Burnham predicted the future would not see us ruled by fascists or socialists. Capitalism would not give way to socialism, as Burnham himself once believed. Instead, the future would bring rule by managers.[389] Managerialism takes management, mixes it with an ideological mindset, and injects a spirit of expansionism.[390] It promises maximal efficiency and peak performance. We can achieve more in our organizations if only we will submit ourselves to the doctrines of modern management, as explained and applied by modern managers.

Burnham believed management was the new ruling elite. Others, too, had suggested[391] civil servants were the modern upper class, but Burnham took it further. A large class made up of managers, directors, consultants, experts, advisers, and academics controlled society.[392] Sovereignty shifted from Parliament to bureaus.[393] Elected officials are only nominal rulers.[394] Elections and new political leaders mean little to management. No matter who forms government, managers hold the reins.[395]

While Burnham's *Managerial Revolution* is dated, it offers a prescient understanding of where the civil service, and specifically health care, would end up.[396] He said professionals would lose confidence in their ability to lead their own professions.[397] They would abandon core, professional pillars, under pressure to work with the managers. Even now, we see some prominent physicians advocating for a shift away from the individual doctor-patient relationship in favour of "accountability to society."[398]

Resisting the general move towards managerialism is futile. Medicare's managerial class assumes the moral superiority of its own opinions. They identify patient welfare with their own interests, quality with their assuming control.[399] They attack individualism, free enterprise, and opportunity as being chaotic.[400] They replace it with planning, coordination, collectivization.[401] Nurses and doctors cannot manage medicare, at least not without special training to turn them into managers. As such, medicare cannot function without the managerial class.[402] "No one who comes in contact with managers will fail to have noticed a very considerable assurance in their whole bearing. They know they are indispensable in modern society."[403]

As we saw in our discussion about control and ownership, in chapter three, Burnham states there can be no ownership without control. "If I cannot, when I wish to, prevent others from entering the house, if anyone else or everyone has the same rights of entry as I, then neither I nor anyone would say that I am the 'owner' of the house."[404]

Owners control access to their own businesses.[405] Medical regulators disagree. The College of Physicians and Surgeons of Ontario passed a rule that physicians must accept all patients who want to join their practice, regardless of what the physician might think. Unless a doctor has closed her practice to all new patients, she must accept everyone regardless of clinical interest, aptitude, or capacity.

Many people support the CPSO ruling. They believe every business must accept all customers, or the business must close.[406] The point is not to debate the CPSO ruling. It is to point out that business owners can no longer make this decision, and that this undermines our understanding of what it means to "own" something to which someone else controls access.[407]

The new ruling elite dictates accountability while being accountable to no one for their own decisions.

The new ruling class will have privileged access, as discussed in chapter five, to obtain care for themselves.[408] At times, Burnham seems to imply support for, or perhaps resignation over, the fact of a new ruling managerial class. Class domination seems inevitable.[409]

On a more positive note, managerialism might eliminate the crises that arise from business cycles: businesses would no longer have freedom to create chaos, notwithstanding businesses' own "constant stream of propaganda."[410] However, managerialism will create its own crises, which will be political and technical in nature.[411] Bureaucracies will struggle with sudden social shifts, such as from war to peace, or with abrupt technological changes.

Finally, Burnham discusses some of the tactics used by managers. He notes that government will need to transition social institutions towards arrangements better suited to a managerial approach. Teams and coordinated programs can be managed; ad hoc groups and social networks cannot. So government will use propaganda to weaken social institutions and bolster its own vision.[412] New laws will have Orwellian titles such as ones we actually have, for example The Patients First Act and The Future of Medicare Act.

Today, managers themselves write articles and books in support of planning and managerialism, which tend to regurgitate and prove Burnham's ideas. This ruling class sits removed from the provision of care. It focuses on data, measurement, and control. Modern managers worry most about media and politics. Power has shifted from the clinicians to the "media and the Ministry of Health."[413] Management focuses on "new ways to collect administrative data and implement controls."[414] This leaves clinicians feeling abandoned in clinical care.

Managerialism continues to spread and grow in popularity with planners. One economist calls for, "not more money, but more management."[415] Another writes that we need to move "from insured services to managed delivery systems."[416]

Frustrated Planners

THUS AN almost unsurpassable gulf yawns between those who work or have worked on the front lines of care and those who manage or talk about it. It seems many of the talkers exist in a land far removed from the real world of patient care. They talk about management of medicare as though it were a factory and praise it as though there was nothing wrong at all.

In 2017, a large group of people working in policy, government relations, communications, and advocacy, including many physicians, attended a health policy event hosted by the Canadian Medical Association, in Ottawa. We listened to two members of government and one speaker who works with government. Given *Chatham House Rules*, we were only allowed to capture ideas, not speakers' identities.

Speaker #1, a former politician, complained that pouring money into healthcare has not changed outcomes.

"This would never happen in the auto or aerospace sector," he said. We "need to measure outcomes better" against "accepted standards ... to enforce outcomes." Governments should "pay for outcomes instead of pay for care."

"We have got to dispel the myth about...the expertise of physicians. These are management decisions."

"We've known for twenty or twenty-five years what needs to be done ...The challenge is with the democratic process and how we get it done."

Speaker #1 promoted the popular devotion to central management. As the late Dr. Michael Bliss, history professor, writes:

> By the 1980s, the whole of the Western world had come to appreciate the flaws of socialist and dirigiste economic management: remove an industry from market conditions, replace price signalling with administrative fiat, outlaw competition, and you create the classic conditions for inefficiency, declining productivity, and gradually increasing consumer dissatisfaction. Not a single county anywhere copied the flawed Canadian "model."[417]

And yet politicians persist in complaining that socialized medicine struggles simply because we do not have enough "administrative fiat."[418]

Speaker #2, an external reviewer, said the province of Ontario wasted $70 million on a diabetes management system and $1 billion on e-health.

"People were afraid to offend people by saying these decisions were not good decisions to begin with."

"Politics and bureaucracy sometimes make the wrong decisions."

In reviewing government, "We [often] found no evidence of how a decision was made. Someone just picked a number." "I see abdication of responsibility by government … no one wants to make the decision."

The data are new, the message is not. Air Canada, Canadian National Railways, and Petro-Canada were once all icons of Canadian distinctiveness which improved when freed from government control.[419]

Speaker #3, a career academic health policy analyst, said he was "surprised to hear the health system was fraught with problems. We need to be way more optimistic." "What a magnificent system we have!"

We spend "too much time on blaming, shaming and 'gotcha' public policy."

"If the healthcare process is broken, then the democratic process does not work. Medicare is the single greatest outcome of the democratic process."

"If the healthcare system is broken, and you all [the MDs in the audience] cause 70 percent of the spending, what does that say about our system and the public policy process?"

This speaker dismissed studies that rank Canada near the bottom.[420] "If you regress to the average, there will always be winners and losers." Canada, "the great loser," still provides good quality. "There's really nothing there [in the studies]."

Indeed. Only socialized medicine reflects democracy. Nothing else will do. If it fails, it is your fault, doctors. Socialized medicine inverts healthcare. Instead of starting with patients and their doctors, medicare starts with governments and tax dollars.

Chapter Eight
A Misplaced Faith in Rational Technique

All political theories assume, of course, that most individuals are very ignorant. Those who plead for liberty differ from the rest in that they include among the ignorant themselves as well as the wisest.
–Friedrich Hayek

[The Rationalist] is not devoid of humility; he can imagine a problem which would remain impervious to the onslaught of his own reason. But what he cannot imagine is politics which do not consist in solving problems, or a political problem of which there is no "rational" solution at all.
–Michael Oakeshott

OUR LEADERSHIP team had been summoned. We were to appear at the central offices of our Local Health Integration Network (LHIN) to report on how we were improving the emergency department. The province had devoted funding to decreasing ED wait times. Our ED had received some of it. We were now being called to report on how we had spent it.

"Your second metric hasn't moved," Fredrick[421] said. His laser pointer twirled a red doughnut on the giant screen. "I'd like you to report on what worked, what didn't, and what you plan to change." A huge designer watch refused to stay hidden under the sleeve of his skinny suit.

My nursing colleagues stared and twitched, lips pressed together. Air rushing through nostrils filled the silence. Frederick's stubble placed him around twenty-one, although his MBA probably made him at least twenty-six: young enough to be their son.

I fired back at Fred to prevent his death by trampling. Our metric was still the best in the LHN, by over 50 percent. He knew that. Furthermore, his data feed had not repopulated with the most recent metrics. He knew that, too.

But we needed Frederick's blessing. He reviewed and approved the performance data for each ED in our LHIN. This was his chance to make an impression, and he wanted big results. We needed Frederick on our side. He was the expert, the guy with the MBA: no Frederick, no funding.

Managers hold a somewhat endearing, youthful faith that every problem can be fixed. Given the right business plan, with definable outcome measures and the right team of experts, they can fix anything. They just need to hold people accountable to delivering change based on key performance indicators.

Given their lack of experience, their ignorance about hospital culture and medical and nursing traditions, as well as their unfamiliarity with any clinical environment, they put all their faith in reason as their sole source of knowledge. This is called rationalism. If they can sit and think of a logical answer, then that answer must be true, barring any empirical detail they may have left out.[422] If clinicians raise a concern that does not fit their system, then it must, by definition, be irrational. Physicians' concerns must be based on nonsense at best, possibly even be proof of traditional hierarchy, unearned privilege, or some other nefarious source of oppression.

The rationalist seeks control and predictability. But new ideas come from unpredictability and human freedom. "Those who extol the powers of human reason usually see only one side of that interaction of human thought and conduct in which reason is at the same time used and shaped. They do not see that, for advance to take place, the social process from which the growth of reason emerges must remain free from its control."[423] The most important parts of care are supra-rational or non-rational. They transcend what we can put into words; we know more than we can tell.[424] We can find reasons to support them, but only after the fact. If we were planning clinical care pathways, we would never include any work or intervention that was not warranted based on reason. This often leaves out the most important elements of patient care.

When I started in emergency medicine, for example, the fastest physician in the department tried to teach me how to be more efficient.

He advised a "one touch" approach. Get everything done in one interaction with a patient, wherever possible. Especially for the frail, most complex patients, who will need to see a consultant, try to make your first interaction your last one. Get a good history. Perform a thorough exam. Order a full work-up. But make sure to tell the patient that the next doctor they see will be the consultant, which may take eight or ten hours.

It would be irrational to pop your head in to explain any minor changes in bloodwork, he said. All old people have abnormal lab tests. You would be wasting time to reassure them their CT scan did not show anything significant. Again, all old patients have *some* findings: atrophy, calcification, or age-related changes. If the patient demands to see you, get the nurse to find out what they want, give the nurse your answer, and keep moving on to see other patients. This approach will maximize patient flow, decrease wait times, and, if you happen to be paid fee for service, will maximize your income. Even if you are on salary, you must focus on the ruthless elimination of all irrational behaviour. To paraphrase *Star Trek*'s Dr. McCoy, "I'm a doctor, dammit, not a therapist."

We could argue that basic human dignity demands that the "one touch" patient should be extremely rare. Patients want to see their physician more than once in a ten-hour stretch. The rationalist might counter that some patients would want their doctor to pop in every fifteen minutes. We have to cut patients off somewhere. Are you suggesting we make a rule, for example, that doctors must reassess their patients every hour? If it is rational to say no to a patient's request to talk with her physician every fifteen minutes during her visit to the emergency department, then it is equally rational to refuse requests at any time, unless there is some material benefit that only a physician can deliver to the patient. If the patient simply wants human interaction with a clinician, a nurse can do it, or call the chaplain if the patient is that needy.

To a twenty-something MBA staring at a spreadsheet in a boardroom, this might make sense. It is LEAN thinking: the efficiency approach championed by Toyota. Eliminate all waste. Only do what adds material value to the instrumental delivery of excellent medical care.

However, service — the intangible goods exchanged in social interactions — is not LEAN. To be clear, LEAN works great in hospitals. It can force emergency teams to finally support shortening a six-page assessment form, if a patient only has a broken fingernail. This can take years to change, in a Canadian hospital. LEAN can help transform every clinical environment. But it works only if the Six Sigma-certified LEAN experts are not rationalists.

Rationalism starts with a misunderstanding of what counts as knowledge. A case in point: Frederick, in the same presentation, twirled his laser pointer around what he thought was meaningful information. He believed his metric captured what mattered. Management meant moving the metric. And he was hired to manage. Aside from having toured through a few EDs, Frederick lacked practical knowledge of management and any real knowledge of the field he was determined to manage. He did not see any need for the practical knowledge required to run an ED, never mind the skill, training, and experience required to provide patient care. He believed he had enough technical knowledge about health policy, funding, and the latest management techniques to solve our problems. Michael Oakeshott's famous essay "Rationalism in Politics" applies here.

> Rationalism is the assertion that ... practical knowledge is not knowledge at all, the assertion that, properly speaking, there is no knowledge which is not technical knowledge. The Rationalist holds that the only element of *knowledge* involved in any human activity is technical knowledge, and that... practical knowledge is really only a sort of nescience which would be negligible if it were no positively mischievous. The sovereignty of "reason", for the Rationalist, means the sovereignty of technique.[425]

Rationalism starts with misunderstanding and "amounts to a corruption of the mind."[426]

Many things in medicine exist as a necessary part of care because of the fact medicine is a human and humane endeavour built up over several thousand years. They have intrinsic not just instrumental value. Medicine is like the English language, not Esperanto, the invented rational language.

Medicine is a social endeavour. It contains habits and patterns of thought that, despite decades of effort to make everything "evidence-based," appear to be nothing more than tradition.

> There is, of course, no question either of retaining or improving such a tradition, for both these involve an attitude of submission. It must be destroyed. And to fill its place the Rationalist puts something of his own making — an ideology, the formalized abridgement of the supposed substratum of rational truth contained in the tradition.[427]

We cannot create evidence for everything. No one will ever do a randomized controlled trial on parachutes. This does not mean we stop experimenting, learning, or trying to find reasons. However, the search for reasons does not mean things that admit no reason are useless. Medicine requires *more* than empiricism and reason alone.[428]

Since rationalism acknowledges only what comes through reason, it cannot fix itself. "You cannot escape its errors by becoming more sincerely or more profoundly rationalistic."[429] Rationalism in politics combines the "politics of perfection" with the "politics of uniformity."[430] When applied to health policy, it shapes legislation, guides managers, and determines which metrics young MBAs should twirl their pointer around.

The need to remove ambiguity through planning and management acquires a moral character. It becomes normative; any debate to the contrary seems mischievous.[431] If the "right" way forward is obvious, it follows that we should apply an authoritarian approach to implement it.[432]

Application of the sovereignty of technique[433] gives us grand documents, such as the Beveridge Report. William Beveridge offered a plan in 1942 to rebuild Britain and address what he called five giant evils: "Want, Disease, Ignorance, Squalor, and Idleness."[434] This plan formed the basis of the British welfare state. Oakeshott called the Beveridge Report a progeny of rationalism.[435] One of Beveridge's team members, Leonard Marsh, wrote the same ideas into a report for Canada, the Marsh Report, 1943.[436] Canada has shelves that sag with similar reports: the Hall Commission, the Lalonde Report, the second Hall Commission, the National Forum on Health, the Romanow Commission, the Kirby Report, and the Naylor Report, to name a few.[437] All bespeaking a "politics of the book."[438]

The rationalist disposition is the only one allowed in a managerial approach mentioned earlier. We prefer "the consciously planned and deliberately executed ... better than what has grown up and established itself unselfconsciously over a period of time."[439] Innovation and creativity always include the element of surprise.[440] Rationalism will have none of it. Unless it is in a book or a guideline, it cannot be allowed.[441]

The most obvious problem with this approach — aside from its repeated failures — is that it ignores most people's experience. Real life is messy, complex. If baking a cake is simple, and sending a rocket to the moon is complicated, then raising a child is complex. Success with your first child is no guarantee with the second.[442] All human interactions are complex. They resist the rationalist faith in technique: "The rationalist faith in the sovereignty of technique is the presupposition both of the notion that some overall scheme of mechanized control is possible and of the details of every scheme that has so far been projected: it is understood as what is called an 'administrative' problem."[443]

Unfortunately, we cannot convince managers who are themselves convinced of rationalism — or perhaps blind to their conviction of rationalism — that it does not work. Each new program they design is still rationalist, just newer.[444]

Rationalism leads us to look in the past for information to build plans for the future. By definition, we assume we already have everything we need to plan,[445] which ties us back to our discussion about the planned economy. The rationalist cannot plan until he knows the demands and prescribes the supply.[446]

We started this discussion with Frederick's confusion about what counts as knowledge. He made up for his lack of practical knowledge by using the supremacy of technique. But we glossed over the difference between technical and practical knowledge. We will pick this up again in chapter ten (about government's ignorance of medicine).

Wrong Facts

HEALTHCARE RESISTS management. Leaders can influence, incentivize behaviours, and shape environments. They can nudge.[447] But healthcare cannot be managed. Attempts to manage it will fail. There is too much information we do not know, and no one is smart enough to handle what we already know. Bureaucracies are a bit like airplanes: the number of dials, switches, and warning lights is proportional to the size the aircraft. Big planes have tonnes of dials. In medicare, this shows up as an obsession to categorize, commodify, and calculate. Everything must be measured, and everyone wants to take part in it. Everyone assumes it helps, and no one stops to consider otherwise.[448]

The capture, measurement, and analysis of data becomes a necessary obsession for planners who insist on planning. They collect data in part, because they can but also because they cannot even start to plan without it. This has led to an obsession with data collection for the sake of collection. If it gets used, "it is used mindlessly." Rarely, does anyone consider the cost of distraction to the clinicians, "plus the costs of the political battles that ensue over who is measuring what, how, where, when, and for whom."[449]

Mark Britnell, having worked around the world as a health consultant, says demands for data not only distract doctors but also can cause harm: "There is overwhelming concern that the increasing number of measures imposed on providers are largely irrelevant and even harmful ... incessant demands for information from regulators, state and federal governments accreditation agencies and professional bodies can impede transparency and accountability rather than encourage it."[450] Even so, politicians continue to advocate fact-based policy and the need for informed public policy.[451]

Henry Mintzberg, professor of management at McGill, suggests we need to question our faith in data, benchmarks, and evidence in general.[452] Instead, we should remember the crucial role of clinical judgment.[453] Clinical decision making always falls in a space filled with incomplete and largely ambiguous information. If everything was crisp, clear, obvious, and data-driven, we would not need physicians. The path towards healing is never clear, always "poorly lit and subject to changes in direction."[454]

Crisp metrics, such as HbA1c levels, blood pressure readings, and surgical complication rates, can never capture more than an artificial slice of clinical medicine. And yet, these are the numbers planners use to define and control. Bureaucracies prefer precise, standard measures, as opposed to accurate ones. A bureaucracy needs simplified, standardized data.[455] States aspire to uniformity and order.[456] "No administrative system is capable of representing *any* existing social community except through a heroic and greatly schematized process of abstraction and simplification."[457]

Medicine applies science, but it is much more than applied science.[458] This leads to a discussion about the nature of medicine, to which we return in chapter ten. The focus here, however, is medicare's obsession with data, which, at heart, is a quest for knowledge.[459] Planners know they do not know enough to plan. In fact, planners can never know enough to assign resources that will meet people's needs, given changing demands for those resources. Friedrich Hayek, Nobel Prize-winning economist, explored this difficulty of central planning for the allocation of resources and services given variable demand. How can central planners know enough to plan an economy? If they could gather enough information, is there anyone, or any team of smart people, able to plan better than individuals are able to plan on their own? He published a landmark paper, "The Use of Knowledge in Society," in 1945, in which he presented a serious challenge that undermined the intellectual validity of welfare economics.[460] No one knows enough to allocate resources, Hayek said. No one is smart enough, and no one has enough data:

> The peculiar character of the problem of a rational economic order is determined precisely by the fact that the knowledge of the circumstances of which we must make use never exists in concentrated or integrated form but solely as the dispersed bits of incomplete and frequently contradictory knowledge which all the separate individuals possess. The economic problem of society is thus not merely a problem of how to allocate "given" resources — if "given" is taken to mean given to a single mind which deliberately solves the problem set by these "data." It is rather a problem of how to secure the best use of resources

known to any of the members of society, for ends whose relative importance only these individuals know. Or, to put it briefly, it is a problem of the utilization of knowledge which is not given to anyone in its totality.

Even staunch supporters of central planning and welfare economics acknowledge the power of Hayek's knowledge problem. Central planners will never have enough information to model or anticipate all the individual decisions and preferences that go into individual decision making. Neither Big Data nor Artificial Intelligence can substitute for millions of people making decisions on their own. The knowledge problem demands epistemic humility. At best, planning, as one writer puts it, "constitutes a case of the blind leading the sighted."[461]

Management of medicare becomes a harried scramble for facts that too often mean nothing, analysed by experts without experience, who write policy few can understand. We are led by "the complex of established civil servants whose expert knowledge can never amount to wisdom, and who are themselves in need of the guidance which no mere body of facts or statistics could provide."[462]

Too often the metrics and figures mean nothing. "Public agencies are very keen on amassing statistics — they collect them, add them, raise them to the nth power, take the cube root and prepare wonderful diagrams. But what you must never forget is that every one of those figures comes in the first instance from the village watchman, who just puts down what he damn pleases."[463]

Wrong Model

"TO A MAN with a hammer, everything looks like a nail." So goes the saying, and it certainly applies to medicare. First, it describes planners' preference to solve all problems using managerialism applied through planning. Second, it describes their assumption about the kind of thing they are trying to whack. Planners assume medicare is something like a machine or a factory. A number of writers have highlighted the problem of managing public agencies. We look at three approaches below.

David Levine, mentioned earlier, argues that governments struggle precisely because they misunderstand the fundamental nature of what they are trying to manage. They assume medicine is a mechanistic bureaucracy, instead of a professional one.[464]

> In a professional bureaucracy, the objectives are external to the organization; for example, making patients well ... There is no best way to provide all the goods and services all the time and the professionals are expected to use their skills and experience to seek the best outcomes using available scientific data.
>
> In a mechanistic bureaucracy, resources are used to provide goods and services ...There is a best practice to produce those goods and services ... The person in charge knows the best practice and, in a clearly top-down approach, implements the management model that will succeed.[465]

Healthcare is not a machine that can be examined and fixed by replacing a part. It is more like a pond or an ecosystem. Most of healthcare will never look like an assembly line, where raw materials enter at one end, are processed, and are spit out as new product at the other end. Healthcare does not have highly predictable inputs, crisp processes, and definable outputs.

Mintzberg describes four types of organizations: machine, entrepreneurial, project, and professional.[466] Machine organizations work like factories. Entrepreneurial organizations, like Apple, revolve around a leader. Project organizations work around teams building novel projects. Medicine and education are examples of professional organizations, which are almost the opposite of machine organizations.[467]

If governments try to manage professional organizations like machine organizations, they create chaos for the organization and the people served by it: detached solutions applied to situations that require nuance and judgment.[468]

James Q. Wilson offers the most in-depth contribution to this discussion. He explains in his classic *Bureaucracy: What Government Agencies Do and Why They Do It* that managers of public agencies face different problems depending on what they have been asked to manage.[469] This seems obvious, but his insight is not. Wilson also suggests his own four organizational types: production, procedural, craft, and coping. In each organization, managers try to manage "operators": the people who do the work. Wilson writes about *outputs* and *outcomes*. I find these words too similar and thus confusing. So I use *activity* instead of *output*. Each type of organization sorts into a group based on whether or not we can see and measure its *activities* and *outcomes*.

A post office is an example of a production organization. We can see the work done (activities, sorting mail) and measure the outcome (letters delivered). *Activities and outcomes are obvious.*

The military in peacetime is an example of a procedural organization. We can see marches and training exercises, but we cannot know about performance until a war starts. *We see activities but not outcomes.*

Professional negotiators are an example of a craft organization. They negotiate in secret, but their deals are public. *Activities are unseen, outcomes obvious.*

Finally, police officers provide an example of a coping organization. Officers keep the peace, but how can we know how much peace has been kept or lost? Furthermore, how does one keep the peace, a metaphysical concept? *We cannot see activity or outcome.*

We need to chew on coping organizations a bit more. In these organizations, managers attempt to manage the unseen, the invisible. But what is an unseen activity? After all, police officers are not invisible. Again Wilson: "Of course some work can be observed some of the time and some examples of results achieved do occasionally come into view ... A police sergeant periodically sees a patrol officer working the street ..." But keeping the peace is intangible. Parades, parties, and picnics each have crowds but present different tasks for officers. Peaceful behaviour at Caribana might be mayhem at lawn bowling.

Schools are coping organizations too. Administrators visit classrooms but cannot measure learning. Tests cannot show whether learning occurred in school or elsewhere.[470]

But is medicine a coping organization? Are the things doctors do, for the most part, unseen? Wilson argues it is such an organization.

The aim of medicine is *"to cure sometimes, to relieve often, and to comfort always."* Doctors can sometimes diagnose, treat, and cure. Managers can measure how many diagnoses led to treatments and then to cures. Cause and effect holds for some diseases. More rarely than patients realize or doctors admit, however.

Doctors work in private. Outcomes appear decades later, if at all. For example, we tell patients to stop smoking. But smoking does not always cause death. Counselling does not always cause quitting. And we cannot know for sure whether counselling, individual effort, or something else played the biggest role in a patient's success. Or a surgeon assesses a sore hip. It is too soon for surgery. But how did he decide? What, exactly, did the surgeon do? How can we manage an assessment that advises no action? Different surgeons might arrive at different assessments.

Statistics offer a pseudo-solution. For example, managers identify more hip replacements in Ottawa than Peterborough. Why does this happen? Do surgeons in Ottawa provide unnecessary care? Are Ottawans obese, causing a preponderance of bad hips? Is access to surgery poor in Peterborough? We might never know. But horse-sense and managers tell us rates should be the same everywhere. Outliers indicate greed or sloth. Modern sense tell us medicine is nothing but scientific technique applied to crisp diagnoses. But Sir William Osler said medicine is a science of uncertainty and an art of probability. Much of what doctors do is invisible, with loose association to outcomes.

Medicine is most often a coping organization (like keeping the peace: *activities* and *outputs* unseen). Sometimes it is craft (like a negotiator: *outputs* seen). Rarely is it production (like a post office: *activities* and *outputs* seen) and never procedure (like the military in peacetime: *activities* seen).

If the best argument supports medicine as being a coping organization, that is the worst case for managers. Managers of coping organizations face an impossible task. Hospitals try to hire the best nurses without any definition of best. Managers shape high-performing cultures without being certain about performance. Hospital leaders field complaints without knowing if a complaint is justified or atypical.[471]

When management fails, managers try to turn coping organizations into procedural ones. They measure and surveil. Even if we cannot know exactly what happens in a counselling session, or whether counselling works at all, we can at least measure how many minutes of counselling took place and review all the notes from the session.[472]

Wilson arrives at a dire but accurate summary for the management of a coping organization like medicine: that it is almost impossible. Given the nature of the organization, and the attempts to manage it, relationships between management and operators become strained, at best.[473] Workers feel they are always being watched, never certain of where or why punishment may come. "Consequently, operators in coping organizations often feel they are treated unfairly by managers who don't 'back them up' or who are 'always getting on their case.'"[474] Workers in an organization in which they feel attacked and nit-picked, without any backup for real needs, will find it hard to remain enthusiastic about the job. When managers try to manage medicine by treating it like a procedural organization, they crush doctors' morale. "The great risks in procedural organizations are that morale will suffer (operators may resent the surveillance, believing they know — even if they cannot show — how to do the job right) and that the surveillance will bias the work of the agency (by inducing operators to conform to rules that detract from the attainment of goals)." Morale suffers. Surveillance increases. Regulation creates a bias to follow the rules instead of serving patients. Attempts to turn medicine into something it is not make doctors focus on meaningless things for unimportant outcomes. They crush professionals' sense of calling.[475] In coping organizations, "The managers and operators will be in constant conflict; the former will focus their efforts on the latter's most easily measured activities, and effective management is almost impossible."[476]

Levine calls medicine a professional bureaucracy, Mintzberg calls it a professional organization, and Wilson calls it a coping organization. Each writer uses different names to highlight slightly different issues, but they all agree on one thing. Disaster awaits those who ignore the nature of what they are trying to manage. Hammering medicine into the wrong model guarantees failure and irreversible damage to those inside. But planners hammer anyway.

Chapter Nine
A Misplaced Faith in Laws and Regulation

Throughout history orators and poets have extolled liberty, but no one has told
us why liberty is so important. Our attitude towards such matters should depend
on whether we consider civilization as fixed or as advancing ... In an advancing
society ... any restriction on liberty reduces the number of things tried and so
reduces the rate of progress. In such a society freedom of action is granted to the
individual, not because it gives him greater satisfaction but because if allowed to
go his own way he will on the average serve the rest of us better than under any
orders we know how to give.
–H.B. Philips

Dying societies accumulate laws like dying men accumulate remedies.
–Nicolás Gómez Dávila[477]

IN THE DAYS before digital copy, medical students lugged around giant
textbooks. *Harrison's Principles of Internal Medicine* and *Schwartz's Principles
of Surgery*—each ran over a thousand pages and represented the pinnacle
of medical knowledge. Excellence meant learning as much as possible from
these giant books, and many others like them. Ignorance guaranteed disaster,
not only on exams, but for real live patients.

Each large hospital in Ontario now has rules, regulations, and
department manuals that together run to several thousand pages. Orientation for new nurses requires a full week of education to get through policies
and procedures, where it once took only a few hours. Physicians must sign a
declaration each year during annual reappointment applications, stating they
not only know and will abide by all the rules, regulations, and bylaws pertain-

ing to their hospital privileges but also have reviewed and understand all the updates and *ad hoc* changes that have occurred over the last twelve months. These rules pile on top of the 380,000 regulations businesses already face in Ontario.[478] No single person knows or could know all the rules and regs.

Americans apparently commit three felonies each day without knowing it.[479] We live in a world awash with rules,[480] which socialized medicine amplifies. Alexis de Tocqueville predicted this, in 1835: "[The state] covers the surface of society with a network of small, complicated rules, minute and uniform, through which the most original minds and the most energetic characters cannot penetrate, to rise above the crowd."[481]

Replacing Knowledge With Power

WHICH LEADS us into the intimidating field of jurisprudence and regulation. Even as non-specialists, we need to hazard some general comments about legislation and how it applies more broadly to regulation in medicare. These comments apply equally to laws and to the overwhelming number of regulatory policies: anything designed to restrict freedom, backed by the state's monopoly on force.

Although policies, rules, and hospital regulations are not laws themselves, many policies carry the force of law. If a physician can lose his licence to practice medicine for breaking a policy, the policy functions like a law. The closer a policy applies to a particular clinical environment — for example, a policy on infection control in the emergency department — the less the policy functions like a law.

We will start by asking why governments legislate to control care in the first place. Then we will look at the character, volume, and impact of regulation in medicare.

No one expects Starbucks to reorganize, or improve service, by having government pass a new law. Starbucks might lobby government to pass a law that puts all other coffee shops out of business, but it would never try to change its business practices through legislation. However, medicare does this all the time.

The idea that we can control outcomes by writing laws represents one particular view of the law. It is so common now, most people take it to be self-evident. Law professors call it legal instrumentalism.[482] Instrumentalism "enables officials to control outcomes one situation at a time."[483] The law is seen as an empty vessel, merely a tool, without content of its own. "Stripped to its core, instrumentalism is not much more than unfettered power to coerce."[484] Of course, this is the opposite of what people mean when they speak about the rule of law: "People are to be ruled by laws rather than by the subjective inclinations of those in authority."[485] We cannot resolve the debate here, but we need to notice that socialized medicine cannot function without legal instrumentalism.

This still does not answer why a government would pass laws to run medicare. Governments need to regulate what they do not understand. The need arises because of their lack of knowledge. "Regulation is an effort to replace knowledge with power." The only way to exert control of something they do not understand is to regulate it — pass laws about what an industry or business can and cannot do. It is an "attempt to substitute for the actual knowledge residing within the company about its operations and markets."[486]

Regulation is rationalism applied to law-making.[487] And as we saw earlier, rationalism relies on knowledge of the past. Regulation uses the past to regulate the future.[488]

Legislators, civil servants, and administrators do not have knowledge of the operators inside medicare, and they have very little stake in the outcomes. Given ignorance, they attempt to regulate everything and turn clinics and hospitals into bureaucracies. Furthermore, governments and regulatory agencies establish their legitimacy by regulating. It defines their reason to exist. And if they under-regulate, it makes people question the efficacy of the agency itself.[489] With every disaster, the public calls for more regulation.[490]

Regulatory Unreasonableness

IF WE think of the law as a tool to solve particular problems, then the only thing stopping us from writing a new law for every problem is not having the political support to do so. The problem is that good laws are hard to write, even if they look simple. Good laws capture unconscious habits of civil society into articulated statements. Law develops over generations. "It has, of course, been as little invented by any one mind as language or money or most of the practices and conventions on which social life rests."[491] For example, "Keep off the grass" captures agreed upon habits that have developed over generations. Long before the "Keep off the grass" law, neighbours knew being a good neighbour meant keeping off each other's lawn. Furthermore, "Keep off the grass" meant you can go anywhere you please so long as you avoid the verge. The instrumentalist version of "Keep off the grass" is "Walk on the sidewalk," do not go anywhere else.[492]

When it comes to legislating to control the medical industry, governments tend to pass legislation that is either really detailed and applicable to specific situations, or really broad, with details to be worked out later in regulatory changes. Passing legislation is relatively hard; changing regulations is comparatively easy. But both approaches presuppose an instrumentalist approach to law: laws need to solve practical problems through legislated control.

At one extreme, for example, Quebec passed a law (Bill 20) against part-time practice for doctors. At the other extreme, the Ontario Liberals passed the so-called Patients First Act (Bill 210), a 200-page omnibus bill that amended or introduced ten different pieces of healthcare legislation. Government gave itself broad powers but offered few details about scope or intent. The bill introduced oversight to "healthcare facilities" but did not define a facility. Without definition, every single doctor's private office could be considered a facility and be open to oversight by an external administrator. Legislators essentially abandoned their duty to lead and left the details to be worked out by the bureaucrats who write the regulations later.

Consider another example. In 2014, the Ontario Conservatives tabled Bill 29, which calls for total transparency and reporting about physicians, including all patient complaints and deaths[493] reported while under their care, as well as complaints and deaths from other jurisdictions. The *Toronto Star* loved it.

While it might seem like common sense to some, the trouble comes when we try to implement instrumentalist laws. Too often, regulators impose new regulation in a legalistic way.[494] This "regulatory unreasonableness" creates an adversarial relationship between regulators and the regulated, which rules out any hope of the cooperation required to fix complex problems.[495] Regulatory unreasonableness itself is hard to measure. Inflexible regulation seems to come from a desire to decrease harm. When industry, tainted by self-interest, complains about regulatory burden, people assume the regulations must be doing a good job.[496] (This also applies to the regulatory colleges, which we address in the next section.)

Returning to Bill 29, we know blame and shame makes providers hide mistakes. Cover-up guarantees that no one learns[497] and other patients will probably suffer the same harm. Furthermore, the law creates its own confusion. Who should be blamed when a patient dies from cancer: the family doc, who knew the patient for years; the surgeon who operated two weeks before; the intensive care doc who cared for the patient in the ICU; or the palliative care doc in the last few days? Palliative physicians care for dying patients. All of their patients die. Does that make them bad doctors? Even if a palliative care doc *is* a murderous physician, how would the public know based on the public reporting? Should we report the naturopathic doc who treated the cancer for eighteen months before the patient finally sought medical attention? Furthermore, would such a bill encourage physicians to care for the very sick or those in greatest need? Most attempts to rescue the dying rest on slim hope. Shall we reward these deaths with blame and shame?

The bill also proposed blame and shame for all complaints.[498] Often, patients with major mental health challenges have the most time to craft complaints. Aside from the obvious ones, many complaints require investigation to reveal that psychosis, delusion, or other cognitive challenges determined the content. Many complaints focus on things out of doctors' control: wait times, legislated reporting about a patient's ability to drive (patients hate this!), the absence of beds in the emergency department, and even the volume of the background music in the clinic and the perfume worn by the front staff. This leads all parties involved to demand even greater clarity and specificity in laws, which makes even less room for flexible application.[499] It makes both sides lawyer up and fight each instance of alleged malfeasance or unreasonableness, which exponentially increases the cost and difficulty of regulation overall.

Legislation Epidemic

THIS APPROACH leads in one direction: more laws and tighter restrictions. "The ratchet wheel of regulatory control can become tighter but cannot easily be loosened."[500] If we simply plot the number of statutes relating to the regulation of medical practice starting in the early twentieth century, and leaving aside all the provisions within each statute, the graph looks like a plot of COVID-19 incidence.[501] Every epidemic either overwhelms the herd it infects or dies off itself. At some point, a system cannot function. A legislative epidemic pits legislators against providers.

In fairness, we cannot blame government for all of the legislation. Too often doctors and nurses and other stakeholders in the system seek to pass legislation to benefit themselves. Economists call this rent seeking. For example, nurse practitioners continually seek to expand the things the state will allow them to do, while blocking the development of other providers, such as Physician Assistants, from practice in Canada. And physicians, historically, have continually sought to restrict other professions in the same way (in the name of patient safety, of course).

An equal amount of lobbying goes into demands for legislation to control patient behaviour: bike helmets, smoking, sugary foods, and so on. It reminds me of a conversation I had with a group of doctors about gambling:

> "You'd never believe the pain some of my patients experience with problem gambling," one doctor said.
>
> "We should lobby government to stop using

revenues from gambling!" said another.

Some in the group frowned and nodded.

"Don't we finance our hospitals with lotteries?" someone asked.

Silence. Blank stares.

"Should physicians dictate morality?" another doctor asked.

More silence. A few of the doctors raised their eyebrows and tried to avoid eye contact.

"When do we stop making laws and start supporting individual freedom?" I asked.

Five or six of them came alive at the same time: "Don't you agree with seatbelts?" one asked. "How about stop signs?" said another.

"Of course I agree with seatbelts and stop signs," I said.

"Well, then you agree with government limiting free choice!"

Granted, this group of physicians reflected a narrow voting demographic not reflective of doctors in general. However, they represented a common theme in the medical politics. The Annual General Meeting of the Canadian Medical Association, until 2018, was four days of motions and speeches about how doctors wanted government to legislate about everything from cholesterol to cats on planes. Again, however, the types of physicians who speak up most at CMA meetings also tend to be from the same voting demographic. They want rules, guidelines, and policy to drive change. Is this because physicians are paternalistic? Do they believe patients cannot decide what to eat on their own? Maybe Canadians prefer rules and doctors just reflect the culture?

Regardless, people who conflate stop signs with prohibitions on cholesterol have confused mutual limits on individual freedom with imposing personal preference on others.[502] It is one thing for us all to obey stop signs for the safety of all. It is something else entirely for elites to impose restrictions on other people's behaviour that have little to do with the elites' own freedom.

Leaving aside the morality of gambling, casinos, and cholesterol, should physicians advocate for laws that limit patient freedom? One physician wrote me, "As long as healthcare is tax funded, and universal, we should limit freedoms of people to keep costs down. If healthcare is private, then you can advocate for individual freedoms."[503] His logic is valid, but is it sound? Another physician wrote, "When the state commits its taxpayers to easing the consequences of its people's actions, then the state has a responsibility to try to prevent those consequences. When socialized healthcare pays for not only the unavoidable frailties of our biology, but also for easing the negative outcomes of our lifestyles, then it is drawn into attempts to alter those lifestyles, even if only for fiscal reasons."[504]

How Law Shapes Medicine

WHEN REGULATIONS are applied with regulatory unreasonableness, doctors are forced to focus on regulations instead of patients. "We are distracted by ever more detailed regulations which give comfort to politicians and officials but fail to secure high quality in a sustainable fashion."[505] In Canada and the US, "healthcare is turning into an industry focused on compliance and regulation rather than patient care."[506] It turns patients into standardized units and undermines the doctor-patient relationship.[507] It makes healthcare more expensive than it would be otherwise.[508]

Government wants to manage doctors but does not want responsibility for outcomes. Politicians want to direct doctors like employees, but they do not want the legal blame when their "employees" underperform. However, when we try to make people accountable for everything, it often makes them less willing to act like responsible citizens.[509]

Innovation, creativity, and excellence in clinical care require freedom to act in the best interests of patients. Legislation never increases freedom. It limits the freedom of those restricted by the legislation. It places the cost of legislation on those being restricted, if they cannot, in turn, pass those costs on to customers.

Peter Schuck, professor emeritus of law at Yale, offers an in-depth look at how law impacts policy-making. The "policy-impairing properties of law are (1) its ubiquity; (2) the simplicity-complexity trade-off; (3) its ambiguity; (4) its discretion; (5) its procedural apparatus; (6) its inertia; and (7) its crowding-out effects on spontaneous, low-cost cooperation."[510] In short, laws are a terrible way to build policy, including health policy.

Regulation prevents doctors and nurses from improving the quality of care and service they try to deliver.[511] It rarely works to lower costs and often introduces inefficiency and unexpected costs.[512] Its uniformity, or "simplicity-complexity trade-off," makes providers feel oppressed by the blunt force of new bills. A former British minister of health wrote, "I am convinced that it is not the rightness or wrongness of the policy decisions that have to be taken by the Minister of Health that exercises the anxiety of the profession, but the fact of the uniform application of those decisions, right or wrong."[513]

We cannot blame politicians for wanting action. Given the chance, doctors would legislate, too. But it runs against any kind of scientific progress, in which ideas are tried, revised, and tried again. Legislation is the imposition of an untried, unilateral, and universal change.

Some governments have recognized the issue. For a time, the federal government, under Prime Minister Harper, had a red tape reduction action plan[514] with a commitment to reducing red tape.[515] However, Harper notes, "It is wrong to assume that all regulation is bad or that deregulation is always good ... Canada was the first country in the world to legislate the 'one-for-one' rule. The end result can be fewer and smarter regulations with lower compliance costs, especially for small-business owners."[516] Even starting with a list of all the health legislation in each province, as Alberta did, would help. I suspect it would stretch beyond many thousands of pages.

Justice Winkler, a retired Chief Justice of Ontario, served as conciliator in the 2015 negotiations between the Ontario Medical Association and the Ministry of Health. In his report, he offered an assessment of negotiations. But he also offered insight that applied more broadly. He said doctors and government "seemed to be on a collision course."[517] He said the current approach is not sustainable.

Medicine has existed for two millennia on abstract rules that defy codification and embodiment in regulations precisely due to the complexity of the medical subject, the patient. We cannot turn medicine into a list of rules for the same reason we cannot turn patients into robots with instruction manuals.

Rules and regulations risk all of the following problems: they stop staff from thinking and impoverish decision making; they make staff hesitate, or freeze with indecision; they mandate a one-size-fits-all approach to individual patients; they cannot keep pace with progress; their creators rarely know the job like front-line workers; rules are often ambiguous and open to interpretation; they cannot account for every possibility; and people cannot remember all the rules. Regulation is expensive; requires hordes of managers to enforce; takes hours to maintain; and crushes ingenuity and personal effort. Regulation undermines leadership, and it cannot create real change. Regulation assumes an air of infallibility and certitude.[518]

Blunt regulation atrophies the resilience required to react in the face of uncertainty. Instead of fostering homeostasis based on feedback loops and adjustment to changing inputs, regulation creates rigidity and an inability to adjust to change or nuance. Regulations are complicated, but life is complex. Healthcare *should* define great customer service for other members of the service industry, but it never will as long as it is over-regulated. Despite all this, governments insist on piling new legislation on old, without ever considering the impact of the load.[519] In 1974, Victor Fuchs, economics professor at Stanford, wrote:[520] "If the past is a good guide to the future, the emphasis is likely to shift to getting legislation that *appears* to serve great and noble purposes. Then, if the system in fact fails to live up to the expectations, the failures can be blamed on the administrators or [underfunding], or on health professionals for sabotaging the programs."

Regulators might do well to consider the difference between enforcing laws vs. solving problems.[521] The whole point of regulation is to decrease risk.[522] But that requires cooperation, which flexibility fosters and legalism crushes. All public policy requires trade-offs only "minimized by promoting and preserving an uneasy equilibrium" between the conflict of values.[523]

How can we get a well-ordered society with respect to medical care? (Hint: it is not with regulation.)[524] We might spend more time considering the huge cost of regulation,[525] and the equally large cost of changing it.[526] Unfortunately, the costs of regulatory unreasonableness are externalized — the regulators pass the costs on to doctors, patients, or the public at large.[527]

Is Self-regulation Dead?

MEDICINE, as a profession, used to work on decreasing risk and maintaining order through self-regulation. This is a form of indirect regulation[528] that still carries the state's monopoly on force to impose compliance. However, self-regulation acknowledges the essential role cooperation plays in guiding behaviour. Patients do best when doctors and regulators work together to improve care and decrease risk.

Self-regulation was supposed to solve problems, not enforce laws. For over a hundred years, it served to make space for the nuance and discussion required to sort out difficult and often abstract ideas about medical competence and professionalism. Times have changed. Legal instrumentalism now infects the regulatory colleges also, especially the CPSO. Over the last two decades, the college has pursued more explicit policies and applied them with less and less flexibility.

Many physicians would describe the CPSO as the apotheosis of regulatory unreasonableness, examples of which could fill many books. In one case, a physician sustained an arm injury that prevented him from writing charts for several months. But he could dictate. In fact, dictation increased the detail and degree of clinical content he could capture in his charts. He sought legal advice and found that current policy allowed charting in either official language — even in Braille — as long as the charts met other criteria such as being contemporaneous, consecutive, and so on. The CPSO policy allowed recorded dictations to be stored in the electronic medical record. After eighteen months of charting this way, the physician had a random, peer assessment by the CPSO. He passed the assessment with a strong recommendation. His arm healed, and he continued using dictation, which created a superior clinical record overall.

Six months later, the CPSO wrote to say they planned to reverse his assessment. Although current policy allowed recorded dictations, the CPSO planned to change its policy to allow only transcribed dictations. In the future, all notes must be transcribed and all dictations over the past several years must be transcribed also, even though the CPSO had said it was not necessary originally. The presented an enormous, unexpected cost for the physician.

After attempting to argue the ruling, the physician's lawyers advised him to abandon the fight. The CPSO has the right to make, change, and enforce its own policy. If he wanted to keep his licence, he must comply. It took the physician over two years to pay off the more than $30,000 transcription fee to get his charts into the condition demanded by the new policy.

Other far more egregious examples exist, some of which cause serious mental health issues including suicide.[529] However, egregious cases do not change the regulatory institution itself. The CPSO simply agrees that tragic outcomes exist from particular failed policies, but those policies no longer exist. Discussion of faulty concepts that underlie the current regulatory approach never take place. Many (most?) physicians in Ontario, especially in the community, live in continual fear of the regulator.

This image actually helps the college. It wants a tough-on-crime persona. It needs to maintain friction with physicians to add to its own credibility with government, media, and other stakeholders. If doctors hate the college's unreasonableness, it must be doing a good job of protecting patients from harm. The regulatory colleges act as an arm of the state, at the pleasure of government. If government believes the CPSO is not being tough enough, government can replace the leadership and take over operations.

Regulatory colleges write the laws, arrest doctors, try them, judge them, and then deliver the punishment. Medical regulators represent the purest form of autocracy in the Western world. Given this, regulatory colleges seem to have abandoned self-regulation, in any original sense of the word. The last registrar of the CPSO wrote in his final address, "I believe the term 'self-regulation' is well on its way to the dustbin of history."[530] "In the future, College work will no longer be described as 'the privilege of self-regulation,' but instead 'the responsibility of medical regulation.'"

I have known many doctors who became chiefs of departments. Chiefs must sign the reappointment letters for each physician in their department, stating that each physician is safe to practice. Chiefs oversee quality. They handle patient complaints. They see problems before they become patterns. Good chiefs try to build safety into a department to prevent problems becoming patterns. Good chiefs try education, encouragement, and incentives as ways to improve quality.

However, chiefs never fully eliminate clinical problems, and many of them start to despair. So they take charge. They make tough decisions. They put their faith in power: rules, oversight, punishment. After ten years in charge, some chiefs are damaged: irreversibly anti-physician. They lose hope in clinical judgment and put their faith in systems instead of people.

The well-known Stanford Prison Experiment assigned students role play either as jail guards or inmates.[531] The two-week research into prison-life psychology was ended six days later "because of what the situation was doing to the college students who participated. In only a few days, our guards became sadistic and our prisoners became depressed and showed signs of extreme stress." Note that the students were acting. None of the inmates were real inmates. They were all innocent. But the guards saw them as criminals. Like most famous studies, the results have been attacked, questioned, and even dismissed, especially by those who do not like the findings.

However if the Stanford Experiment holds true for other situations, then those at the CPSO, who believe self-regulation is dead, will see themselves as medical regulators. They will not see themselves as helping an honourable profession to self-regulate. They will assume authority. Their ethos will change. But maybe that change started long ago?

If self-regulation is dead, then regulatory colleges are dead. If self-regulation is dead, then we have government regulators. Physicians should stop pretending their licence fees are for "the privilege of self-regulation" and start calling them a tax paid to their regulator.

The separation of power is a basic prerequisite of the rule of law.[532] A king could act as judge, jury and executioner. Western states separate those powers. Developed countries assign separate roles to those who create laws, those who enforce laws, and those who decide whether a law was broken. Monarchs and dictators assume all three roles. They have control without blame — agency without liability. It always leads to tyranny. Physicians should demand that regulatory colleges operate on the shared values of our parliamentary democracy. Canadians need clear boundaries between those who create the laws, those who enforce the laws, and those who mete out punishment in medicine. Canadians need this to protect patients, not physicians.

The retiring CPSO registrar raises fundamental questions: How should we structure society? Should we have laws to define limits and allow freedom? Or should we have rules and regulations, with overseers to monitor every move and keep us in line with "best practices"? One way gives us Western, parliamentary democracy. The other gives us rule by a small group of elites: oligarchic tyranny.

In fairness, regulatory unreasonableness is not a necessary feature of socialized medicine. We could envision this kind of bad behaviour in any political system. However, regulatory unreasonableness grows best in the environment created by the concepts that socialized medicine supports and would stand out as foreign and repugnant if it were not so reflective of the unreasonableness required by socialization itself.

Self-regulation makes sense only in community. A standard of care can never be codified. It is always changing. Doctors keep in touch with it by keeping in touch with each other. However, socialized medicine encourages atomization between individuals and the state. Even in artificially defined "teams," physicians do not need relationship to survive the way they did pre-medicare. "Bureaucratic employment ... weakens professional identification with colleagues ..." which ultimately "destroy[s] colleagues' relationship and neutralizes the controls which an autonomous profession imposes on its members."[533]

Freedom can exist only in direct proportion to the internal moral restraint of the people for whom freedom exists.[534] Self-regulation, the essence of professional freedom, works only when we encourage and exercise the disposition required for freedom. If we build a system that removes the need to exercise the disposition, we are left with men without chests; *homo economicus*, money-making animals; technocrats; rule followers. When we exchange a system of liberty for a system of rules and regulations, we change the character of those inside the system.

Instead of keeping the muscles of disposition sharp and in shape, disposition takes second place to a reflexive deference to rule following. *What regulation applies?* becomes more important than, *What ought we to do?*

Chapter Ten
Government's Ignorance of Medicine

The Hippocratic Oath, even in its original form, represents not a triumph of science but a triumph of moral absolutism.
–Jonah Goldberg

The truths of science, endowed with an absolute authority, hide the truths that matter, and make the human reality imperceivable.
–Roger Scruton

FAMILY DOCTOR Lynsey Bartlett made the national news in 2017 when she announced she would let 200 patients go from her practice near Ottawa.[535] One of her patients, Fred Martin, had taken his frustration at "being dumped" by his doctor to the media. CTV News reported that the patients had been unceremoniously informed by mail. "It's very impersonal," said Martin.

Bartlett had selected patients who were stable and free of acute health issues. Her letter included an apology and noted that the "current political reality of practicing medicine in Ontario has made our practice model unsustainable." Martin called Bartlett's office. "Her assistant said I should call my member of Parliament," he said. "I don't understand why I should do it. It's not me. I'm basically a taxpayer paying taxes. The fight is with the doctors not with me."

I spoke to Dr. Bartlett right after this happened.[536] This was her first experience handling media; most doctors have never had media training. Not wanting to create more hassle for herself, she cautiously shared what the media left out.

Most nights Bartlett had been working on her clinical charts until midnight, after seeing patients all day. She devoted more than a third of her day to complex mental health patients who needed specialty care. On top of this, she could not afford to hire more staff. She was simply overwhelmed. Bartlett mentioned how hard it was to care for really sick patients without specialist backup. She was seeing some patients twice weekly until a specialist could take over. "I was not trained for this. I am doing my best, but there are just not enough resources in the system." She had extended office hours to keep up with demand, but that still was not effective.

Dr. Bartlett and I talked for close to an hour. I found her passion for sick patients humbling. She had agonized over her decision. She had identified patients she could safely retire: none of them had major mental health or medical issues. Many of them lived in another city and would be best cared for by a doctor in their own area.

We talked about the media camped outside her office. She chuckled about trying to wait until they left so she could go home unnoticed. Doctors just want to care for patients. They are not trained to handle reporters.

Many physicians do what Bartlett did, but they do it quietly. They trim office hours or join larger groups. Patients end up waiting longer for next-available appointments. But no one sees it in the news. Access changes, like the tide, quietly and slowly.

We need more physicians like Dr. Bartlett. She welcomes the sickest. She stays late and cares deeply. She extends her office hours, but she also knows her limits. Trying to save the world is a tragic heroism; no one should have to take the risk in the first place. If we do not improve things soon, doctors who are simply overwhelmed will be forced to change or quit.

A few days after I spoke with her, Dr. Bartlett phoned to let me know that, contrary to media reports, she had let only 40 patients go, and the total might hit 75. But it did not matter. The media had their headline. She was the heartless, impersonal doctor.

How to Motivate Doctors

When doctors complain about government-run medicine, they are not just whining. They are trying to protect the essential ingredient of great care.[537]

On an assembly line, process and efficiency determine performance. Standards can be set, and workers incentivized to work faster or held to account for slowing down. In a knowledge industry, performance rests, in large part, on motivating knowledge workers. Knowledge workers, in every industry,[538] behave according to *intrinsic* motivators. Intrinsic motivation offers the secret to supporting creativity and innovation.[539] *Extrinsic* motivators — carrots and sticks — play a much smaller role, for knowledge workers. High-performing organizations in knowledge industries need to provide challenging and meaningful work. They need to enable learning and career advancement, ensure adequate resources, recognize contributions, and create a supportive environment.[540] Businesses must manage these intangible assets or suffer low performance and poor staff retention.[541]

Motivating physicians is no different. Physicians are moved by intrinsic motivators such as: attention to mastery (comprehensive knowledge, skill improvement, career advancement, recognition, status); autonomy and power (control over one's work environment; control over work with other team members; personal influence); relatedness (affiliation to a program or team; peer support); social purpose (helping patients, doing the right thing; helping, supporting, and protecting coworkers); hygiene factors (work-life balance, avoiding stress and anxiety, making work easier, job security, ease of doing work, financial stability); and financial motivators (salary linked to performance or status, additional financial reward for shared savings, etc.).[542]

Socialized medicine inverts each one of these motivators. For example, instead of supporting the quest for mastery, medicare makes it hard to advance or change careers within medicine. Retraining options are closed, and residency positions are rationed. Medical students much choose a path they cannot change (except in rare cases) long before they have experienced fields in medicine or matured as individuals. When doctors do not cooperate with political agendas, politicians take turns attacking physicians in Parliament and the media — precisely the opposite approach required in managing knowledge workers.

The state chips away at physician autonomy a little more each year. Governments decide the staff physicians must work with, and administrators seek to decrease physician influence in hospitals and healthcare in general. Planners arbitrarily disrupt hospital affiliations by closing or transferring programs with little notice. Physicians find it increasingly difficult to do the right thing, without the resources to do so.

Central planning almost seems determined, by design, to negatively impact hygiene factors: work-life balance becomes impossible with increasing accountabilities and decreased support. Government rarely makes medical work easier,[543] and random cuts create uncertainty and turmoil. The primary motivation is financial: volume at fixed prices; not status, shared savings, or any other element. Given all this, it is no surprise quality improvement becomes especially challenging. Improvement is best achieved when it is built around things physicians care about.[544] Financial incentives, too often, do not create lasting change. As A. Donabedian, a well-known health quality pioneer, has said, "The secret of quality is love."[545]

Governments can have a positive or negative impact at a basic level of involvement in medical care: for example, providing raw materials for medical care. But at higher levels of functioning, it loses its ability to help but retains its ability to harm. The state cannot enhance intrinsic motivation from a central office, but it can crush it. When we consider government involvement, the stakes get higher the farther up we move on Maslow's hierarchy of needs.[546] Using carrots and sticks, government planners dictate the distribution of medical care and regulate its delivery, without any notice of their impact on the intrinsic motivation to care. With respect to carrots, economists say physicians are rational beings. But then they also say they are nothing but robotic rationalists. "Having conferred upon us the dignity of reason [the economist] renders it useless by describing *homo oeconomicus* as nothing more than an amalgam of rational choices."[547]

From here, economists build a case against doctors using all the same arguments thrown at capitalists since before Marx. For example, "Strong economic incentives [exist] for the physician to overemphasize the supply of his own services to the exclusion of substitutes and to bias the patient's 'choice' of services towards those which yield the highest net revenue per time unit for the physician."[548] This feeds the urban legend that doctors care only about money.

The assumption of rational self-interest demands control of self-interest. But as contract theorists have argued extensively, contracts can never overcome the problem of regulation. Contracts cannot solve the free-rider dilemma, in which people overuse a shared resource. Furthermore, contracts cannot solve the prisoner's dilemma either, in which people acting in pure self-interest create a worse outcome than if they cooperated. The pursuit of rational self-interest always leads to the tragedy of the commons: for example, a community will tend to decimate a public pasture through overgrazing. "Social contract theorists, from Hobbes to Rawls, have attempted to overcome this problem, but always they come up against some version of the original difficulty: why is it more reasonable to bide by the contract than to pretend to bide by it?"[549]

Medicine figured this out several thousand years ago. It did not start with rational self-interest. Galen of Pergamon wrote in the second century that physicians can practice for a love of humanity, honour, glory, or money. He thought the love of humanity was best, which, to his mind, made doctors philosophers.

No doubt, doctors possess a blend of motivations: between one doctor and another, as well as within individual physicians over time. Saddled with school debt and seeking to pay off a mortgage, doctors, like most young people, will probably focus on working hard to earn as much as possible. As their debts decrease, most doctors lose the drive for more. They can practice for the love of the craft and the patients they get to help. Maximizing rational self-interest plays a minor role, at best, for most physicians.

Planners know this but rarely admit it. New fee codes (a raise!) take two years for physicians to start using on a regular basis. It is almost as if most doctors do not notice the new fees at first. Governments do not create fees because they like physicians. They do so to incentivize different kinds of care. Fees are supposed to be carrots, but they often work poorly and take too long for physicians to adopt. So planners turn to sticks. We discussed this at the system level in the last chapter. Planners create rules for doctors and repackage the same rules for everything else: after-hours care requirements, surgical outcomes, in-patient lengths of stay, etc. But better rules do not guarantee better patient care. Better rules make doctors focus on rules, not patients.

Rules change behaviour the way speed limits change driving habits. People perform to the limit of what goes unpunished.

This is not an argument for anarchy. We need rules. But rules without relationship create perverse outcomes. No tactic works all the time for all people. Tactics work only as well as the relationships they leverage. Simply "tightening accountabilities" without addressing relationship will not change behaviour. Without relationship, nothing changes. We will return to this in the next chapter.

Motivating physicians falls into a broader discussion about accountability. Planners define goals, which they need physicians to accomplish. Government starts by offering physicians new fees codes — carrots — to achieve a new goal, for example, increasing the number of flu shots. Usually, the goals are partially achieved but rarely to the level hoped by government or promised by physicians during negotiations.

So government calls for greater accountability in a general sense: accountability to society, or physician accountability to their "social contract." (The CPSO even sends out instructional material advising doctors of their responsibility under social contract theory: a contentious, partisan political idea.) Too often, provincial ministries of health demand accountability without paying for it, and physicians expect incentives with very limited accountability. Accountability without payment is slavery. Payment without accountability is robbery. This creates a whole new quest to find meaningful incentives, clear accountabilities, and "value-added care."

In all of this, we cannot ignore the fact that accountability presupposes freedom. It is nonsense to increase accountability without reducing red tape at the same time. We need to give providers freedom first, then we can demand accountability. (In the same way, society cannot exist on social contracts; contracts can exist only if a society first exists to support the development of contracts.) Accountability must be inverse to the regulatory burden. If payers micro-manage every system process and detail, and remove freedom from providers, they have no right to demand accountability on outcomes.

This debate could take place at the bargaining tables around physician contracts. But neither government nor physicians have time to really consider it. Both sides focus on money and service agreements: carrots and sticks.

Reducing care to rules and accountabilities frustrates doctors and corrupts patient care. It will not change doctors' behaviour. As others have said, those who are regulated too often gain control of the regulators — something called regulatory capture. Healthcare labour unions are expert at it. Placing our faith in rules, as a solution for every complex problem in healthcare, leads back to our discussion about managerialism.

Medicine is hard, at the best of times. One old doc warned me, before medical school: "Many things, I would gladly do for free. Others, you could never pay me enough to do, but I do them anyway."

Doctors need to function in an environment that fosters and rewards the desire to serve. Doctors are not magical wells that spring forth eternal passion, service, and good will. Neither are they greedy black holes that suck up every last dollar in sight.[550] Physicians are peculiar. They combine a natural bent to solve problems, help, and serve with the capacity to learn and apply the material required to do so. The combination is fragile and priceless. It is a gift to society much like any other gift of generosity or genius found in other professionals: teachers and scientists, musicians and authors.

The Nature of Medicine

SOCIALIZED MEDICINE misunderstands the nature of the thing it seeks to control. In our earlier discussion about managerialism, we considered medicine at a higher level, as an organization in part of an industry. Here, we look at the nature of the practice of medicine. At its core, medicine is humans caring for other humans; as such it cannot be reduced to clean definitions and cold measurement. This resistance is neither belligerent nor arbitrary. As we mentioned earlier, any attempt to reduce a complex system into a merely complicated one eliminates what we are trying to reduce in the first place.

Socialized medicine cannot manage what it cannot understand. Its plans for distributing and regulating care do not fit the care it hopes to control (or the care patients need). Political solutions need to fit the problems they aim to fix. If not, the solutions require force to make them fit, like ramming pudgy feet into glass slippers or — using the hammer of management, mentioned earlier — like pounding square pegs into round holes. Unlike children, politicians and planners do not tire of pounding square pegs. When solutions bend sideways, they reach for bigger hammers and blame the round holes for not being properly square.

David Suzuki made millions telling Canadians about the nature of things, starting with his TV show by the same name. He mixed science with storytelling to promote everything from environmentalism to globalism. His descriptions became prescriptive. He told us what is, and we inferred what ought to be. Regardless of what you think of Suzuki's politics, his methods work. So far, medicare's *Nature of Things* has been written and produced largely by people outside medicine. Physicians who enter the business of describing the *Nature of Things* assume the nature offered by socialized medicine. Then they blame medicine for not accommodating the solutions they envision. Medicine is not a thing. Neither is patient care. Medicine is not a list of fees and procedures.

Consider one example. During the COVID-19 shutdown, a patient came to the emergency department to get swabbed, because a family member had tested positive. The physician asked his patient how the patient's family member was doing. Not well, the patient said. After the patient left, the physician reviewed the family member's chart (regulators would cringe!). He noted that, given new treatment protocols for COVID, the family member now required different treatment. The physician spoke to the specialist on call, who agreed: the family member needed to be in hospital.

The physician called his patient at home and suggested his family needed to come to the hospital. The patient said he would try, but the family member was tired of going to hospitals.

The family member finally called back and asked to speak to the physician. He reviewed everything with the family member, then alerted the next emergency physician on duty, as well as the admitting specialist, that the family member was coming to the hospital.

Someone needed care. An emergency physician and a specialist made sure the patient got care. Both physicians worked fee-for-service, and neither one saw the family member, so neither physician got paid. This does not warrant praise. It is not even noteworthy beyond our purposes here. And yet this is what it means to be a doctor. A fee code cannot capture it. It would be absurd to try to assign one. We should be surprised if this behaviour did *not* happen.

I asked the emergency physician why he did it. Why did he call the patient at home? Why did he speak to the family member? He came up with something that sounded rational, but it could not begin to capture why he did what he did. His behaviour flowed from a mix of professionalism, training, duty, social expectations, tradition, curiosity, concern, habit, and a dozen other things. He broke rules and policies to do what was right. Regardless of why he did it, we both agreed it is precisely what we would expect any other physician to do in his place.

Debate over the nature of medicine goes back thousands of years, so it is no wonder people continue to struggle with defining it. Aristotle called it an art, like philosophy or mathematics. As such, physicians should practice for the love of the field, without pay, as philosophers did in those days. Others preferred to see it as a "practical craft" and still see it that way today.[551]

The attempt to define medicine is not academic. How we define and describe it will shape what we do to distribute and regulate it.

Medicine is a social enterprise. It is a complex, overlapping movement of science, technology, language, history, morality, culture, sociology, anthropology, philosophy, and political science. Socialized medicine focuses on attempts to define medicine as a market based on fixed prices. It is the only way it can gain control.[552]

Most of the crucial parts of being a physician cannot be tied to fees at all. We expect physicians to do the right thing, payment or not. We expect them to answer questions from nurses, clerks, and colleagues all the time. Physicians who did not do this would be castigated by their colleagues. It would be an affront to the profession.

If we cannot understand and explain what it is doctors do, we should not attempt to pay them for it. It becomes a fool's game. The medical associations' schedule of fees, which doctors used as a rough guide before medicare, was acknowledged as both: rough and only a guide. It was an arbitrary framework — a *pro forma* template — designed so doctors could point to something. It was not designed to capture and codify what doctors do. But in the hands of the planners and rationalists, the schedule of fees becomes reality. Instead of a *pro forma* template, it becomes scripture, with elaborate systems of punishment for transgressing any jot or tittle. What was once a dynamic, open-ended discussion based on relationship and mutual exchange between patient and physician now has deteriorated into a rigid entitlement system fueled by government's begrudging payment and doctors' resentful submission.

The point is to highlight what it is doctors do. Regardless of how we pay them, we need doctors to be doctors. This is an entirely different thing from the payment mechanism we apply, regardless of the one applied.[553]

Socialized medicine is built on the mistaken notion that patient care can be packaged in aliquots and redistributed. Economists reduce medicine to material processes. Then they assign a material reward for the processes they just invented. Having defined doctors as nothing but rational self-interest maximizers, economists can observe physicians as furious hamsters on socialized wheels chasing material rewards for invented processes. All that remains is to adjust the brakes on the wheel, change the size of the material incentives, and criticize the hamsters when they run in the wrong direction.

The view that fees or salaries can be attached to quanta of care and applied equally to all assumes care is definable and static. But medicine is an amalgam of ideas, attitudes, experience, moral codes, mental heuristics, cognitive processes, habits, character, and a hundred other non-material things.[554] Assuming this thing called medicine can be seized by the state, redistributed, and regulated is the materialist superstition.[555] Explaining medicine, and doctors' behaviour, in terms of economic incentives is a bit like trying to explain the existence of cathedrals with economics.[556]

Physicians start by exploring the experiences of individual patients. Each episode of care links to the last and the next. Measuring performance by one event, without considering the whole string of events, distorts care. It often leads to meaningless conclusions. A broken wrist is never just a broken wrist. It is always individualized and context specific: a ninety-five-year-old who lost his balance, a five-year-old who fell off a swing, or a fifty-year-old who was pushed down the stairs by her boyfriend. Medicine addresses patients in the first person singular.

Even in the context of a patient visiting the emergency department for acute care, their visit consists of a string of events with fees arbitrarily attached to some of the things a physician may do at certain points during the visit. Episodic care works well for young healthy people with rare acute illnesses or trauma. But medicine now deals largely with chronic disease. We educate and motivate instead of diagnose and treat.

Whereas physicians used to develop relationships with patients spanning decades, such that one fee for a particular episode of care was weaved into the larger relationship, socialized medicine has ripped that fabric and forced an arbitrary uniformity based on a reduction of the relationship to single events. Salary would eliminate the reductionism of events but not replace the fabric that existed before the state instilled itself into the relationship. Salaried physicians cannot save us.

Giving, Not Taking

MEDICINE ITSELF is based on a system of exchange — giving and receiving — and when it functions best, it is more like the free market than a soup kitchen.[557]

Medicine starts inside physicians, with passion and ideas, with hearts and minds.[558] Medical school builds on students' curiosity and passion for discovery.[559] Physicians learn how to "cooperate, compromise, and discipline themselves to practical tasks."[560] The desire to explore and learn and help people is fragile. People do not simply grow up to become effusive, energetic dreamers of new and inventive ways to give — in this case, to give care — without an environment and incentives that foster this precious and essential passion.

Survival of the fittest seems to rule for getting into medical school, but it most definitely fails after training. Physicians must cooperate and compromise, not only with other physicians, but also especially with nurses, house staff, and administrators.[561] The solo, *Little House on the Prairie* approach to medicine disappeared in the nineteenth century, if it ever existed at all. Medicine cannot function without a complex, overlapping system of relationships, each requiring nuance and compromise, all directed towards achieving the communal task of caring for patients.[562] Indeed, woe betide if medicine does not find a way to immunize itself against the popular social trend towards collectivized divisions of victims and oppressors. If medicine does not protect doctors' deep commitment to work together, ignoring social differences, in order to serve patients, it risks irreparable fracture itself.

Michael Novak, the late American philosopher and diplomat, wrote an extended study on the moral framework required for free enterprise to function. His argument applies to medicine. "High moral discipline" determines success, not the economist's drive to be a rational self-interest maximizer of material goods.[563] "Among those attitudes [required for success] are not merely industriousness, enterprise, sound work habits, and a willingness to live under the rule of law, but also a sense of cooperation, attentiveness to customers, openness to strangers, and alert curiosity."[564]

The communal task of caring for patients did not develop by design. It grew up over centuries with millions of social interactions. The norms and standards — the "moral depth" — required several thousand years to hone, and they still are not ideal.[565] But that does not mean we should discard or ignore the fabric, faulty though it may be, in favour of an arbitrarily rationalized central structure. For example, planners will plop a new centralized referral program onto a community to solve access problems without any understanding of problems the old system functioned to solve.

Socialized medicine does not see this. Reducing doctors to rational self-interest maximizers deflates the energy required to provide care in the first place. Socialized medicine also reduces patients to standardized quantities, categorized, measured, and lined up neatly down a hospital hallway, with number signs taped to the walls.[566]

The defining characteristic of free enterprise is surprise.[567] How can we improve what we offer? How can we do better for those we hope to serve? The defining characteristic of socialized medicine is the *elimination of surprise*. How can we avoid unforeseen events? How can we guarantee the same product, based on historic trends, without increasing costs?

George Gilder tackled the practical and moral issues that drive free enterprise in his international best-seller *Wealth and Poverty*.[568] Here again, Gilder's assessment of the driving forces behind free enterprise also apply to medicine, better than the socialist alternative. For example, medicine "is more an information system than an incentive system. Increasing revenues come not from a mere scheme of carrots and sticks but from the development and application of productive knowledge."[569] Medicine, like every service industry, starts from the desire to help — to give, not to get.[570] "The gift comes first."[571]

Health economists often complain doctors create their own demand: they dream up new (read: unnecessary) ways to provide care, which drives up costs.[572] Economists point to Say's law as proof that doctors — driven by greed — produce their own demand for services. According to the French economist, Jean-Baptiste Say, in 1803, production of a product or service creates its own demand. But the health economists seem determined to have us miss the point. Say's law demonstrates that we need to give before we get. Supply comes before demand.[573] We see this with iPhones and innovative medical procedures. Perhaps we should focus on whether a particular service benefitted the patient in question, instead of trying to read the mind of the doctor who offered the care.

Society runs on reciprocal exchange, on the basis of trust and good will between neighbours and friends, doctors and patients. "The understanding of the Law of Reciprocity, that one must supply in order to demand, save in order to invest, consider others in order to serve oneself, is crucial to all life in society."[574] We cannot reduce the Law of Reciprocity to doctors' greed. Those who accuse doctors of driving wasteful consumption through an artificial increase in unnecessary demand misunderstand, or choose to ignore, the Law of Reciprocity. They assume that the doctor-patient relationship is more like a railway train that goes one direction, from doctor to patient, whether the patient wants it to or not.

The drive to serve, to care, and to dream of new and better ways to help patients cannot be reduced and repackaged into a master plan. Two identical hospitals in the same region with similar patients often will have drastically different results. Everyone in the community knows which of the hospitals to avoid. This happens in other industries also. One drive-through coffee shop will continually struggle with slow speed and spotty service, while its sister franchise will offer fast service. Everyone knows which one is always fast, no matter how hard the franchise tries to standardize the experience. Virtually identical businesses often have radically different performance.

Gilder describes the work of Harvey Leibenstein, economist at Harvard, to explain this difference. Leibenstein came up with something he called "X-efficiency."[575] The key factor in the different performance between firms derives from management, motivation, and spirit. Armies win or lose depending on their level of "desire to fight and to face danger." The willingness to innovate and seek new knowledge will make one firm eclipse another. Examination of inputs or raw material cannot reveal the cause. Gilder calls it "the spirit factor." A doctor's heart and drive to serve and care — to really impress her patients, their families, and her own colleagues — comes from a bigger understanding of human motivation than the typical health economist allows. "It is impossible to create a system of collective regulation and safety that does not finally deaden the moral sources of the willingness to face danger and fight, that does not dampen the spontaneous flow of gifts and experiments that extends the dimensions of the world and the circles of human sympathy."[576]

Complex patients present enormous risk to those who attempt to care for them. We need to foster a system that encourages physicians to embrace that risk; to rush into danger instead of avoiding it. Socialized medicine, with its uniform, standardized, one-size-fits-all approach to risk, payment, and regulation, crushes the desire to embrace the uncertainty presented by our most challenging and most vulnerable patients.

How Doctors Think (A Phronetic Guild)

WE NEED to pause for just a few paragraphs to consider how the way doctors think creates an insuperable barrier to planning. Kathryn Montgomery, professor of medical humanities and ethics at Northwestern University, has spent the better part of three decades in medical education. She writes that calling medicine a science is not just wrong, it "does not begin to do the profession justice."[577] We damage patient care when we picture medicine as a field of "physical certainty [as] taught in grade school and presented in the media."[578]

> What characterizes the care of patients, however, is contingency. It requires practical reasoning, or *phronesis*, which Aristotle described as the flexible, interpretive capacity that enables moral reasoners ... to determine the best action to take when knowledge depends on circumstance. In medicine that interpretive capacity is clinical judgment.[579]

Contingency, interpretation, inference, clinical judgment — these things do not fit with details and rule-governed consequences of a Newtonian science. That is not to say there are no details or consequences in medicine.

Rather, medicine requires much more. Montgomery goes on to describe how, too often, we hold to an outdated understanding of science in a positivist sense, which we apply to medicine.

> This is Newton's science: science as the explanation of how things work, how they really are. It gives us the facts, which are understood to be certain, replicable, dependable. Science in this sense is an egregious straw man, but a straw man with very powerful legs. The positivist idea of science — science as the uninflected representation of reality — pervades our culture. In the media, journalists not only use "science" in this simplistic way but take it for granted in reporting on medicine: cost containment, technological breakthroughs, malpractice, and, especially, new therapies."[580]

Montgomery suggests that *phronesis,* or practical knowledge, offers a better sense of how doctors think. She interprets Aristotle's description of phronesis in the *Nicomachean Ethics* as "the intellectual capacity or future that belongs to practical endeavours rather than to science."[581]

Consider anatomy, the most concrete and "knowable" body of medical information. A surgeon's knowledge of anatomy must go far beyond what he can read in a book.[582] Even if we cut a room full of cadavers into one-millimeter cross-sections in order to learn all the variants of normal anatomy, and then we did the same for the thousands of disease states, we still need the surgeon's imagination to reconstruct the three-dimensional image in his own mind. Even if surgeons used 3-D computed tomography and the electronic renderings of a patient's internal anatomy, they still require their own mental image, or they operate blindly. Once a belly is opened, full of purulent exudate (pus) and infected tissues, the entire shape collapses, like a deflated balloon. Surgeons need a tacit, "inarticulate intelligence" of landmarks and anatomy to save their patients. They must know more than they can tell. "Everyone experiences far more than he understands. Yet it is experience, rather than understanding, that influences behaviour."[583]

Anthropologists spend decades not only learning a language but also immersing themselves in a culture. Every language includes prejudgments and meaning beyond the level of the words themselves. This is one reason why it is so hard to understand jokes in a second language, even if we speak it well enough to do business. Language and prejudgments trade within a particular community of norms, beliefs, traditions, and so on.[584] For example, physicians follow a particular approach to problem solving for each new patient: history and physical exam followed by lab tests, and so on. The physical exam of a particular patient is usually an individualized abbreviation of an idealized notion of examination. Physicians then package this information into a recognizable formula when they record their thoughts: identification, chief complaint, then history of present illness. While doing this, they perform in light of (rather rigid) norms of objectivity, honesty, and more. At the same time, clinical medicine contains a warmth and messiness entirely foreign to the cold, artificial clarity of the policy-makers' process. All of this, and more, bakes into the social enterprise of medicine.[585] Physicians continue to hone and master their knowledge and abilities within this enterprise, especially during their first five years in practice.

This is not to suggest non-medical observers of medicine have nothing valuable to add. They do. Often the non-medical observer can spot things a physician could never see. But brilliant observation and insight do not qualify someone to run the whole medical industry, if that were even possible. An ability to talk about medicine — a rational understanding of the language — does not qualify someone to lead it.[586]

This discussion brings us back to our earlier comments about rationalism. There are many types of knowledge, but planners need only one. We can read about cooking in a cookbook, but we will never become master chefs by reading.[587] "Practical knowledge can neither be taught nor learned, but only imparted and acquired. It exists only in practice, and the only way to acquire it is by apprenticeship to a master — not because the master can teach it (he cannot), but because it can be acquired only by continuous contact with one who is perpetually practising it."[588]

Practical knowledge stands on a tradition of thought, an approach to patients. It does not fit into the neat mould planners require. A tradition of ideas and patterns of thought — indistinct behaviours based on clinical judgment — do not work for planners.

Plans require clarity. They need definition and logic, not approaches or principles. The ideology of socialized medicine, informed by a positivist understanding of medicine, promises the clarity needed to plan. Ideology can be crisp and self-contained, unlike the impossible tangle of tradition. "[Ideology] can be taught best to those whose minds are empty: and if it is to be taught to one who already believes something, the first step of the teacher must be to administer a purge, to make certain that all prejudices and preconceptions are removed, to lay his foundation upon the unshakable rock of absolute ignorance."[589]

Perhaps doctors do not see economic materialism as strange or foreign because they have spent decades training in scientific materialism. Physicians need to see and understand what medicine does beyond bedside physicalism, or they will remain unintentionally supportive of the economic materialist's superstition.[590]

Philosophical Zombie Doctors

POPULAR DESCRIPTIONS of ideal physician behaviour sound less human, more zombie-like. Philosophical zombies look and act like regular humans but do not have conscious experience or feeling.[591] We understand them entirely in physical terms, as super-advanced robots. Doctors should be objective; empathetic but psychologically unphased, infinitely malleable to their patients' wishes and worldviews.

Planning works best if physicians behave like philosophical zombies. Zombie doctors follow guidelines faultlessly. They never veer from standards of practice for unscientific reasons such as patient individuality. If planners or legislation call for action, zombies obey without question. If a patient requests a legal treatment, doctors mechanically deliver referrals the way vending machines serve candy bars.

Patients never have to worry about zombie doctors acting unprofessionally. Zombies do only what is expected, without variability. Zombie doctors learn ethical guidelines and apply them with computerized regularity. They do not have opinions, debate nuance, or wrestle with inconvenient social dilemmas. Zombie doctors do what they are told and always act in patients' best interests as defined by the social collective.

The zombie defence might explain why Canadian doctors supported the Sexual Sterilization Act between 1928 and 1970.[592] This is an egregious failure; one we should not forget. Patients deemed unfit to reproduce — for example, people with low IQ, no money, alcoholics — were sterilized against their wishes,[593] sometimes without their knowledge[594] during an unrelated procedure. A zombie defence might explain how the head of the Toronto Psychiatric Hospital served in the Eugenics Society of Canada during that period and received the Order of Canada.[595]

But do patients really want zombie doctors? Or do we want thinking, feeling doctors who act on strongly held personal beliefs? More importantly, who can adjust and adapt to serve their patient.

Doctors denounce,[596] and refuse requests[597] for, female genital cutting[598] even though most jurisdictions don't prosecute parents who take their young girls out of country for the procedure. Most doctors denounce sex selection[599] even though there are no laws against[600] it in Canada.[601] If sex selection and female genital manipulation became legal, we hope most physicians would refuse to have anything to do with either of them.

As Dr. Margaret Somerville, the founding director of the Centre for Medicine, Ethics and Law at McGill University, said recently, "Do you really want to be treated by a doctor who doesn't care if he thinks that he's doing something unconscionable or unethical or immoral? There will always be some tension between the moral convictions of an individual medical professional who adheres to his or her own worldview and the different procedures that are legally available in a pluralistic society."[602]

(Clear laws *can* help remove uncertainty. But Martin Luther King, Jr., reminded us to "never forget that everything Hitler did in Germany was legal." Since WWII, "just following the law" has become known as the

Nuremberg defence. And history has shown the need for those who are willing to think more broadly, and challenge accepted thinking.)

Life is great when other people do what we want them to. But utopian dreams blur imperceptibly into nightmares. A civilized society should not force anyone, including doctors, to do what they find morally reprehensible, even if it is legal. Unfortunately, socialized medicine is designed for zombie-doctors rather than free-thinking patient advocates.

Medicare Changes Doctors

MEDICINE STARTS with service: to help everyone who asks, no matter how trivial the request might appear. The desire to serve mixes with a passion for discovery. For some, the quest to know swells larger than the desire to serve, especially during training. By the end of training, the quest to know wanes and becomes overshadowed by a focus on fixing problems. The work of medicine is to apply knowledge, skills, and experience to fix and improve problems for other people.

Socialized medicine, in contrast, starts with a plan to sort, distribute, and regulate necessary care. It starts from the assumption that needs are known, and the state can meet them. Any demand for care that exceeds the supply offered by the state is, by definition, unnecessary. When government controls healthcare, and physicians are given little input into management, doctors care less about how the system runs. If medical care is "free," it can be only correct or negligent. "Value added" holds less meaning. Doctors insulated from patients' ability to pay tend to worry less about costs. With increased regulation, doctors avoid regulators' wrath by ordering more tests. Doctors worry less about avoiding patient harm and more about avoiding trouble. Medicare makes doctors appreciate payment from government instead of requests for care from patients. Doctors become thankful to government, less beholden to patients. Third parties define when and where patients should seek care, and from whom. Patients' opinions are devalued. When government pays for all care, reimbursement becomes an expectation from government instead of a payment from grateful patients.

Every decade politicians and bureaucrats work to reshape social-ized medicine in their own image.[603] Eventually, the system will not toler-ate the professionals it was created to fund. Physicians must change and become something different, something better designed to exist inside a socialized framework. Brian Lee Crowley, writer and managing director of the Macdonald-Laurier Institute, emphasizes this point for all Canadians, not just doctors. In his bestseller *Fearful Symmetry: The Fall and Rise of Canada's Founding Values,* 2013, he writes:

> While some think that the character of individuals is simply given, that it is beyond the reach of governments and policy, anyone who has seen the effects of decades of Eastern European communism on individual behaviour, or the damage done to individual behaviour by lawless, corrupt, and arbitrary regimes such as Zimbabwe's or Nigeria's or Pakistan's will know that there is an unbroken continuum between individual behaviour and the institutions under which one lives. Under some regimes, it is quite impossible to live honestly and honourably.[604]

Doctors bring assumptions about work, performance, effort, knowledge, and character into their training. Practice deepens those ideas and hones new attitudes and behaviour. For example, physicians hold a deep faith in delayed gratification and hard work. They generally believe reward must be earned, excellence exists, and all workers are not identical. Physicians see knowledge as growing and building on the past. They think new infor-mation should inform current practice, innovation breaks some rules, and we should follow where the evidence leads. Doctors hold a firm belief that actions have consequences. They believe in self-reliance — you write your own exams and perform your own lumbar punctures; confidence — make a decision and act on it even in the face of limited information; and self-control — keep emotions in check, be calm in crisis, practice decorum.

All professionals, not just doctors, possess a unique bent. Profes-sionals — knowledge workers — function best in places that presuppose the values and tendencies that contributed to their becoming professionals in the first place. Workplace form should follow provider function and advance professional purpose. Much like our earlier discussion of intrinsic motivation, forcing professionals to function in an environment, constructed without attention to the natural bent and peculiarities of the professional themselves, reduces performance, crushes morale, and in many cases causes irreversible damage to the professional.

We do not hire sumo wrestlers to work as jockeys, or morticians as cheerleaders. We want stockbrokers to think and act differently than kindergarten teachers. We hope firemen follow fewer rules than building inspectors.

Physicians are every bit as frail as the patients they serve. Given a culture of sorting patients according to need, defined by experts, physicians learn to scowl and scoff at worried moms with fussy babies: "They should know better than to come to the hospital for such a useless complaint. What do they think this is?"

Before medicare, everyone assumed that more than 30 percent of physicians' work would be charity. That assumption fostered a particular attitude among doctors. It elevated professional duty over payment. Indeed, the system could not function otherwise. The reverse is also true. A system that pays 100 percent of the time creates the expectation of it. It turns doctors' orientation towards payment.

Medicine was never a strict supply and demand market. Money never balanced the equation. Doctors supplied care to meet the demand regardless of whether any payment followed the supply. Market economists state that the demand determines the price: high demand means high price. But for physicians, the price often dropped to zero despite often the highest demand for the most vulnerable.

Misunderstanding Frustrates Planners

Experts have an answer for everything. When it comes to problems in healthcare, the usual response is straightforward: blame doctors. "The most popular, yet simplistic, approach is to select a villain, usually the medical profession, and to assume that, if its powers were curtailed, greater equity would be achieved."[605]

The well-known champion of medicare Dr. Danielle Martin offers a case in point. Speaking on national TV, Martin said: "And frankly, when they [patients] are admitted to hospital four and five and six times a year, often it's because people like me aren't doing a good enough job of keeping them out of hospital and managing their illness well in the community."[606] She also worries about how well doctors choose medications for their patients. Private drug insurance plans "give licence to doctors to prescribe more expensive medicine when less expensive ones are just as good, resulting in high costs for no reason."[607] Too often, doctors prescribe medications "off-label," for conditions a drug was not originally designed to treat.[608] Martin highlights the need for guidance "about the most appropriate choice for a given condition."

Given this, it makes us wonder: How often do patients suffer because docs aren't doing a "good enough" job? Should the CPSO punish doctors if patients end up in hospital? Michael Decter thinks so. The former DM of Health in Ontario says this about diabetes care:

There's a standard of care here. If you meet it, there's an incentive. But you can't go on as a physician licensed by a college and not meet a professional standard of care. And I think in some cases, the profession has let itself off too easily on some of these things.

There is an acknowledged right way to treat and manage this disease and I think at some point the College of Physicians and Surgeons is gonna have to step up and say, Okay, ya know, malpractice isn't just, ya know, taking off the wrong breast.

Malpractice is also not organizing your practice to support a patient with diabetes ... but we shouldn't be bashful about saying some things are unacceptable. And not tackling diabetes until it's an amputation is not acceptable.[609]

Decter has been saying the same thing for over twenty years. "We should increase accountability — whether with physicians or nurses — at the front line, for managers and workers."[610] But he never mentions accountability for government or patients (that I am aware of). He criticizes doctors for making patients wait[611] but also criticizes them for increased utilization.[612] All things being equal, decreased waits tend to increase utilization; the faster doctors see patients, the more patients will want to be seen.

Martin and Decter identify from opposite ends of the political spectrum but share the same viewpoint. Amputations are doctors' fault. Admissions to hospital are doctors' fault. We could bend the healthcare cost curve, if doctors would just do their jobs.

Too often, planners possess a fundamental misunderstanding of the work physicians do. Non-physicians, and many academic physicians, have never run a clinic, outside of an academic centre. They are ignorant, in an academic sense. They lack knowledge, awareness, or information about something in particular. There is little harm in experts sharing ideas with each other. But in positions of power, political demands push these same experts to rearrange healthcare without a clear understanding of how their decisions can harm patients.

At one time, all senior government officials dealing with medicine or public health were physicians. As the state inserted itself into the control of medicine, senior government officials were replaced "by non-medical (chiefly financial) experts."[613]

Outside of data and statistics, medicine involves real patients, who have a say in what happens to their bodies. Patients get to choose whether they take their medications, change their diet, exercise, or do anything to impact health outcomes. Doctors see diabetic patients for twenty minutes once every three months, if we can convince patients to come in that often. For 130,000 minutes until the next appointment, patients make their own choices. It is absurd to blame doctors for everything that happens with a patient's disease based on a doctor's input into 0.015 percent of it. Even enthusiastic, keen, self-motivated patients can end up with poorly controlled diabetes. Some patients need amputations. Blaming doctors and patients shows an ignorance of real-life patient care and a profound insensitivity to what patients manage in their lives besides their diabetes.

Experts see poor outcomes and assume doctors are responsible. Doctors must be slacking off. Doctors did not explain diabetes clearly enough or in enough detail. Doctors are the focus and the problem. Planners incentivize doctors for twisting the arms of patients to achieve ends that experts have decided are good. What if a patient does not want to visit his doctor for his diabetes every three months? What if a patient gets tired of ten-, twenty-, or thirty-minute visits about diabetes four times a year? Maybe a single mom of two kids with special needs has to focus on other things besides her Hb A1c. Mom might have her hands full worrying about her kids arriving home alive. Her doctor should support her where she is at, not badger about lab values. Hopefully the lab values will improve later. But some never do. Experts do not get that.

... And It Burns Out Doctors

AND SO WE return to Dr. Lindsey Bartlett, from the beginning of this chapter. Desperate to do a great job, she simply could not keep up. In the updated final chapter of his magisterial review of health insurance in Canada, Malcolm Taylor draws attention to how government impacts care. Taylor filled his "definitive history" with harsh denunciations of physicians that, in many ways, contribute to the anti-physician bias we mentioned above. However in the updated edition of his book, he seems to soften a bit. When it comes to patient care, he admits that quality is fragile. It rests on physician competence which itself rests on physician morale.

> Quality is clearly a fragile attribute of human services. It depends not only on competence but also in large measure on individual morale, on how one feels about the system, on how confident one can feel about one's career and the conditions surrounding its pursuit. When, for example, governments act without notice or adequate consultation to introduce drastic changes or cuts in resources, morale is seriously lowered and, inevitably and perhaps unconsciously, quality is adversely affected.[614]

Taylor's comments would not warrant mention if they were not so often ignored. Maybe governments feel they cannot avoid major changes, even without consultation or warning. Or perhaps planners and politicians assume forced, unexpected change will not matter. Or maybe they think temporary harm to physician morale will not do long-term damage.

Damage to morale is like infidelity. It has lasting impact. Aristotle suggested politics should be like relationship. Oakeshott suggested it should be like conversation. Relationships and conversations can recover from occasional missteps. But politics means trade-offs between competing goods. Missteps are not just unavoidable but appear baked into the necessary design of political function. If that is so, and if physician morale is a vital element to great patient care, then the solution is clear: we must remove politics from patient care.

Chapter Eleven
Government's Failure of Medicine

The role of the state is, or ought to be, both less than the socialists require,
and more than the classical liberals permit.
–Roger Scruton

"Understand Frodo, I would use this Ring from a desire to do good. But
through me, it would wield a power too great and terrible to imagine."
–J.R.R. Tolkien[615]

"HOW LONG do *you* plan to stay?" she asked. My patient had many children and had watched several doctors cycle through our rural clinic. The latest politically induced crisis had raised alarm.

Long before they experience the chaos, patients start to worry. Kathleen Wynne, former premier of Ontario, had launched an historic rampage against doctors and healthcare, in 2015. Her government had succeeded in making Ontario the most indebted subnational government in the world. We were famous.

Julia Munro, our long-time and well-loved local MPP, called me in a panic. "Four doctors just left our building!" she said. "That office has been there for thirty years. The pharmacy depends on them. My office is in a unit in the same mall. The landlord doesn't know what to do. Any suggestions?"

Around the same time, a colleague shared how his elderly parents were worried about their rheumatologist retiring. They had the same specialist for years. "Who will take care of them when he leaves? There's no one else around."

At two separate offices, staff asked me, "Are you going to come and work with us?" Their jobs depended on physicians having somewhere to work.

The Ontario Palliative Care program, which represented two years of work at the provincial and national level, was virtually frozen overnight by Wynne's cuts. Yet patients desperately need palliative care. A Medically Complex Patients project had started important work for vulnerable patients. It involved new physician services. How would it run with the new, rigid cap on the physician services budget?

In every program threatened by cuts and uncertainty, thousands of staff went into limbo. The government put programming on hold, stopped new projects, and abandoned preparations for new care. No one knew what would happen.

In the face of financial crisis created by political mismanagement, people look for quick solutions: cut services or increase taxes. Too few look to change government itself. "In a system where government is the steward, governor, manager, regulator, funder, negotiator, evaluator, planner, distributor, executioner, paymaster, surveyor, policy-leader, procurement regulator, implementor, vendor ... Maybe we need more government accountability?"[616]

Everything we have discussed so far in this part of the book — inefficiency, central planning, managerialism, over-regulation, and misunderstanding of medicine — ultimately ties back to the political process. Although every arm of the state injects its own dysfunction, in socialized medicine everything leads back to government. And government injects an additional level of dysfunction all of its own.

We can start digging into this dysfunction by looking at how the Ministry of Health works, at how an idea becomes a policy. Then we need to consider the unique challenges government faces when it tries to manage given that governments were built to balance interests, not run industry. This will lead us into a brief look at the theory of government failure as the lesser-known cousin of the theory of market failure. We end this section with a few comments on unions, a unique challenge in a socialized approach.

How the Ministry of Health Works

GOVERNMENTS ARE designed to balance power and avoid rash decisions. They are not built to capture new ideas, experiment, and then implement the best. Ideally, governments should promote peace by reconciling competing interests.

Imagine you have an idea that could improve care. Let us assume that you are an expert in your field, your idea is backed by the very best evidence, and this new idea will save the system money. How can you get your idea put into action?[617] The following process comes from a lecture given by a seasoned civil servant. To be clear, he was not criticizing the process. He simply outlined the challenges involved given government design at that time.[618] Ask yourself, would any business be able to survive if it adopted the following approach?

First, you write a note to the minister of health outlining your idea. The minister's office will write a note back thanking you for your idea.

Remember, the minister of health works for the constituents in her local riding. Those people elected her. She must perform for *them*, not for the whole province in her role as minister of health.[619]

The minister will send your note to the deputy minister of health. (Notice that it is not clear what kind of experience the DM requires. Some DMs come with experience from their time working in hospitals, others from a career in the civil service. Over 65,000 people work in the public service. DMs usually last two to three years in their position.)

The DM will send a note back to the minister saying thank you and register your idea in the government project tracker. The DM will hand off your note to an assistant deputy minister of health. ADMs usually last between three to four years on the job.

The ADM will give your idea to a director. (Most directors spend up to one-third of their time managing human resource issues and not dealing with new projects.)

The director will pass the idea along to a manager. The manager will give it to a senior analyst. If you are very fortunate, the senior analyst will have received the same note that you delivered to the minister of health initially.

The analyst will analyse your idea, add research, and offer analogous ideas that might align with your initial concept. Then, the senior analyst will feed your modified idea back up through each step of the chain, returning it to the minister of health. A number of other ideas will get added in at each step of the process.

The minister of health will then send your idea to a cabinet committee. It will be altered and then finally arrive at cabinet. Note that the public service cannot speak to you about your idea. Public servants take an oath not to speak to the public, a practice that originated initially with the military.

Cabinet will ask for changes. The minister will have had ten minutes to present your idea, but it will still be changed to create a new idea. The new idea will go to the finance committee to determine costs. Then finance will send it back to cabinet.

Cabinet will decide whether the idea requires any changes to regulations or legislation. If it does, then it will require an order-in-council if necessary or it will be sent for outside advice. If cabinet decides that there is no need to change any regulations or legislation, the idea will be sent to the policy department.

The policy experts will send the idea to communications to develop a communications plan (in the two official languages). Policy will also work on implementation.

The final policy will be sent out to everyone in the Ministry of Health, Health Promotion, Health Quality Ontario, Cancer Care Ontario, Public Health, all of the Local Health Integration Networks, as well as any agency that might, in any way, be impacted by the new policy. Each of these organizations will then go through the same process of analysis and policy development all over again.

Government Cannot Manage

POLITICIANS IN Canada, of all political flavours, compete to see who can say almost the identical things about healthcare while trying to sound a little bit different. They each pledge allegiance to medicare and the principles upon which it stands. Every politician wants to make medicare better, stronger, and more efficient. And, once in power, they each work to make their mark, without making substantive change. They rearrange the pieces on the board, as quickly as the political process will allow, but they do not change the game.

When it comes to medicare in Canada, every political party is conservative on socialized medicine: they all want to keep it; liberal on faith in planning; they all want to manage it better; and progressive on services covered: every citizen should get every service they want, for the most part.[620] We cannot even differentiate parties on their preferred speed of change. At one time, the Conservatives were just the slow Liberals, but not anymore. Everyone rushes to bat and swings at every pitch.

Minister of Health remains one of the most coveted positions in cabinet, equalled only by Finance. But despite the prestige associated with a budget that eats up half of provincial spending, ministers of health can do very little. Their budgets are already assigned.

John Roberts served federally as a Liberal cabinet minister in a number of portfolios in the Pierre Trudeau and also the John Turner governments. He has also taught at a number of universities. In 2003, Roberts wrote a chapter in *Searching for the New Liberalism: Essays in Renewal.*[621] He noted that, throughout the last half of the twentieth century, governments held to three basic assumptions: (1) economic management could sustain growth, (2) "government could be good at administration, at running things," and (3) "large-scale expenditure programs" could fix poverty, social security, and inequality.

By the 1980s, these three beliefs had lost credibility. Canada was open to other markets; other countries' decisions often impacted our economy more than the policies we made. And performance by any measure — unemployment, inflation, productivity — did not support the case for government management. Things looked bad for government.

> Nor with the passage of time did the government appear to be an efficient manager. From the 1930's on, when government departments multiplied and expanded, and a plethora, almost uncountable, of crown corporations was established. Government

was poor, however, at managing for a variety of reasons — the political processes of government militate against flexibility, decentralization and the delegation of responsibility; personnel management, an essential instrument of management, remains largely outside the hands of political direction; government does not have profit as a bottom line objective and therefore finds it difficult to apply as a means of bureaucratic control; the objectives of government are as mixed and as varied and as contradictory as the members of society. These amorphous purposes, the lack of precision in purposes, make public management cumbersome rather than streamlined.[622]

Government resists flexibility, decentralization, and delegation. Government struggles with personnel management. It has no bottom line for bureaucratic control (unlike profit in business). There are too many objectives. Purposes are amorphous and imprecise. Politics, meanwhile, achieves outcomes, not solutions — two entirely separate things. Even Malcolm G. Taylor, medicare's chief historian and hagiographer mentioned above, highlighted the difference and its impact on health policy, quoting Graham T. Allison, a political scientist best known for his work on the Cuban missile crisis:

The decisions and actions of governments are essentially … political outcomes: outcomes in the sense that what happens is not chosen as a solution to a problem but rather results from compromise, coalition, competition, and confusion among government officials who see different faces of an issue; political in the sense that the activity from which the outcomes emerge is best characterized by bargaining.[623]

In other words, government cannot make decisions like a regular business. Voters expect government to deliver results like private industry (better!), but government is not designed to do so.

Donald Savoie, mentioned earlier, refers to three phases of government development. The first phase focuses on building infrastructure: roads, canals, and post offices. We might include medicare in phase one. The second phase of government development around the Western world is the pursuit of Keynesian economics: "the desire to smooth out demands in the economy, and the willingness to intervene in many sectors."[624] Medicare experienced this beginning in 1977, with the federal end to 50 percent cost sharing, which led to increasing intervention by provincial governments into the management of medicare. Savoie suggested that, by 2015, most of Canada had entered the third phase, in which "governments are trying, with mixed results, to rationalize their operations and deal with stubborn deficits and growing debt."[625] Medicare seems to have been solidly in phase three since just after the 2008 fiscal crisis and perhaps long before. Given government's intractable expansion into medicine, we need to explore why government fails so often.

Theory of Government Failure

GOVERNMENT MANAGES medicare. Patient care depends primarily on government's, not on doctors' and nurses', performance in socialized medicine.

Government can shape and influence the other actors within the state. Regardless of politicians' protests that they cannot control the state themselves, they nevertheless hold the greatest and farthest-reaching authority that impacts patient care. Unfortunately, government failure does not garner the interest it should. Peter H. Schuck, professor emeritus of law at Yale, has written many books on government. In *Why Government Fails So Often, and How It Can Do Better,* published in 2014, Schuck notes, "Political scientists... publish four times as many works on distributive issues than on studies of government effectiveness."[626] Even so, a respectable body of work offers far more than we can summarize in a book about socialized medicine. Much like our cautious comments about the intimidating world of legal theory, we need to hazard a few pages about government failure.

While most people have heard about "market failure," few have considered the equally compelling work on government failure. "[The] assertion that both government and markets can fail is true but misleading as it implies a false equivalence: failed products quickly exit the market; failed programs, like diamonds, are forever."[627] Former prime minister of Canada Jean Chretien said much the same thing:

You can start from the premise that government can be a force for good. That's my position. Others on the right of the political spectrum have a different view. I can give you many, many examples where government became an instrument for the good. But an instrument to do good can wear out. Government is good at coming up with instruments to do good. Government is not as good at deciding that the instrument has done the job and when it should be done away with.[628]

Schuck calls for good government, not the abolition of government. Some approaches almost guarantee failure; for example, "The more social programs are designed to change individuals, the more likely the net impact of the program will be zero."[629]

Policy-makers analyse and write policy for a living. It is no surprise that they produce more of it. Schuck suggests that policy-makers should intervene only when their intervention will correct a known and significant market failure.[630]

Government intervention almost always creates an increase in bureaucracy. "Agency bureaucratization … often produces predictable pathologies: tunnel vision, middling competence, limited imagination, fear of controversy, and obsession with process."[631]

It is not only the process of bureaucratization but also the people who end up attracted to work in that environment that gives the culture its character. David Levine, mentioned earlier, notes that the large and complex bureaucracies do not deal well with creativity or original thinking.[632] Innovation and risk are not encouraged or supported.[633] The public sector offers secure (often boring) jobs that can "attract people who are relatively rigid and risk averse."[634]

Government creates an unusual work environment, in which, "Risk is dampened. So is opportunity. Rewards at the top are not all that different from those below. Nearly all workers, from janitors to governors, earn middle-class salaries. Unions thrive. Change is gradual. Layoffs are rare. Promotions come slow. The role of money — as a motive and as a symbol — is circumscribed."[635]

Every public policy is run through a bureaucracy. This bureaucratization changes policy simply because the policy becomes a product of the bureaucracy that created it.[636] Any idea created by a clinician to improve care comes back crushed by the policy press of bureaucracy. Checklists, reporting guidelines, double sign-offs, passwords that expire, and a thousand other accoutrements make the idea slower and more painful than the one it was invented to improve. Bureaucracy itself ends up determining performance, not the policy idea.

Improvements and solutions that appear obvious to clinicians, and also often to civil servants, are denied, or fail on implementation, when run through the bureaucracy that determines whether a particular service is allowed.[637] Milton Friedman noted this in the US with the tendency of the Federal Drug Administration (FDA) to not approve medications. The only real choice faced by FDA civil servants was between approving a bad drug or denying a good one. In the first instance, patients come to harm and people lose their jobs over it. In the second, no one knows any better, including the patients who missed out on a potential cure.

Government failure, or non-market failure, "*is a systematic, incentives-based tendency of government policies.*"[638] Just as markets create "externalities," for example, pollution, government create "internalities." Internalities are private goals that do not relate to government's public mandate. They could be anything from protecting an agency's budget to civil servants protecting their own position. The internalities arise because the products of non-market activities are often hard to define; quality is elusive; outputs are created often by legal mandate by a single provider; and no criteria exist to evaluate their effectiveness.[639]

Schuck agrees with PM Chretien from above: government can do many good things; he reviews a number of notable government successes, for example, social security, the food stamp program, the National Institute of Health, and others. Having reviewed failure and success, he draws a number of conclusions, which we can apply to healthcare.

"*To succeed, then, the programs largely needed to engage the actors' self-interest; they did not need to create new values or transform deeply rooted behaviours.*"[640] Too often, the focus in socialized medicine seems bent on turning physicians into public health specialists, or social contractors, who focus on populations before individual people. For better or worse, medicine is an old institution, stretching back several millennia. It embodies the *deeply rooted behaviours* Schuck says to avoid.

Government's pilot projects often work because they are run by true believers. They go on to fail in the real world. Schuck writes that a focus on incentives, over values transformation, increases the likelihood of success.[641] A lifelong supporter of Democrat presidents, Schuck is not a right-wing anarchist. He knows government can be a force for good. We just need to be realistic about what it can achieve, he says, and be aware of the "the risks of tinkering with complex, poorly understood human systems."[642] He concludes his review by saying:

> Many, perhaps most, governmental failures are *structural*. That is, they grow out of a deeply entrenched policy process, a political culture, a perverse official incentive system, individual or collective irrationality, inadequate information, rigidity and inertia, lack of credibility, mismanagement, market dynamics, the inherent limits of the law, implementation problems, and a weak bureaucratic system.[643]

Public Interest vs. Self-interest

A SITTING member of federal Parliament once offered the public some advice during a political campaign: "Politicians are vote-maximizing machines." Public choice theorists argue politicians will do whatever they can to keep their jobs. Similarly, bureaucrats will always seek to increase the size of their bureaucracy. And civil servants often confuse their own interests for the interests of those they serve.[644] Regardless, public choice theorists argue that civil servants will always put their own interests before the public's interest.[645]

However, public choice theory explains too much and thereby risks explaining nothing at all.[646] Difficulties with the theory include: "Exaggerated claims to universality, fragile empirical foundations, tautological use of 'self-interest', excessive focus on collective action problems, reductive accounts of human interactions, and inability to exclude competing explanations."[647] The theory does not explain how people vote, does not predict politicians' behaviour, and does not match the evidence.

Having said all that, public choice does a better job of predicting how policies will be implemented than its main rival, the public interest theory.[648] Circular thinking and resistance to testing apply even more to public interest theory. "Rational self-interest ... unquestionably drives most political behaviour most of the time. Only the cloistered idealist will regard this as altogether pernicious."[649] Political actors build institutions and policies for their own benefit.[650]

Clinicians have complained about this for years. Politicians seem to care most about what matters to their jobs not to patient care. Administrators pay closest attention when their own positions are at risk. Long waits for care do not worry any individual civil servant, as long as there are similar concerns in everyone else's portfolio of responsibilities. As one of our hospital CEOs often said, "Everyone is trying to be the tallest of the seven dwarves." A little bit better but mostly the same.

Economics professor Randy T. Simmons offers a readable summary of this theory in his updated book *Beyond Politics: The Roots of Government Failure*, published in 2011. Simmons explains why government cannot run a medical industry, or any industry for that matter. Governments were never set up to manage. For example, politicians avoid making forthright statements or clear commitments about care. Instead, they send up "trial balloons" to gauge public satisfaction before committing to any particular path of improvement.[651] "Politicians find it highly rational to engage in obfuscation, play-acting, myth-making, ritual, the suppression and distortion of information, stimulation of hatred and envy, and the promotion of excessive hope."[652]

Health economists, as we have seen, love to argue that physicians create demand for their own services. Leave aside the fact that most patients like to avoid seeing the doctor. Even if we allow that physician-induced demand may happen, civil servants create much greater demand for their own services.[653] Politicians, voters, and bureaucrats form "a kind of benevolent conspiracy, or in the popular phrase, an 'iron triangle.' "[654] William A Niskanen, Jr., noted in 1971 that bureau budgets were "twice the size of an analogous private firm operating under competition and three times the size provided by a private monopoly."[655]

Absent the constraints of market competition, government bureaus need other branches of government for oversight. In socialized medicine, this means meetings, consultations, approvals, and public hearings, and even then one forgotten veto vote can block a multi-year process.[656]

When governments cut agency budgets, agencies cut the programs most likely to harm those served by the agency. This creates pressure to reinstate the budget.[657] Simmons calls this the Washington Monument strategy.[658] Faced with cuts to the park service in 1968, the Monument closed the elevator and told tourists to take the stairs. Tourists were directed to complain to their members of Congress. This is the opposite of what a firm would do in a competitive market. In a competitive market, firms do everything to maintain or, if possible, even improve their level of service. If cuts must be made, they cut things that make the smallest difference to customer service and satisfaction. Public agencies do the opposite. Central government makes the decision to cut funding, but the funded agency gets to decide where to apply the cuts. So the agency applies the cuts to services that will cause the greatest dissatisfaction for customers. This creates pressure on the central government to maintain funding. In other words: "Competitive firms protect their market share by improving consumer satisfaction while bureaus, at least in the short run, protect their budgets by *decreasing* customer satisfaction."[659] We see this in medicare, for example, when home-care cuts nurses instead of managers.

Economists spend their careers building demand curves, but it is impossible to build a valid curve for goods promised by politicians. A demand curve plots the relationship between the price of a particular item and the amount consumers demand of that item at a particular price. "Whereas the [businessman] asks *how much* people want something, the equivalent of asking what they are willing to pay, the politician asks *how many* people want something. Politicians count majorities first, and intensity of preferences and beliefs second, and indirectly."[660] Politicians want to know whether voters will support medicare, not how much tax voters are willing to pay for it. It turns a continuous variable (demand) into a discrete variable (votes). This is like asking a hungry diner whether he wants to order everything on the menu or nothing at all: please vote yea or nay.

Medicare suffocates from the inefficiencies injected by the political process itself, such as, "(1) perverted incentives; (2) collective provision of private wants; (3) deficient signaling mechanisms; (4) electoral rules and the distortion of preferences; (5) institutional myopia; (6) dynamic difficulties; and (7) policy symbolism."[661]

Without prices to direct supply, governments resort to "price ceilings and floors, subsidies, tariffs, barriers to entry, quotas, make-work rules, rationing." Governments can threaten "rent extraction," if parties refuse to support government plans. We see this often in physician-government negotiations: support our plan or risk cuts to funding.

Can't Handle Change

IT SHOULD come as no surprise that government finds it extremely hard to change. It is "hopelessly sclerotic."[662] Every new program attracts vested interests that fight to expand its size and guarantee it never shrinks or disappears.[663] Program costs spread to all taxpayers, but the benefits accrue to a small group of well-organized interest groups. All taxpayers contribute a small amount through increased taxes (diffuse costs) to provide a windfall for a small, vocal group of voters (concentrated benefit). [664] Change either takes years and becomes almost impossible, or we cycle between regionalization vs. centralization, or block funding vs. payment per procedure.[665]

How do planners know which programs to cut and which to increase? Every program teams with dedicated workers who are equally passionate about their program and keeping their jobs. "Governments are not entrepreneurs. They cannot create better, cheaper ways of accomplishing important goals. Rather, the role of government is to prevent fraud and abuse, help the needy, and provide transparency."[666]

Market Failure a Concern; Socialized Medicine Not the Solution

MANY PEOPLE support socialized medicine because they worry about market failure. Medical care is not like other goods and services: physicians have more information than patients; certain types of care are very rare; fear of illness makes patients irrational; individual decisions about care can impact a whole community; and so on. Economists write long lists of troubling concerns, each scarier than the last (allocative inefficiency, monopoly power, merit goods, bounded rationality, negative externalities, information asymmetry, and more). In other words, medicine clearly needs tight government control. Much of the academic literature paints such a worrisome picture of free enterprise it is a wonder businesses are allowed to exist at all.

The market vs. government debate sets up a false dichotomy. Neither one can exist alone, despite socialists and anarchists who argue otherwise. The answer lies in good government supporting an environment of economic liberalism, a discussion to which we return in the conclusion.

All the major concerns about market failure can be overcome for the bulk of care that most people will ever need, without the "heavy regulation" socialists call for. Governments should focus on what they do best: refereeing. In order to justify government intervention:

> Policy makers should have to answer four questions in the affirmative: (1) Does a market failure exist? (2) Is that market failure large enough to justify an intervention, given the costs that it will impose on actual or potential market actors and on taxpayers? (3) Are substantial public values at stake that the market default cannot adequately advance? (4) Is the intervention likely to succeed, given the possibility that the intervention may itself constitute a government or "nonmarket" failure that could not readily be corrected or dislodged?[667]

If we do not limit government to what it is good at, government becomes a battle of interests, not of ideas, as originally intended.[668]

Unions Shut Down the Medical Centre

IN SOCIALIZED MEDICINE, unions inject an additional level of descent into government dysfunction. It is impossible to even begin a discussion about hospital performance absent unions' influence.

For many people, unions are either good or bad. They are saviours of the working class or the scourge of society; protectors of freedom or full of selfish tyrants.[669] Unions have great potential for good and for corruption. At their best, unions offer an organic social group that helps support the fabric of civil society. Unions offer association to buffer the space between the almighty state and the atomized individual. Vigorous, voluntary unions that focus on building worker solidarity and commitment to a shared vision of excellence and pride can bring out the very best in people and the work they perform. Great unions know they cannot exist unless their members have equally great companies to work for. Unions can elevate a company or run it out of town. For all these reasons, Lenin focused on eliminating unions along with all other voluntary associations.

At their worst, unions can become corrupt, tyrannical, and short-sighted. They seek monopoly control of a labour market, while union bosses pamper themselves at their members' expense. Too often, modern unions promote outrage, protect incompetence, and sacrifice new, enthusiastic members on the altar of wage increases for the old, slothful, and cynical.

The Law's Support of Unions

On a foggy morning in early August 2018, a mob formed around a small private medical building in Thunder Bay, Ontario. Canada's largest private sector union, Unifor,[670] had brought in hundreds[671] of unionists from across Ontario and Manitoba to surround[672] the Port Arthur medical clinic. Unifor represents over 315,000 workers. It had assets of over $263 million in 2014.[673] The Port Arthur clinic lists approximately thirty physicians on its website, a number of whom work part-time.[674]

The local union workers had been on strike since April. This new mob was different. Unifor strongmen set up fences around all the entrances. Police left the new unionists alone and refused to escort doctors into their offices.[675] The courts issued an injunction to stop the illegal activity. Unifor defied it and went further:[676] they filled door locks with glue, cut power lines and phone lines, and shut down WiFi. Now doctors had no way to check labs remotely; no way to inform patients about critical results. Banked sperm threatened to thaw without refilling the cryo, which meant parents might never get genetically related siblings. Patients wait over a year to see some specialists. They need to book time off work, travel from out of town, and often spend a night in a hotel. This action stranded some of them.

Unionists do not care about the law; it is on their side. Police did not enforce anti-trespassing or forcible confinement laws. And the judge did not enforce the injunction to remove the fence. Unionists just moved the fence out a few feet away. The judge had offered the injunction but only if parties agreed to talk. Law was just a means to her social end.

Western democracy rests on the rule of law, but when government refuses to enforce it, chaos ensues. When media promote union messages, without condemning the impact to patients, chaos ensues. The unionists spoke to the core assumptions of socialized medicine. So the authorities let them do it.

Unionists have shown they have no qualms about harming patients in their march towards power. They will fight anything that appears to undermine their privilege. They will attack anything that falls slightly outside the lines of government paying for all medical services in facilities staffed by unionized employees.

This is not a new issue. As early as the 1970s, "stricter health and safety regulation, along with a growing union movement and a consequently higher wage environment, squeezed the lifeblood out of Quebec's private hospitals."[677]

Do Unions Help Patients?

AT A LEADERSHIP BBQ, I asked the group of nurse leaders I worked with at the time what they thought about the impact of unions on patient care in our hospital. Did the unions improve care? The group sat in awkward silence for long moment. Then they erupted with a visceral outpouring:

"It's terrible!"

"Ruining the hospital."

"Total waste of time."

"Starts fights."

"Continual nitpicking."

"The union was good at first. It got us on the pay grid. Thirty years ago salaries were so low we had to share rooms in apartments. So the union was good for that. But those days are gone."

Unions bully hospitals. Management worries before making decisions. "We don't want the Union Bus parked out front!" the nurses said in fear. The bus means endless meetings and bad media. It kills approvals for government funding.

Unions protect workers. They do not protect patients or improve efficiency. They do not fight for patient care unless it benefits their members. A nurse leader said: "New nurses used to spend one hour with the union rep during orientation. Most of us did not even know who the union rep was. Now, reps spend a whole day with new staff members. Everyone knows the rep, and the rep makes sure that nurses know their rights."

Reps spend their shifts hunting for ways that work processes might possibly infringe on collective bargaining agreements. They need issues to justify their roles. Unions recruit people who can foment discord. It is all about fights, rights, and "No way I'm doin' that!" Many union reps model entitled, distrustful, overly critical attitudes. Too often, they poison culture with a hard, scoffing demeanour towards work and management. They need never worry about hospitals losing money and leaving town, like a regular business would. So conciliatory skills in a public sector union leader are nice but not necessary. This is the opposite of what patients need: compassionate, encouraging, hopeful attitudes from providers committed to meet needs that do not fit neatly around break-times and end-of-shift. Union reps, paid by the hospital, used to try to see patients, but they ended up spending most of their shift on union issues. Most departments have given up and simply pay a full-time RN union representative just to do union work and not see patients.

Unions create their own level of bureaucracy in hospitals. A platoon of nurse leadership and human resources staff spend hours managing unions. Not employees, unions. If they knew about this, would the public support this extra cost?

Our emergency department scheduled regular meetings with the unions to make sure we had buy-in before any decision. Success depended on how happy we could make them, more than any other single factor. Union reps had *de facto* veto power. If reps were happy, things went well. If not, they tortured the program VP, who would then punish our nurse leaders for making her job so hard.

As mentioned earlier, with a fixed pie everything becomes a zero-sum game. The only way to get more money is to form a union and fight. The unionization rate for hospital staff is over 95 percent. In the broader public sector, it is around 66 percent. In industry, unionization rates have been dropping and currently sit under 20 percent.[678]

Concentration of power in a large union or association stamps out diversity. Everyone follows the same rules regardless of patient need. Pay reflects crude ratios of nurses to patients, without nuance for acuity or level of care. Differentials for productivity or skill do not apply. Unions resist change unless it can be shown to clearly benefit union members.

Private organizations go bankrupt when unions become too strong. Public organizations just use more tax dollars. Medicare already struggles with over-regulation; it makes no sense to have powerful unions restrict management even more.

We might improve the value unions offer if we were to:

- Report the total cost of union-generated administrative work (number of hours, number of administrative staff required, etc.).
- Report the number of staff holding union positions per hospital.
- Report the number of hours hospitals pay providers to perform union activities instead of caring for patients.
- Include performance incentives in every contract.
- Limit the number of grievances allowed per week.
- Allow dismissal of frivolous and vexatious grievances.
- Allow workers to not be union members; or at least charge dues only for negotiation-related activity.

What have unions done for patients in the last five or even ten years? In a publicly funded healthcare system, does it make any sense to have unions? Don't government jobs already have good salaries and benefits? Have unions increased efficiency? Have they improved customer service, quality, innovation, or patient choice? Do unions improve anything other than salaries and benefits for their members? In a world of evidence-based decision making, is there any proof that unions add value for patients? We should examine the impact unions have on patient mortality and morbidity due to unions refusing care unless wages go up or work effort goes down.[679] Michael Decter makes a fair point: "Because the system is built around distributing wealth rather than creating it, bargaining agents must take some responsibility for the process that creates wealth."[680]

People help patients. Organizations, governments, unions, and associations may or may not help patients. We need to debate whether the labour movement helps them. Columnist Jeffery Simpson, in his book *Chronic Condition*, takes aim at nurse and physician organizations: "Nor can they [hospitals] break union rules that make surgeries happen to fit the convenience of providers instead of patients ... A system that boasts brilliant surgeons ... accomplished staff, wonderfully furnished facilities but uses them only a fraction of the available time in the face of unmet demand is a system straitjacketed by ideology."[681]

It does not need to be so. As we said above, unions can be a force for good. But without a natural competitor, unions take over their environment. Healthy business ecosystems hold union and business interests in balance; each thrives without choking the other. In socialized medicine there is no balance, only union growth and aggression. Unions represent a massive and intimidating problem for socialized medicine,[682] one no one has yet had the courage or ability to fix.

Conclusion:
Towards a Cure for Canadian Medicare

Act in such a way that you treat humanity, whether in your own person or in the person of another, always at the same time as an end and never simply as a means.
    –Immanuel Kant

If we are to make the best and sanest use of our laws and liberties, we must first adopt a sober view of man and his institutions that would permit reasonable things to be accomplished, foolish things abandoned, and utopian things forgotten.
    –James Q. Wilson

THE INDIGNITY of soggy diapers in hospital hallways demands a response. How can we rescue patient care from being used as a means to achieve some other end? Patients should not be pawns in the "bold political vision"[683] of anointed social reformers, who seek to redistribute wealth or win elections or reshape the values of Canadian society.

When we find ourselves walking in the wrong direction, the most rational and obvious thing to do is turn around and go back the opposite way. Unfortunately, for more than fifty years, socialized medicine has run faster and faster in the same direction. Restoring the moral fabric of medical care in Canada requires thinking and doing the opposite of much that we have done so far.

Governments keep trying to change healthcare at the wrong level of dysfunction. Recall the four levels introduced in chapter one: care, coordination, culture, and concepts. Care is what patients experience; coordination refers to politics and programs; culture reflects the ideology of socialized medicine; and concepts create a worldview. Each political party tinkers at the level of care and coordination. When in power they introduce a new program or tweak a spending formula. Aggressive governments regionalize care only to have the next government centralize it all again. Some of the time, the Conservatives centralize, which runs against their typical platform of free enterprise and local control. At other times, the Liberals decentralize, which makes *them* look like the party devoted to localism and free enterprise.

Canadian governments have mastered medicare transformation without making any major positive difference to patient care. Failure no longer surprises us; it should not have surprised us in the first place. Even if reform ideas show promise to create change, socialized medicine swallows them without a hiccup. The ideology of socialized medicine neuters anything new. It is like giving a teenager a dress shirt only to have him turn up the collar and untuck the tail. He reshapes the shirt to match his look.

Real reform to medicare requires thinking upstream, at the level of culture and concepts. This is harder and less obvious than it sounds. Governments focus on spending, programs, and structure. They do not have time to ponder political ideas. Patrick Moynihan, an American senator who served with four Presidents, once said, "I do not believe I have ever heard at a Cabinet meeting a serious discussion of political ideas — one concerned with how men, rather than markets, behave."[684] Politicians need practical ideas, something actionable.

What might offer a better approach? What does a great healthcare system need? Although these questions warrant a book of their own — one I plan to write — some issues jump to mind and demand mention. We will tackle these next. It's well past time to start building a path towards something better.

Embrace Abundance

THE OPPOSITE of a socialized industry is a free, open, diverse, and abundant one.[685] The opposite of socialism is liberal democracy; the opposite of a planned economy is an innovative, organic, complex, free, and unplanned economy.[686] "We are a free and happy people, and we are so owing to the liberal institutions by which we are governed, institutions which we owe to the exertions of our forefathers and the wisdom of the mother country." Thus said Sir Wilfrid Laurier, in 1877. We need to re-emphasize the ideas that gave Canada the wealth and stability required to consider sickness insurance in the first place. Canada stands on a political tradition that runs deeper than political party. We either embrace thinking that builds prosperity or follow "the illusions which wait for the ignorant and the unwary."[687] Initiative and entrepreneurial spirit built our country. We should celebrate them, not view them with suspicion. Most people love the things they enjoy; they feel attached to them with a sense of ownership. People do not want to throw away what they value for a vision they may never see. As they say, the things that matter most cannot be measured or managed. Canada's history is one of courage, hope, and freedom, not raised fists fighting for a bigger slice of a fixed pie.

Writers devoted to the medicare establishment maintain a large lighthouse on the shoals of the "slump-and-boom cycles of the market mechanism."[688] Beware free enterprise. But even their own guiding light, Karl Marx, taught that "the bourgeoisie, during its rule of a scarce 100 years … has created more massive and more colossal productive forces than have all preceding generations."[689]

This does not mean that we should let down our hair and unleash laissez-faire on our patients. Nor should we jump on internal markets, public-private partnership, trusts, fund-holding, healthcare savings accounts, or any other financial silver bullet.[690] These may work. But jumping to fix coordination issues would repeat our error. We need first to tackle culture and concepts, ideology and worldview.[691] We should not fall for the trap of offering a plan before we know whether a plan is possible or needed for the problem in question.

A well-known story of a conversation between the last president of the Soviet Union, Mikhail Gorbachev, and British prime minister Margaret Thatcher is instructive. Gorbachev asked the PM, "How do you see to it that people get food?"[692] and her answer was that her role was not to see that citizens got all the essentials necessary for life. She had to provide for some, just as we will always have some people who cannot care for themselves. And government had to provide some goods and services, even though it did not try to provide all of them. Medicare tries to provide all medically "necessary" care to all people, before we know if we need medical care or something else.

Canadians need two things. First, more care. Never mind the latest technology or boutique procedure. Canadians need more of the basics: home care and wound care; basic medications, medical appliances, dental and vision care; almost every kind of hospital bed; and of course, doctors, nurses, and an army of allied providers.[693]

Canada currently pays for over 99 percent of what doctors do but only a third of all the drugs and services patients need in the community. Every hospital in Canada uses gift shops, coffee stands, and overpriced parking to raise money from sick people and their families. Our rigid Canadian dogma of paying for 99 percent of doctors and hospitals means there is nothing left to pay for everything else and no pressure to improve what we have now. Perhaps we might want to reallocate some of what we spend on doctors and hospitals and devote it to medications and appliances instead.

However, focusing on the kinds of care we need carries its own risk. A focus on *what* care we provide, and how we pay for it, leads us to emphasize amount, distribution, and technical quality.[694] It places medical care into the world of things, not people. Patients become objects to be fixed, not humans to be helped. They become instruments without intrinsic value of their own. A focus on *how* we provide care leads us to emphasize dignity. A focus on *how*, paradoxically, leads us to provide more of *what* we aimed to provide in the first place,[695] which brings us to the second thing patients need. They need to be treated well.

Focusing only on *what* we provide would be like Starbucks obsessing over the quality of coffee beans, the temperature of espresso steam, and the precise way to make latte foam while ignoring all the other components of good customer service: friendly staff, clean stores, pleasant music, and so on. Starbucks' customers bypass other equally expensive coffee shops for more than just quality coffee. Starbucks offers service and experience. Customers know Starbucks wants them there.

Experts have defined quality care as being effective, efficient, equitable, patient-centred, safe, and timely. But none of that means outstanding patient service. "Patient-centred" comes close, but it still includes too much provider. Only the patient can define outstanding service, and each patient defines it differently. Great service needs diversity and choice so patients have someone else to see when their physician cannot deliver the service they expect.

Currently, Canada has the opposite approach. Patient service is an afterthought. Doctors and nurses are expected to provide good patient service to each patient simply because that is what doctors and nurses do. Good service quickly descends to, "You should be thankful you aren't still in the waiting room."

This is not about consumerism. Nor is it about "shopping for our healthcare," as those who oppose choice imply.[696] Neither is it crass pandering to individualist, libertarian, or any other maligned motivation that anti-freedom apologists employ.

We should pursue patient choice because it is an essential part of human dignity. This is a moral decision. We should not champion choice simply because it promotes efficiency or diversity or any other good thing. Choice may or may not deliver these other ends.[697] We should promote choice for the sole reason that it is inhumane to do otherwise.[698] From this one decision — do we give patients choice or not? — flows most of the other decisions made inside medicine.

No question, patients are happy to relinquish choice in dire situations. Furthermore, patient choice does not mean shopping for a bit of blood-pressure treatment here or a bit of MRI scanning there. Medicine should never function like a supermarket. But that does not mean it must function like the post office. We will return to the notion of shopping for care below.

Appetite Expands, Benefit Shrinks

AS MEDICINE improves, its marginal benefit shrinks, and costs go up. We get less and less benefit from something that costs more each year, for which we seem to have an insatiable appetite. Furthermore, the benefit we chase is often not even a benefit to treatment of a disease, *per se*, but rather a benefit to *health* and *well-being*: a state of comfort and happiness.[699]

Medicine offered its biggest benefits starting with antibiotics, in 1935. Heart surgery, anti-psychotics, and the elimination of polio in the following decades made big differences to how long people lived and how well they enjoyed life.[700] Medicine advanced between 1935 to 1970 an order of magnitude greater than it has in the last fifty years. Advances such as CAT scans (1973), coronary angioplasty (1979), and LASIK eye surgery (1989) arrive less frequently, at higher cost, and make smaller changes to people's lives. The golden age of medical care focused on saving lives and treating disease. Now, it focuses largely on managing chronic conditions.

Socialized medicine developed at a time when medicine could do far less than today but offered a greater impact overall. Today, medicine can do more. However, spending more on medical care has a smaller impact on life expectancy or ability to function[701] compared with spending on other needs. Studies suggest that nutrition, housing, and support for mental health might play a bigger role in people's lives, especially for the poorest people in society, than spending more on medicine. Medicine was once a major factor in health, when we could do very little. Now it seems less so.

What is worse, as we try to offer more, newer, and better medicine, we sacrifice the essentials of saving lives and treating disease. Fancy, expensive operations for conditions that never cause death or disfigurement — treatments that redefine the original definition of medical necessity — now make front-page news. Dazzling, often politically correct, subjective needs soak up resources from boring, objective things such as fixing fractured hips. No one has courage to ask whether all the "medically necessary" care we offer is necessary or medical. This requires a book of its own also.

As we said earlier, we could find useful ways to spend Canada's entire GDP on medical care.[702] Our appetite expands for a benefit that shrinks. Given this, does it make sense to continue our rigid attachment to government funding for 99 percent of the care that doctors provide? The reality of rationing in our medical system became obvious to Canadians with COVID-19, in a way we had never experienced. Hospitals warned previously healthy eighty-year-olds, before they went on a ventilator for COVID, that they would be extubated if a younger patient needed it. After keeping themselves healthy for eight decades — taxed for over sixty years, barely using any medicare — does it make sense to outlaw any other options for them?

In the 1960s, socialized medicine seemed to offer a cultural transition, like going from horses to cars. But it has left us with lease payments on a Lamborghini, as our only vehicle, in a country covered in snow six months of the year.

More Than Markets

THE OPPOSITE of planning and control does not lead us to *laissez-faire*. The market cannot save us by itself. Markets are just shorthand for "many people trading things." People, not markets, and definitely not organizations or governments, provide care. Allowing people to behave as they wish — giving them the freedom to make their own decisions — may turn out looking like a market. Or it may not.

Discussion about markets in medicine quickly becomes polarizing. The anti-market crowd emphasizes what is being traded as a means to disparage how it is traded. The pro-market crowd emphasizes how trades happen, as a means to celebrate the dignity of the traders. Both sides have a point. The anti-market crowd points to the theory of market failure. Patients who are in severe pain, fearful of death, and ignorant of medical science will find it impossible to participate in a supermarket of medical care. But if we were to embrace freedom and economic liberalism in medicine, it need not — indeed, could not — mean patients must comparison shop for ceramic hips vs. titanium implants.

Shopping for hip implants is a straw man.[703] With any other professional service, for example, dentists, accountants, or lawyers, we do not expect people to shop for bits and pieces of the professional service in question. We do not expect patients to pick fillings and crowns, or wills and real estate contracts, the way they shop for shoes. Professional service requires relationship. In this sense, professional services do not demonstrate the "widespread cooperation through anonymous interactions with others"[704] that forms the basis of a true market.

Two Ways to Dance

THOSE WHO champion markets in medicine have a point, but not one about invisible hands and self-interested bakers. We face a choice about how to create great care and outstanding patient service in the same way we might choose how to organize a dance for a gala. We could hire professional dancers, closely matched in skill, experience, and training. Professional choreographers could craft a performance and then direct the dancers. Once properly selected, trained, and supervised, the troop could put on a dazzling show for twenty minutes. Or we could turn down the lights, have the band play a waltz, and let the magic of imagination create an event that lasts all evening. The first approach aims for uniformity and perfection; the second for diversity and participation. Both scenarios require behavioural norms, skills, and experience. The waltz requires even more informal rules and traditions than the first dance, in order for dancers to navigate the infinite combinations of twirls, turns, and toes to avoid. The first dance focuses on getting it done; the second on keeping it going. The first uses experts; the second imperfect dancers. The first is military, the second magic.

Some things in medical care can be militarized. Vaccinations, neonatal blood screening, and pap smears come to mind. We could create a one-page instruction sheet for each of these, then teach technicians to execute care with regimented accuracy. But most care resists militarization. As Sherwin Nuland puts it, "Disease never reveals all of itself."[705] It takes years just to learn how to hear what patients want and let them reveal the disease to you, never mind learning about the diseases in the first place. Most medical care looks less like a military parade and more like a farmer's market in May.

Functioning markets presuppose far more than their name implies. Trading only works with trust, good will, a desire to serve, attention to the needs and wishes of those we hope to serve, honesty, integrity, waiting our turn, and a million other things, each more necessary than the market itself. Traditions and taboos play as big a role as prices and profit. This is why so many societies that have the individual components of a free market — prices, profit, competition, and trade — cannot recreate a free market.

Perhaps those who champion free market healthcare actually mean we need all the institutions, traditions, norms, morality, and relationships required to make the market happen. If so, then, sure, let us have free markets for medical care. But too often people mean none of that. They see free markets through the same reductionist lens as the controllers and planners in socialized medicine.[706] The only difference is that the free marketers want freedom. Both sides of the debate see each dance as nothing but moving bodies, one controlled, the other not.[707]

Medicine has always functioned as something other than capitalism or socialism, markets or bureaucracies. Like most other social endeavours, medicine requires common values and beliefs, guided by a tradition around standards of care and professionalism.[708]

We err with both worship and contempt of markets, the Scylla and Charybdis of health policy. The theory of market failure does not rule out markets in all areas of medicine, just as the theory of government failure does not rule out government. Fundamentalism in either direction does not help patients. Unfortunately, in Canada anti-market fundamentalism rules the academy and much of medicine. We tolerate capitalism outside medical care, but only as the cow that supplies the capital for care.

Happy Anti-Capitalism

WHEN THE CBC, *Toronto Star*, or *New York Times* denounces care for profit, most readers agree with the basic message. Profit seems a dirty word. What does business have to do with medical care? Everything should be publicly funded, or at least non-profit. It is immoral to think otherwise. Government has its problems, but at least it escapes the taint of profit from patients' misfortunes.

Medicare survives, in part, because most Canadians know little of wealth creation or profit, and what they do know, they despise. Most people, including many physicians, think wealth comes from income. Someone pays us for doing a job. It feels unfair[709] when business owners seem to work less and make more than their employees.

Consider a man, for example, who parks cars for a living at Gretzky's Restaurant.[710] Valet parking costs $30, and a valet can park one hundred cars in a ten-hour shift at $10 per hour. The valet collects $3000 per shift but keeps only $100 in salary. Why should Gretzky get $2900, and the valet $100? Why should Gretzky earn twenty-nine times the valet, when he did not do any of the work?

Gretzky had the idea; he took the financial risk, and Gretzky knows how to manage the business. The cost to build and maintain the parking garage may take years just to break even. The whole parking venture might even cost more than the total income generated. It might be a "loss leader" used to attract customers into the restaurant. If the business does not make money, it goes bankrupt. Mr. Gretzky loses any personal assets he used to start the business. If he loses investors' money, he will struggle to find investors for his next venture, if he succeeds at all. He may be ruined. Either way, the valet goes home with $100 at the end of the shift, even if no one needs valet parking.

Earning an income is the opposite of creating the wealth required to supply the income in the first place. Earning an income does not require a novel idea; it does not require substantial personal financial risk; and it does not require the skills, knowledge, and experience required to run the business. School debt is the closest most of us come to true financial risk.

Since parents and governments pay for schooling most of the time, the majority of students never see school debt as a financial risk.

Physicians learn a unique set of prejudices against free enterprise.[711] Unless we can overcome the bias of anti-capitalism, we can never consider options outside the state system. This does not mean we must rush into the arms of big business and *laissez-faire*. But we do need to see the bias.[712] As a British NHS manager once put it: "without business there would be no buildings, no drugs, no machinery, no beds, no scrubs — just a lot of doctors and nurses in a field in their underwear."[713]

Too few social elites care to pay attention. A gulf widens between those who understand business and intellectuals who write and teach about the welfare state,[714] with players on both sides expressing contempt for each other.[715] Love of socialism is often simply a hatred of business. With a mixed bag of motives, statists, anti-capitalists, socialists, unionists, physician organizations, bureaucrats, and many others all want socialized medicine. They depend on Leviathan for their income.

Not only does socialized medicine see no role for the risk-taking, innovative entrepreneur, it also views these kinds of people as parasites.[716] It can tolerate individuals who find better ways to provide care, just as long as there is zero benefit to the person who found the way. If the person happens to make more money, or expend less time and effort doing so, then we must view them with suspicion. We are happy for entrepreneurs to take the risk, at their own expense. God forbid they should ever benefit from it. That would be profit, which by socialist thinking is money stolen from some poor worker. We should "expropriate these parasites."

So instead of innovation and progress, Canada becomes the land of pilot projects. We cannot scale up good ideas because they are either economically unviable or they generate "surplus value," which we cannot allow.

Offensive Relationships

RELATIONSHIPS ARE anti-equalitarian. At minimum, relationships are voluntary, exclusive, privileged, restrictive, organic, and anti-utilitarian.

They rest on mutual sacrifice, commitment, and a level of devotion not shared with those outside the relationship. People expect help from friends and family in a way they could never expect from a stranger. Relationships build on immaterial privilege and a sense of ownership. Relationships place expectations on us. We cannot do or say whatever we want without risking the health of our relationships. No one stays in a relationship to serve the greater good. From root to branch, relationships reverse or dilute every essential feature of socialism.

Medicare would not exist without medically necessary care, which itself is the outgrowth of the doctor-patient relationship. The technical development of tests and treatments remains outside the provision of those technical elements of care. At the heart of socialized medicine lies a structure — relationship — inimical to socialism.

Relationships cannot be forced. They are most definitely *not* like teacher-student interactions in public schools.[717] Doctors cannot get an accurate history of present illness without the nuance inside relationship. Young, rationalist physicians want to get to the details as quickly as possible: Fever? Fatigue? But they cannot get them as efficiently — or perhaps ever — without relationship. Patients offer details voluntarily, within a covenant of trust, or not at all.

Voluntariness, trust, and confidence take effort to create. They are fragile, easily destroyed by forced reporting, arbitrary data collection, or awkward inspections. Relationships happen even in brief, interrupted clinical interactions. It all builds the clinical relationship which transcends an individual episode of care. This is not just the art of medicine; it is medicine.

Too often, we dismiss relationship as mostly emotion; something that makes youths giggle and pine. Relationship, however, is hard and tangible. It demands and excludes.

Accountability within relationship drives behaviour that no rule could ever enforce. It is the reason people so desperately want to "know a guy" when they have a problem; we want a relationship before we need it. Showing up in need, without relationship, never works as well. And as we saw in the chapter on privilege, relationship creates the special liberties found in any system that lacks liberty, which guarantees that equal care for all can never exist in medicare. As such, maximizing everyone's opportunity to choose relationship is the only insurance against privilege based on fame, wealth, or any other social currency.

The doctor-patient relationship has been medicine's solution to market failure for over three thousand years. It forms the centre of medicine, and from it patients and doctors work together to determine what investigations and treatments seem best. Patients search for good doctors in the same way they search for good dentists or lawyers. Patients need technical competence, but more importantly, they need someone they can trust.

The anti-market, pro-central-planning crowd knows this. Relationships undermine attachment to the state. Everything about them threatens and offends those who seek social levelling based on broad social contracts. Relationship offends the utilitarian model of society held together by contractual obligations.[718] "Sophisters, economists, and calculators" cannot allocate and redistribute relationship.[719]

So the planning crowd seeks to undermine the doctor-patient relationship. Attacking doctors in the media, for some, is not just journalism but an attempt to weaken patients' trust in their physicians and increase trust in the state for care.[720] Which leads us back to the discussion we already had about planning and the planners' desire for more of it.

Equity vs. Excellence

RELATIONSHIPS FORCE us to confront our fascination with equality. Modern equalitarians separate equal treatment from equal outcomes. They call equal treatment equality; equal outcomes equity. Thus, equity demands *unequal* treatment: some people need special privileges to achieve what others can achieve on their own.

As we discussed in chapter five, socialized medicine lost the moral high ground on equity decades ago. Even so, authors continue to promote it as a righteous intention, regardless of our inability to achieve it.

When a teacher hands out candy canes to her students, most people think it would be unfair if any student got nothing. Every student should get the same outcome. However, while this works for teachers giving treats, it does not work for students earning grades. Take group projects, for example. Larger groups multiply free riders, so high performers cut back.

At a superficial level, medical care appears to function somewhat like a teacher handing out treats. Everyone should get the same access; no one earns care. But the pursuit of equity falls apart if we want to help those in need. Doctors put priority on the sickest patients. Physicians do not think about equality or broader social utility. If they did, patients would never trust them. Doctors devote enormous resources to the sickest patients in order to achieve a small marginal benefit. This is normal and good, in medicine.

Furthermore, excellence requires inequality. We do not get professional athletes, or musical genius, or any other gift to society, by holding back high performers or giving them the same reward as the rest of us. Equality is the death of progress.[721] Someone needs to progress beyond the crowd.

This does not remove our responsibility to help the less fortunate. The fact that we need inequality to achieve progress and excellence creates a mandate for charity. It multiplies our responsibility. The reality of inequality mandates charity as an inescapable social policy. We judge societies on how well they care for their most vulnerable members. But that does not mean we must treat all vulnerable patients the same, even if it were possible.

If we pursue progress, some of our most vulnerable patients will receive the latest, cutting-edge, experimental therapy in order for care to improve for all, over time. Equity always exists in an inverse relationship to excellence. More equity means less excellence. People cannot pursue excellence and equity at the same time.[722]

W E C A N now return to content of parts one and two of this book to guide us towards building something better. Following are nine steps towards that end.

1. Provide Care Regardless of Ability to Pay

D O C T O R S H A V E always provided medically necessary *care regardless of ability to pay*, and did so long before medicare existed. Canada could easily have universal care right now, including first-dollar coverage, without our one-sized, single-payer, centrally controlled approach.

In the 1940s, more than two decades before medicare, Canada already had *one* viable option to achieve universal care, without the need for state medicine. Medical associations across Canada had created non-profit insurance programs. They were extremely popular with the public and physicians. By the 1960s, over 50 percent of Canadians had joined one of the plans. The plans offered predictable premiums and universal care to anyone who joined, and physicians supported the fee schedules. On top of this, the plans ran with an extremely low overhead. Physicians designed, built, maintained, and abided by the requirements of the plans themselves. They supported the plans because insurance removed the barrier of payment between patients and medical care. And the care offered by the plans matched the standard of care, not a political vision or a special interest group's goal. As such, insurance also removed the primary reason to socialize medicine in the first place.[723]

Governments could easily have subsidized citizens who could not afford the premiums. In many ways, these companies shared more in common with prepaid medical plans, rather than the risk-adjusted, survival-of-the-fittest approach of corporate insurance we see in some countries.

Physician support for the insurance model played a major role in their later support of the government's own medicare insurance model.[724] Aside from Saskatchewan, which had a large number of British physicians who had escaped socialized medicine in the UK, most Canadian doctors already supported the concept of insurance and had no personal experience with socialized medicine to tell them otherwise. Doctors found it easy to work with the handful of Canadian insurance plans. Canadian physicians saw government insurance as simply one way to insure everyone. They were not trying to escape hundreds of different insurance companies, a common motivation driving calls for single payer in the US. One of the only major worries about the government insurance plan was whether it could match the efficiency and performance of what already existed in the physician-led plans.

In fact, public support for the whole concept of an insurance model pushed governments towards insurance and away from other approaches, such as the one in Saskatchewan's own Swift Current Health Region, in the 1950s. The Swift Current approach functioned more like the Post Office with a government-owned and -operated clinic. It was managed care before health maintenance organizations existed. Swift Current's user fees were not popular, and farmers worried about higher land taxes that would be required to fund the government approach.[725]

The point is that there are many ways to provide universal care, requiring a book of its own to examine and detail them. Insurance offers one example. But new ideas can only come after we remove the barriers to considering them.

2. Adopt One Purpose: Patient Care

CANADA SHOULD pursue one goal using multiple approaches. Instead, we have pursued multiple goals using one approach. The Canadian approach to medicare is like having one state-provided brand of tissue paper to be used for everything from kitchen spills to bathroom cleanup. We see multiple types of tissue paper as being wasteful. We must flip this around. Why not allow dozens of different approaches to the provision, funding, and coordination of care, in order to achieve one goal, great patient care? Let the best approaches emerge from actual performance serving real patients, not pilot programs serving political visions. Canadians already believe we should care for patients for no other reason than that patients need care. This is both simple and hard — something we have discussed at length and need not develop further here.

Care pursued as only a means to another end—wealth redistribution, political support, nation building, fiscal federalism—can be traded, cut, hijacked, distorted, and corrupted beyond repair. Canadians must not allow it or patients will suffer. It does not need to be more complicated than that. Patients are already familiar with different processes for prescriptions, eyewear, and dental treatment. The public can handle much more variety than the medicare activists allow. Society thrives on variety.

3. Provide What You Promised

CANADIANS SHOULD demand integrity from politicians. For example, the prime minister of Finland resigned when his party failed to deliver on healthcare promises. "Isn't the idea of public responsibility for health care the very point of having a public health care system?"[726] If we promise to provide hip surgery in three months, then we must provide it. Sweden promised hip replacement within three months or paid for the procedure to be done privately if that target was not hit. That is a real promise. Figuring out how to deliver on our promises is easy. Deciding to follow through on our promises is hard. But if we do not, broken promises will continue to erode support for any government involvement in care.

The problem is that medicare purists cannot tolerate structural accountability in anything other than a bigger public system. True accountability cannot exist within a monopoly. The only way to achieve accountability is to allow choice (choosing a new government every four years does not count). If we can never hold governments accountable to their promises, then we should never allow governments near patient care. You cannot promise care and not provide it. You cannot assume responsibility and ignore that responsibility. The courts call that negligence when doctors do it. Canadians need to demand a similar level of accountability from the civil service. Freedom without accountability is anarchy, chaos. Agency without liability is tyranny.

We all make mistakes. Some promises cannot be kept. And some of our best efforts to help cause harm. Regardless of why we had to break a promise, or what our best intentions were for helping in the first place, we must take responsibility for our own mess. We must fix or pay for our failures.

We cannot allow governments to promise to provide medically necessary care and then ration it with wait-lists. If governments intend to offer rationing, wait-lists, and privileged access to workplace injuries, then politicians need to say so. Rationing by stealth is dishonest.

4. De-institutionalize Privilege and Patronage

LIKE THE POOR, privilege and patronage will be with us always. The only way to limit privilege is by giving everyone a chance to get some. When it comes to medical care, privilege comes from relationship, as we discussed above, not individuals paying money for care or wielding power. People with money and power use them to form relationships in order to access care. If we promote relationships for everyone, we remove the need for money and power. It levels the field. Promoting relationships for everyone does not mean paying for more relationship. It means making relationship easier. It means making relationship a precious resource to protect. If we compromise, undercut, or create arbitrary constraints on relationship, then we harm the most vulnerable people who need it.

Anything that we heap on top of the doctor-patient relationship — data collection, coding, reporting, rule-following, record-keeping, rationing, population health, system accountability, and a million others — makes relationship harder to form and harder to keep. It increases the cost of relationship. This creates an opportunity cost to the formation of relationship. Those with money and power then have the greatest ability to overcome the cost, form a relationship, and get the care they need. Those who have no other currency with which to artificially leverage a relationship, will go with less or without. Again, this happens with the intangible currency of privilege, not through the physical exchange of money or material goods.

The more difficult it is to form and maintain the doctor-patient relationship, the more likely those with privilege will benefit most. Privilege runs rampant in a system built on restraints that reward people for getting around them. The current approach creates insiders and outsiders.[727] We need a radical commitment to off-load the doctor-patient relationship; to free it up so regular people can get great access, too.

5. Align Incentives

IF WE commit to a system designed to deliver patient care, then every single person in the system must benefit to the degree to which she delivers. Performance incentives should not just apply to senior executives. Everyone needs performance incentives.

How can we reward knowledge workers who perform duties that no one can see to achieve outcomes that no one can measure? For the most part, we do not even try.

At the hospital level, medicare planners try to measure performance through wait times and service volumes. Then they track service and quality with patient satisfaction scores and complication rates or hospital lengths of stay. The trouble is that satisfaction scores can be gamed; complication rates only apply to specific procedures;[728] and lengths of stay end up measuring how heartless the hospital staff are at sending sick people home to recover.

Incentives align only to the extent that the chance of success or failure exists. If failure is never an option, then no one will get too excited about avoiding it. At the same time, people inside the organization need the opportunity to participate in success beyond a piece of a cake at a staff appreciation event. They need to know that, at some level, they own the outcome. This ties back to our earlier discussion about intrinsic motivation.

Organizations must feel motivated to succeed or to avoid failure based on whether they can provide outstanding patient care. This cannot be imposed from outside. It only happens when patients have the opportunity to choose places that develop a reputation for great care.

6. Support, Not Plan

THIS POINT combines the material covered in chapters seven through nine: central planning and a misplaced faith in rational technique and regulation.

Planning creates a vicious cycle. When we start to plan other people's lives, people are less likely to find their own solutions. This increases the need for us to plan for them. No one is smart enough to make all the decisions required for people's health — or to fix medicare. No one knows enough, and no one can know enough.

I spoke to a physician who, after his colleagues retired, ended up with over five thousand patients in his family practice. He had to innovate quickly. By hiring nurse practitioners, nurses, and more office staff, he created a system whereby his patient satisfaction scores beat everyone else's in his area. But he was scared. His practice was three to four times the size of many of his colleagues. Would the college come after him? Would the government notice his incredibly high capitation payments?

If a civil servant came up with the same solution, he could never implement the solution. Implementation requires the passion of the person who tackled and solved the problem. If governments insist on being involved with healthcare, they might focus on making sure all the supplies to provide care are available to do so instead of trying to tell doctors and nurses how to provide. If politicians and planners started from an assumption that they can never know enough, it would change the way they approach management. Instead of chasing data and analysis, they would focus on influence and support. Instead of goals and plans, they would focus on incentives and constraints.

Academic publication rewards rationalism, new data approaches, and novel management techniques. This works well for academics, but it fails those who look to the literature for guidance. The approach that rewards academics, as they advance in their careers, tends to feed the assumptions of managerialism, which already influence the civil service. When civil servants turn toward the literature for ideas and wisdom, they absorb the approach that rewarded the academics in the first place.

The desire to plan, combined with the assumption that we are smart enough to do it, leads well-meaning people to create laws to solve problems. In the face of uncertainty, most people look for control. We want brakes before gas pedals. We humans restrain anything we cannot understand. Security and freedom have always been at war. Although most people choose freedom for themselves, they choose security in the form of restraints for everyone else. Thus, politicians and planners, in the face of a medical industry they do not understand, make regulations and pass laws. This will not stop until people push back. This requires us to think deeply about the law, its role in public policy, and how we might improve regulation. Regulation exists to solve problems. Are we regulating to placate public outrage or are we trying to understand ways to maximize cooperation with those we hope to regulate, and all while working to avoid regulatory unreasonableness?

Perhaps a commitment to a one-for-one approach, where every new law requires an old one to be removed, would help. Maybe a five to one ratio would be more appropriate. This, too, will require concerted thought and effort by those who understand law and medicine.

7. Leverage Doctors' Unique Value

MEDICINE RELIES on doctors' passion not on the technical delivery of care. If governments could learn to leverage doctors' innate passion, there would be much less need for planning. But passion is not just another lever to squeeze out performance. The real substance of medicine lies beyond what we can see. Again, we need a broad and deep effort to understand medicine far beyond the technical, measurable aspects of care. A revival in the philosophy of medicine could defend against the onslaught of managerial medicine.

Physicians, for the most part, are practical people. They use medicine — a social enterprise — to solve tangible problems. But the social enterprise itself is not tangible. Like any institution, it has a complex and nuanced language, history, and social structure. Medicine is a bit like parenting. Academics continue to study parenting, but parents cannot wait for research; they must get on with it. How do we help parents? Most people would laugh at measuring parental performance as a way to help parents and their offspring. The same applies to medicine. Given the difficulty of articulating all that goes into medicine, physicians tend to focus on doing the work of being a doctor.[729] But just because doctors must get on with helping patients does not mean that medicine is nothing but the medical work we can see and measure.

8. Government Should Focus on What It Is Good At

GOVERNMENTS insist on trying to do what no one has ever done or will do. They try to be the buyer and seller of the same item at the same time. It cannot be done.

If you walk into a coffee shop to buy coffee, you are the buyer. You can complain, comment, and even bribe management to change the shop, but you remain the buyer. Only the seller can change the shop.

But what if you are the only buyer at this shop? Would you not then have control over how the shop runs? The coffee shop owners would definitely pay attention to your wishes, but you are still the buyer and they are still the seller.

What if you are the only buyer and you can write laws about how to make coffee and can send inspectors in without notice? This would clearly give you great control. But the owners would still make decisions that impact the coffee. Owners get sued for coffee burns and slippery sidewalks. Multiplying laws, inspections, and oversight will only frustrate them, make it harder for them to work, and frustrate you in never achieving a perfect cup of coffee.

The only way for a buyer to achieve true reform is to buy the shop. Become a seller. Even then, it will require skill and nuance to manage the coffee shop. There is no guarantee the coffee will turn out well. But it is foolish to attempt to make real change to the coffee and how it operates unless you are the seller of the coffee.

Governments buy care. Governments pay for medical services that patients demand and doctors supply. Can you think of any other buyer-seller relationship in which the buyer successfully innovates the service or product that a seller supplies?[730] "Successful innovations are produced by entrepreneurs, *challenging* conventional thinking — not by bureaucrats *trying to implement* conventional thinking."[731] These so-called demand-side reforms fail, because they try to innovate from the wrong side of the supply-and-demand equation. As long as physicians are independent contractors, governments and doctors will remain locked in a contest to control care. Again, this is not about intractable petulance. Doctors carry the legal risk of providing care. Governments carry the political risk of paying for it. Chasing regulation frustrates both parties and hurts patients in the process.

Furthermore, Western governments are democratic. Organizations are not. High-performing organizations use many management techniques; democracy is not one of them. Management must tell workers what needs to be done. Government cannot run medicine like a democracy. Canadian governments try to give the impression that they consult and win the support of doctors and nurses before making decisions for healthcare. This gives the appearance of democracy, but it is not democracy.

Canadian governments are caught. When Canada socialized medicine, it took control of managing the medical industry. This means provincial governments must behave like organizations. So we expect democratic provincial governments, which hold monopolies on the use of force, to behave in a democratic manner to manage medicine: a logical impossibility. What could possibly go wrong?

We must stop believing in the magical land of *private practice, public payment*. That dream ended when Pierre Trudeau passed the Established Programs Financing Act (1977), which put an end to federal blank cheques for healthcare. Without limitless funds from the federal government, provinces cannot afford *public payment* for *private practice*. Given the federal government's conditions on federal funding, under the Canada Health Act, provinces cannot experiment with anything beyond public money for care. If they do, they lose federal support. Thus, provinces cannot let doctors to do whatever they think patients need, because government cannot afford it. Provinces must control costs and that means controlling doctors. Heavy regulation is a fool's game; it never accomplishes the level of control government requires, never mind the insult to democracy.

If Canada wants to maintain *public payment*, then it must have *public practices.* Hire doctors on salary. Build medical care organizations around a salaried model centred on intrinsic motivators. Include performance incentives, gain-sharing, and so on. This approach will face all the challenges of any other government service, such as the post office or military. But at least we will know what we are getting into.

If Canada wants to maintain *private practice,* then we must allow some element of *private payment.* This would require massive deregulation, otherwise it would only change where money came from and do nothing to change how care happens. This approach will face its own challenges, but we can use the experience from dozens of European countries that have figured it out.

Finally, transparency, efficiency, integration, or any other concept we pursue so often cannot fix medicare. They may improve the nobility of our pursuit, but they will not change its purpose.[732] Canadians can be thankful that socialized medicine is not more efficient or organized: waits and rationing might be worse than they are now.

Government plays a crucial role in healthcare as a referee.[733] However, like any actor, it cannot play multiple roles at the same time. We need government to create the context in which medical care can flourish.[734] Context requires a commitment to a particular view of political action. Medicine needs trustees, not executives; conversation, not command; and "friendship rather than the pursuit of a common cause."[735]

9. Do Not Try to Fix Medicare

GIVEN AN obvious problem, most of us try to fix it.[736] It takes many parents twenty years to learn that this does not work. Some never learn. Children need parents to support, guide, monitor, and do a dozen other things, but parents must, at some point, stop trying to fix their children's problems.

We cannot change medicare by trying to change it directly. The cost of change is too great. Vested interests fight to keep what they have already fought to win. Change takes too long — much longer than most governments last. Too much of the change required in medicare has to do with changing government itself, and like the legislation ratchet, medicare change is path dependent. Monopolies never change; they just externalize costs. Revising old policies is boring, and change often harms patients, when public agencies work to maintain their budgets. In all of this, unions resist all change unless it benefits unions. Finally, no government will relinquish control of a program that represents half (or more) of its annual budget.

Governments feel political pressure to *do something*. But fixing medicare is like trying to be happy. We can achieve happiness only by trying to accomplish other goals. Medicare will improve only when we try to change the environment in which it exists. We need to treat medicare more like a child and less like a puppet. We need to create the environment for care to flourish and take a shape that matches patients' needs, instead of forcing it to grow in a political science laboratory.

Patient care should be pursued for its own sake, not to achieve some other purpose. This is obvious and true in the same way that putting politics before patient care is wrong. Medical care in Canada will never improve until governments commit to what most Canadians know already: that medicare is supposed to meet patients' needs, and not the needs of doctors, nurses, politicians, planners, lobbyists, governments, or anyone else.

Epilogue

Utopian movements succeed because they tell people something they wish
desperately to hear. Whether or not the message is true is beside the point.
It speaks to a deeply felt need, and that is enough.
–Roger Kimball

MOST OF this book took shape during the COVID-19 lockdown. As I write now, tree buds force open while the rest of Canada is forced closed, afraid and growing more frustrated each week. Many predict COVID-19 will either mark the start of a new era in healthcare or will fade from memory, like SARS, Swine flu, bird flu, and all the others. Fewer people have died in Canada than predicted. Most of our ICUs did not overflow. And so far we do not know how many people have been hurt by cancelled surgeries and treatments.

COVID hit the mainstream media in Canada less than one week after the city of Brampton, Ontario, declared a state of emergency due to hospital overcrowding. By the time the country was shut down in mid-March, hospitals had cancelled all booked surgeries and any medical care that could be delayed. Some hospitals in eastern Ontario and Quebec filled up with COVID cases, but most hospitals remained far from crowded, their corridors haunted by staff in PPE. A colleague texted me to say that Toronto Sick Kids Hospital, despite drawing patients from across Ontario, had not had a single severe case of COVID.

Academics will write about this for a very long time, armed with stacks of data and analysis. In the meantime, we can hazard a few early comments based on hearsay and anecdotes.

First, the public loves doctors and nurses. While public support waxes and wanes, it has never waxed as full and bright as it has over the last two months. Communities have organized mini parades. Honking cars filled with happy children form long lines around the hospital. Hospital staff post tearful emojis on Twitter. Signs and banners expressing gratitude hang outside homes and businesses.

Fear always enflames love for those who go to fight for us. It pulls us together and builds cohesion. Regardless of how well or poorly socialized medicine performs, we will probably pull through the pandemic and emerge with something like post-WWII optimism. We will have conquered The Pandemic.

The public sees doctors covered in personal protective equipment, and they assume that medicare did that. They see medical success as medicare success. The public sees care and coordination, and it gives credit to culture and concepts. Voters see success even when medicare fails. Bad things have happened during this pandemic — more on this below — and, still, people will give medicare the credit for not allowing the disaster to be worse. It is too distasteful to think anything different. During our moment of greatest need, we want to believe we are safe, that a great system takes care of us. No data could convince us otherwise.

Doctors and nurses donned PPE in countries without medicare also. Canadians do not see that, for now. Conflation of medicine and medicare creates a happy comfort. This might change as we try to catch up with all the cancelled surgeries and treatments, but probably not. Fear makes change virtually impossible.

Second, people can live for a long time without doctors. Walk-in clinics are closed. Lab tests and x-rays have plummeted. Patients feel relieved to delay until the fall, if they can possibly get away with it.

On the one hand, when we finally create a graph of the utilization of medical services during COVID, it will show a dip — no, a gaping crevasse — during the lockdown. It will offer economists and statisticians wonderful fodder for all manner of fancy arguments about why Canadians do not need all the care they used to receive. And the economists would be right. Patients could go without much of the care doctors provide. Doctors could even advise against much of the care and testing we do, if we were not so worried about getting into trouble for the one patient who comes to harm because we skipped a test.

That is the crux: it is always cheaper to not provide medical services, and most people come to no harm. Most things get better with a nap and an Aspirin. In the community, doctors spend most of their time ruling out disease or managing chronic conditions. Outside acute care settings, though, caring for acute or new disease forms a tiny part of what doctors do.

On the one hand, the dip in utilization during COVID will provide an irresistible case to spend less. Matched with the desperate fiscal situation created by deficit spending and pandemic debts, governments might not have a choice. Cuts to medicare funding will work fine for a short time, and for most patients, but it will haunt us years later as missed diagnoses and the impact of delayed treatment pile up. On the other hand, the dip in utilization will hide the incredible impact on our most vulnerable patients. Elderly patients lay on rubber mattresses along hospital hallways before COVID. The same patients bore the brunt of lockdown. Seniors who lived alone but managed with the help of family before COVID became abandoned and isolated during the outbreak. Tenuous situations became dangerous, when supports were cut off, literally, overnight in mid-March. Simple things, such as remembering to drink enough fluids, become life threatening without family around. We need to judge care by how well we perform for our most vulnerable. We can hope the public will remember this during the post-COVID analysis.

Finally, medical practice changed overnight also. After years of pushing for it, COVID forced new fees for virtual care. Pre-COVID, most doctors dabbled in or avoided virtual care. It was not worth the effort. The telemedicine platforms hosted by government were slow, unreliable, and painful. Government refused to pay for any virtual encounter but its own. However, within a week of lockdown virtual care took off.

But something else happened that was not obvious. Suddenly, doctors were scrambling to find work. Walk-in clinics closed. Long-term care homes refused to allow doctors to attend at more than one home at a time; the risk of transferring infection was too high. Operating rooms closed. Elective care was postponed. Hospitals had no trouble finding willing doctors to sign up for new COVID assessment clinics or to serve as back-up for ICUs. No doubt, altruism, professionalism, and a sense of duty drove much of the behaviour. But many doctors felt desperate — a common feeling for most small business owners, but new for doctors.

We could use COVID as a study case on how centralized control works, or does not work, with respect to public health. However, the case is not ideal. Public health is like the military. Medicine, I have argued, is more like farming. We could militarize farming, but it failed in all the countries that tried it. Public health deals with risks to populations that can have medical consequences. Public health and medicine overlap, but they are two separate areas of expertise.

This does not mean we should be anti-military or anti-public health. We need the military when we face problems that cannot be solved without it. The military operates at a higher level, behind the scenes, ready to act, but invisible most of the time. Public health does its best work in the same way. Monitoring, preparing, and training for the next threat, public health works best when it does not insert itself into people's lives at every turn. Unfortunately, too often public health prefers the latter and ignores the former. Too many public health officials would rather design other people's everyday lives than prepare and stockpile for an unknown threat that may never come during their own careers.

In many ways, public health meshes perfectly with the thinking of socialized medicine. I have never met a public health physician who does not advocate a stronger role for government, more central control, and comprehensive monitoring of population health. Indeed, that is why public health exists.[737]

I THINK COVID will mark the change of an era in health care, much like 9-11 did for security measures. Medical protocols will never fully return to the old normal.

Voters sense this. They expect things to be different. The public will give governments more latitude for finding creative ways to deal with the COVID backlog of postponed surgeries, treatments, and investigations, than they would have pre-COVID. Provinces are already looking at innovative ways to deal with the backlog of surgery and postponed treatment. But we face a narrow window. Hopefully, governments will pursue courageous change that focuses on outcomes, not ideology. They will need to act fast. Public enthusiasm to support care will fade as we settle into a new normal.

Medicare failed to protect the dignity of our most vulnerable patients pre-COVID. It seems unreasonable to expect it to perform any better with the post-COVID backlog and beyond. I hope this book will help give politicians and decision makers the resolve they need to look forward for innovative solutions, not backwards for more of the same. It will require space for freedom and experimentation. Creativity always comes as a surprise. And who knows? Maybe COVID will open space for change that will eliminate waiting altogether and return dignity to all patients.

Endnotes

Chapter One

[1] Hall, E., et al. *Royal Commission on Health Services, 1961 to 1964. Canada.Ca.*; 1964.

[2] Canadian medicare is European. Sir William Beveridge wrote the blueprint for British healthcare in 1942. Canada hired Leonard Marsh, a Beveridge team member, to create the same thing for Canada (1943). Marsh, L., Moscovitch. A. *Report on Social Security for Canada: New Edition.* McGill-Queen's University Press; 2018. It looked much like the Beveridge report of 1942. By the time Canada built what it had copied, Europe had moved on to something better.

[3] Formerly the British North America Act 1867.

[4] For example, the federal government:

- Funded provinces for healthcare services with the 1948 National health grants program. It created a hospital building boom that lasted well into the 1970s.
- Promised to pay 50% of all hospital and diagnostic services (Hospital and Diagnostic Services Act, HIDSA 1957).
- Promised to pay 50% of all necessary medical care (Medical Care Act, MCA 1966).
- Grew tired of paying 50% of everything switching to block grants instead (Established Programs Financing Act, EPFA 1977).
- Promised clawbacks from provinces that allow user fees or extra-billing (Canada Health Act, CHA 1984).

[5] Richer, J. "'We Will Not Be Dictated To': Quebec Premier Warns Feds Over Health Care." *CTV News.* https://www.ctvnews.ca/politics/we-will-not-be-dictated-to-quebec-premier-warns-feds-over-health-care-1.4177649. Published November 14, 2018. See also Whatley, S.D. "The Most Responsible Politician: Who's the

MRP for Health Care in Canada?" August 2019. Accessed August 3, 2020. https://macdonaldlaurier.ca/files/pdf/MLI_MostResponsible_Whatley_FWeb.pdf

[6] It gets even more complicated. To finance WWII, the provinces gave up corporate and personal tax room to the federal government, in a temporary tax-rental agreement, 1942. https://www.thecanadianencyclopedia.ca/en/article/intergovernmental-finance A government's essential power rests in its ability to tax. Thus, transferring tax room to the federal government essentially was a transfer of power to the federal government. In return, the feds gave provinces a per capita rental payment. Thirty years later, the Carter commission brought peace but still never returned taxation to pre-war arrangements.

[7] Taylor, M.G. *Health Insurance and Canadian Public Policy: The Seven Decisions That Created the Canadian Health Insurance System and Their Outcomes.* McGill-Queen's University Press; 2009, p. 375.

[8] Shlaes, A. *Great Society: A New History.* Harper; 2019, p. 1.

[9] Rogers, A., Ingebritson, M., Sebetic, B., Munro-Ludders, G., Halvorson, E. "Socialism Is Back — But What Is It? And What Should One Make of It?" *Wall Street Journal.* February 26, 2019.

[10] Ukueberuwa, M. "Boomer Socialism Led to Bernie Sanders." *Wall Street Journal.* https://www.wsj.com/articles/boomer-socialism-led-to-bernie-sanders-11579304307. Published January 17, 2020. Accessed August 3, 2020.

[11] Francis Fukuyama described the end of the cold war as the end of history in his book by the same name. After the fall of socialism, all that remained was liberalism. Fukuyama, F. *The End of History and the Last Man.* Free Press; 2006.

[12] "The familiar communist slogan — who is not with us is against us." Scruton R. *Fools, Frauds and Firebrands: Thinkers of the New Left.* Bloomsbury Continuum; 2019, p. 135.

[13] Schumacher, A. "A Prescription for Health Care Reform: From Myth to Dialogue to Solutions." Canadian Club of Canada. Monday, March 19, 2001.

[14] "Dr Charles Wright, former VP at Vancouver General Hospital, wait-list consultant to the BC Ministry of Health, Health Council of Canada member, and recipient of an $850 000 grant to study wait lists, stated, 'Administrators maintain waiting lists the way airlines overbook. As for urgent patients in pain, the public

system will decide when their pain requires care. These are societal decisions. The individual is not able to decide rationally." Day, B. "The Future Is Not What It Used to Be." Editorial. *BC Medical Journal*. 2016;58(7):353.

[15] Decter, M. *Healing Medicare: Managing Health System Change the Canadian Way*. McGilligan Books; 1994, p. 209.

[16] Jonathan Lomas, Executive Director, Canadian Health Services Research Foundation, from Day, B. Dr. Brian Day Official Site. Health Care Quotes. Accessed August 4, 2020. https://www.brianday.ca/health-quotes/

[17] Ralph Nader, the American author and political activist, quoted in Sowell, T. *The Vision of the Anointed: Self-Congratulation as a Basis for Social Policy*. Basic Books; 1995, p. 71.

[18] Evans, R.G., Barer, M.L., Stoddart, G.L., McGrail, K., McLeod, C.B. *An Undisciplined Economist: Robert G. Evans on Health Economics, Health Care Policy, and Population Health*. McGill-Queen's University Press; 2016, p. 105.

[19] Anglin, H. "Canadian Health Care Is Even More Restrictive Than Communist China's." *Toronto Sun*. October 6, 2016.

[20] Decter, M. *Healing Medicare: Managing Health System Change the Canadian Way*. McGilligan Books; 1994. Decter writes of a "persuasive case for a vision of health based on broad population health, rather than a narrow treatment of illness" (p. 21), and states: "Promotion of health and prevention of disease are better than cure" (p. 200).

[21] "The individual is the single most important obstacle that all bureaucratic systems must overcome, and which all ideologies must destroy." Scruton, R. *A Political Philosophy: Arguments for Conservatism*. Bloomsbury; 2006, p. 168.

[22] Edmund Burke: "In the manifest failure of their abilities, they take credit for their intentions."

[23] "Managers" includes politicians, administrators, civil servants, physician leaders, and many others.

[24] Canada's system was ranked second last overall in Davis, K., Stremikis, K., Squires, D., Schoen, C. *Mirror, Mirror on the Wall, 2014 Update: How the U.S. Health Care System Compares Internationally*. Commmonwealth Fund Study, 2014. On a repeat of this study in 2017, France fell to second last place, pushing Canada up to third last. Schneider, E.C., Sarnak, D.O., Squires, D., Shah, A.,

Doty, M. *Mirror, Mirror 2017: International Comparison Reflects Flaws and Opportunities for Better U.S. Health Care*; Commonwealth Fund Study; 2017.

[25] Tuohy, C. "What's Canadian About Medicare? A Comparative Perspective on Health Policy." *Healthcare Policy | Politiques de Santé*. 2018;13(4):11-22. doi:10.12927/hcpol.2018.25497

[26] Scruton, R. *Fools, Frauds and Firebrands: Thinkers of the New Left*. Bloomsbury Continuum; 2019, p. 24.

[27] "Not consciousness that determines life, but life determines consciousness." Ibid., p. 22.

[28] "I have discovered that the most important differences people have over health policy have little to do with facts, reasoning or logical arguments. The most important differences stem from differences in fundamental world views." Goodman, J.C. *Priceless: Curing the Healthcare Crisis*. Independent Institute; 2012, p. xvii.

[29] Cassel, C.K. "The Patient-Physician Covenant: An Affirmation of Asklepios." *Connecticut Medicine*. 1996;60(5):291-93.

[30] Pooled risk remains popular with Canadians as a way to protect themselves against the potential expense of all kinds of possible threats. A discussion about insurance — moral hazard, adverse selection, premiums, etc. — usually comes up first in a discussion about healthcare. This leads to a long conversation about funding and finance. Funding leads to debates about vertical and horizontal equity, progressive vs. regressive taxation, transfer payments, and much more. Debate about funding overshadows the ideas that guide the funding discussion in the first place. Instead of discussing the ideas on which funding stands, we assume all the ideas and get to the important work of discussing funding, which leaves the ideas unchallenged and unchanged. For this reason, I have left the important funding discussion for my next book.

[31] Reid, T.R. *The Healing of America: A Global Quest for Better, Cheaper, and Fairer Health Care*. Penguin Press; 2009, p. 73.

[32] Naylor, C.D. *Private Practice, Public Payment: Canadian Medicine and the Politics of Health Insurance, 1911-1966*. McGill-Queen's University Press; 1986, p. 26.

[33] Beauchamp, T.L., Childress, J.F. *Principles of Biomedical Ethics*. Oxford University Press; 2013.

[34] It might seem tempting to bolster this argument with rare hard cases. That would

be a mistake. For example, hospitals stop treating the sickest patients when it appears futile to continue. Usually, doctors, nurses, families, and everyone involved can agree when to stop treatment and let a patient die. However, some families want to continue no matter how futile things appear. In Canada, the latter families have no place else to go. When the state decides it is over, it is over. But rare, difficult cases probably would not convince the whole country to change medicare. As they say, hard cases make bad laws. See, for example: www.heritage.org/health-care-reform/commentary/the-moral-costs-socialized-medicine

[35] Fuchs, V.R. *Who Shall Live? Health, Economics, and Social Choice.* Basic Books; 1974, p. 147.

[36] "Dr Charles Wright, former VP at Vancouver General Hospital, wait-list consultant to the BC Ministry of Health, Health Council of Canada member, and recipient of an $850 000 grant to study wait lists, stated, 'Administrators maintain waiting lists the way airlines overbook. As for urgent patients in pain, the public system will decide when their pain requires care. These are societal decisions. The individual is not able to decide rationally.'" Day, B. "The Future Is Not What It Used to Be." Editorial. *BC Medical Journal.* 2016;58(7):353. Accessed August 4, 2020. https://bcmj.org/editorials/future-not-what-it-used-be

[37] Walkinshaw, E. "Patient Navigators Becoming the Norm in Canada." *CMAJ: Canadian Medical Association Journal.* 2011;183(15):e1109. doi:10.1503/CMAJ.109-3974

[38] Boozary, A., Laupacis, A. "The Mirage of Universality: Canada's Failure to Act on Social Policy and Health Care." *CMAJ.* 2020;192(5):E105-E106. doi:10.1503/CMAJ.200085

[39] Scruton, R. *Fools, Frauds and Firebrands: Thinkers of the New Left.* Bloomsbury Continuum; 2019, p. 123.

[40] Burnham, J. *The Managerial Revolution: What Is Happening in the World.* Greenwood Press; 1941, p. 185.

[41] Ibid., 128.

[42] Referring to Brian Sinclair and Laura Hillier.

[43] Mulgrew, I. "Province's Medicare Expert Pummelled." *Vancouver Sun.* July 12, 2019.

[44] Picard, A., tweeted: "On health reform, Canada needs a kick in the ass, not a pat on the back." In reference to his article. "Mr. Sanders, Complimenting Our

Health System Is Nice, but Not Helpful." *Globe and Mail.* October 30, 2017. https://www.theglobeandmail.com/opinion/mr-sanders-complimenting-our-health-system-is-nice-but-not-helpful/article36765869/?utm_medium=Referr er:+Social+Network+/+Media&utm_campaign=Shared+Web+Article+Links. Published 2017. Accessed August 4, 2020.

45 Lum, Z-A. "Bernie Sanders Wants Canadians to 'Be a Little Bit Louder' with Health Debate." *HuffPost Canada.* Published October 29, 2017. Accessed August 4, 2020.

46 Jancelewicz, C. "Jim Carrey Educates Americans on Canadian Health Care in 'Real Time' Rant." Globalnews.ca. Published 2018. Accessed August 4, 2020. https://glo-balnews.ca/news/4437597/jim-carrey-canada-health-care-video/

47 Or as D. Furlong said, "Not much is wrong with the system." FP in rural New Brunswick for 30 years, then 1999-2003 the MLA for northern NB. Two years as Minister of Health. Furlong, D.J. *Medicare Myths.* Dream Catcher; 2004, p. 1. This brings to mind the story of the man who thought he was dead. His family tried everything to convince him that he was alive. Finally, the man's family took him to see a psychiatrist. The psychiatrist also failed to convince the man. So the psychiatrist taught the man all about blood and circulation. Eventually, the man understood that dead men do not bleed. "Are you convinced?" asked the psychiatrist. "Dead men do not bleed?" "Yes," the man said. "I now know, for sure, that dead men do not bleed." The psychiatrist grasped one of the man's fingers and plunged a needle into the tip. A red puddle welled up. The man's eyes widened. "Dead men *do* bleed after all!"

48 Crowley, B.L. "Why Health Care's Broken and How to Fix It." March 2014, Com-mentary, Macdonald-Laurier Institute.

49 Nisbet, R., Douthat, R. *The Quest for Community: A Study in the Ethics of Order and Freedom.* 2019 ed. ISI Books; 1953, p. 31.

50 "So far, however, universality in Canada has successfully met the repeated chal-lenges thrown up by professional ideology and self-interest, and the much less serious grumbling by the ideologues of the market." Evans, R.G., Barer, M.L., Stoddart, G.L., McGrail, K., McLeod, C.B. *An Undisciplined Economist: Robert G. Evans on Health Economics, Health Care Policy, and Population Health.* McGill-Queen's University Press; 2016, p. 143.

51 Philosophers call the process of making a thing out of an idea reification.

[52] Canadians live trapped in a live version of *Rapunzel*. Mother knows best. Do not leave the Tower. Evil men will take advantage of you and leave you penniless. Suffering, bankruptcy, and untreated injury await outside. Government knows best. You are free to leave, just don't come crying back to Canada. Those who repeat the story and maintain the tower are those who stand to benefit from it. Economists call them rent seekers. Canadians enjoy predictability inside medicare. It is not perfect. And there are other ways to provide care. But Canadians should be grateful. It comes down to values and identity. Are we willing to trust mother? Or are we wayward, ungrateful? children who leave the tower and ruin everything? The Arne-Thompson-Uther folktale type 10, otherwise known as "The Maiden in the Tower," 1790.

Chapter Two

[53] Crowley, B.L. *Fearful Symmetry: The Fall and Rise of Canada's Founding Values.* Key Porter; 2010, p. 50.

[54] Reid, T.R. *The Healing of America: A Global Quest for Better, Cheaper, and Fairer Health Care.* Penguin Press; 2009, p. 127.

[55] Naylor, C.D. *Private Practice, Public Payment: Canadian Medicine and the Politics of Health Insurance, 1911-1966.* McGill-Queen's University Press; 1986, p. 137.

[56] Ibid., p. 138.

[57] Hiscox, H. "And the Greatest Canadian of All Time Is …" CBC Archives. Published 2004. Accessed August 4, 2020. https://www.cbc.ca/archives/entry/and-the-greatest-canadian-of-all-time-is

[58] "Many of the leading lights of progressivism around the turn of the twentieth century … were children of Protestant clergymen. The premise of Christian theology is that we are fallen creatures who either do not know what we want or want the wrong things (e.g., golden calves), and hence need to be governed by moral auditors." Will, G.F. *The Conservative Sensibility.* Hachette Books; 2019.

[59] Douglas, T.C., Thomas, L.H., Higginbotham, C.H. *The Making of a Socialist: The Recollections of T.C. Douglas.* University of Alberta Press; 1984, p. 7.

[60] For example, D. Martin et al., wrote in a 2018 *Lancet* article, "Canada's Universal Health-care System: Achieving Its Potential": "In the early 1900s, Thomas Clem-

ent 'Tommy' Douglas, then a young boy growing up in Winnipeg (MB), nearly lost a limb to osteomyelitis because his family was unable to pay for care." Martin, D., Miller, A.P., Quesnel-Vallée, A., Caron, N.R., Vissandjée, B., Marchildon, G.P. "Canada's Universal Health-care System: Achieving Its Potential." *Lancet.* 2018;391(10131):1718-1735. doi:10.1016/S0140-6736(18)30181-8

[61] Naylor repeats the story in his book: "If my parents had been rich, I'd have had the best doctor in Winnipeg." He went on to say that medical services should be "an inalienable right of being a citizen in a Christian country." Naylor, C.D. *Private Practice, Public Payment: Canadian Medicine and the Politics of Health Insurance, 1911-1966.* McGill-Queen's University Press; 1986, p. 181.

[62] Douglas, T.C., Douglas, L.H., Higginbotham, C.H. *The Making of a Socialist: The Recollections of T.C. Douglas.* University of Alberta Press; 1984, p. 6.

[63] Ibid., p. 7.

[64] For example, T.R. Reid writes: "Surgery was indicated, but surgery in those days was a luxury for people who had far more money than the struggling Douglas family." Reid, T.R. *The Healing of America: A Global Quest for Better, Cheaper, and Fairer Health Care.* Penguin Press; 2009, p. 124. And: "When Tommy Douglas's Scottish family settled in Canada shortly before World War I, the rich Canadian had access to medical care and the poor Canadian did not, except at a few widely scattered public clinics." Ibid., p. 129.

[65] Douglas's story pops up in every policy text, but most medical schools do not mention it. "If I hadn't been so fortunate as to have this doctor offer me his services gratis, I would probably have lost my leg." And: "I felt that no boy should have to depend either for his leg or his life upon the ability of his parents to raise enough money to bring a first-class surgeon to his bedside."

[66] Even with the legalization of medical aid in dying (euthanasia), protecting life and limb still represents the touchstone of medical care. As one reviewer has added, it seems interesting that when life and limb are beyond salvaging, then we prioritize dignity.

[67] Decady, Y., Greenberg, L. Ninety Years of Change in Life Expectancy. Statistics Canada; 2011. https://www150.statcan.gc.ca/n1/pub/82-624-x/2014001/article/14009-eng.htm

[68] Lebel, A., Hallman, S. Mortality: Overview, 2012 and 2013, Statistics Canada.

https://www150.statcan.gc.ca/n1/pub/91-209-x/2017001/article/14793-eng.htm

[69] Decady, Y. Changes in Causes of Death, 1950 to 2012, Statistics Canada. https://www150.statcan.gc.ca/n1/pub/11-630-x/11-630-x2016003-eng.htm;

[70] Hurley J., Grant, H. "Unhealthy Pressure: How Physician Pay Demands Put the Squeeze on Provincial Health-care Budgets." School of Public Policy, Research Paper, University of Calgary. 2013;6(22). doi:10.2139/ssrn.2304393 https://www.policyschool.ca/wp-content/uploads/2016/03/grant-physician-income.pdf

[71] Prior to medicare: "They competed professionally with each other; the physician across the street or down the road was a colleague but also a competitor. They were happy, and eager, to see any patient walk into their office for service." "Most physicians were extremely fortunate when they received fifty percent of accounts receivable." Furlong, D.J. *Medicare Myths*. Dream Catcher; 2004, p. 84.

[72] Doctors provided substantial non-remunerative work at least as far back as the early 20th century: e.g.: "In 1929, 77.5 percent of work done was remunerative; but in 1932 half of the patients were non-paying." Naylor, C.D. *Private Practice, Public Payment: Canadian Medicine and the Politics of Health Insurance, 1911-1966*. McGill-Queen's University Press; 1986, p. 59.

[73] Manitoba Historical Society. College of Physicians and Surgeons of Manitoba. Accessed August 4, 2020. http://www.mhs.mb.ca/docs/organization/collegephysicianssurgeons.shtml

[74] Beck, A.H. "The Flexner Report and the Standardization of American Medical Education." *JAMA: The Journal of the American Medical Association*. 2004;291(17):2139-2140. doi:10.1001/jama.291.17.2139

[75] Atwal Gawande wrote in *New Yorker* about "the 1946 Toronto *Globe and Mail* report of a woman in labor who was refused help by three successive physicians, apparently because of her inability to pay." As a world-famous writer and scientist, Gawande would not normally stake his reputation on one story reported in a newspaper that hinges on "apparently." It passes because it aligns with the grand narrative. Gawande, A. "Getting There from Here: How Should Obama Reform Health Care?" *New Yorker*. Published online January 2009. www.newyorker.com/magazine/2009/01/26/getting-there-from-here

[76] Pipes, S., Fraser Institute (Vancouver, BC), Pacific Research Institute for Public Policy. *Miracle Cure: How to Solve America's Health Care Crisis and Why Canada*

Isn't the Answer. Pacific Research Institute; 2004, p. 145.

[77] Jedwab, J. "Sources of Personal or Collective Pride in Canada." 2019. Accessed August 4, 2020. https://acs-aec.ca/wp-content/uploads/2019/06/ACS-Sources-of-personal-or-collective-pride-in-Canada-EN.pdf

[78] "History of Health and Social Transfers." Canada.ca. Accessed August 4, 2020. https://www.canada.ca/en/department-finance/programs/federal-transfers/history-health-social-transfers.html

[79] Gunn, A. "Survey Shows Atlantic Canadians Most Pessimistic About Health Care." *The Guardian.* https://www.theguardian.pe.ca/news/local/survey-shows-atlantic-canadians-most-pessimistic-about-health-care-311157/. Published May 13, 2019.

[80] "Our system is less 'public' than many people think (remember, only 70 percent of health care is financed with public dollars)." Martin, D. *Better Now: Six Big Ideas to Improve Health Care for All Canadians.* Penguin Random House; 2017, p. 37. And again in a *Lancet* review, 2018, of the Canadian healthcare system, Martin, D., Miller, A.P., Quesnel-Vallée, A., Caron, N.R., Vissandjée, B., Marchildon, G.P. "Canada's Universal Health-care System: Achieving Its Potential." *Lancet.* 2018;391(10131):1718-1735. doi:10.1016/S0140-6736(18)30181-8

[81] Martin, D. *Better Now: Six Big Ideas to Improve Health Care for All Canadians.* Penguin Random House; 2017, p. 19.

[82] Canadian trust in government was nearly 60 percent in 1968, but only 28 percent in 2012, according to a public opinion survey. Savoie, D.J. *Democracy in Canada: The Disintegration of Our Institutions.* McGill-Queen's University Press; 2019, p. 7.

[83] Taylor, M.G. *Health Insurance and Canadian Public Policy: The Seven Decisions That Created the Canadian Health Insurance System and Their Outcomes.* McGill-Queen's University Press; 2009, p. 2.

[84] "It was for several decades assumed that the state had the right and the duty to 'manage', not only the economy, but the education system, the relief of poverty, the pattern of settlements and the industries that furnish them with labour, the terms and conditions of employment — in short, just about everything on which the well-being and security of the people might seem to depend." Scruton, R. *The Meaning of Conservatism.* St. Augustine's Press; 2002, p. 114.

[85] "The role of government is no longer limited to providing necessary public ser-

vices like a legal system and national defence. Instead, government is expected to use its power to cure social ills that are not adequately addressed by private markets." Simmons, R.T. *Beyond Politics: The Roots of Government Failure.* Independent Institute; 2011, p. 29.

[86] Tuohy, C. "What's Canadian About Medicare? A Comparative Perspective on Health Policy." *Healthcare Policy | Politiques de Santé.* 2018;13(4):11-22. doi:10.12927/hcpol.2018.25497

[87] "The design of Canadian medicare was an elite project." Ibid.

[88] Lewis, S. "Does the Canada Health Act Matter Anymore and Could It?" Lecture at University of Ottawa, Faculty of Law. Published 2015. Accessed January 10, 2019. https://www.youtube.com/watch?v=gWQAy5lWXFY

[89] Stein, J.G. *The Cult of Efficiency.* House of Anansi Press; 2002, p. 192.

Chapter 3

[90] Quoted in Nuland, S.B. *The Uncertain Art: Thoughts on a Life in Medicine.* Random House; 2008, pp. 8-9.

[91] "One could be forgiven for thinking that the design and implementation of health care institutions, processes, and agreements are all about improving health care. At best they are the product of the political zeitgeist: a reflection of what goals political actors deem to be important and the resources they have at their disposal. At worst, health care reforms are not really about health care at all but merely serve as means of achieving other political objectives." Fierlbeck, K., Lahey, W. *Health Care Federalism in Canada: Critical Junctures and Critical Perspectives.* McGill-Queen's University Press; 2013, p. 45. Using people to achieve one's own end reduces people to means. "Coercion is evil precisely because it thus eliminates an individual as a thinking and valuing person and makes him a bare tool in the achievement of the ends of another." Hayek, F.A., Hamowy, R. *The Constitution of Liberty: The Definitive Edition.* University of Chicago Press; 2011.

[92] Picard, A. *The Path to Health Care Reform.* The Conference Board of Canada; 2013, p. 17.

[93] Evans, R.G., Barer, M.L., Stoddart, G.L., McGrail, K., McLeod, C.B. *An Undisciplined Economist: Robert G. Evans on Health Economics, Health Care Policy, and*

Population Health. McGill-Queen's University Press; 2016, p. 101.

94 Litz, B.T., Stein, N., Delaney, E., et al. "Moral Injury and Moral Repair in War Veterans: A Preliminary Model and Intervention Strategy." *Clinical Psychology Review*. 2009;29(8):695-706. doi:10.1016/j.cpr.2009.07.003

95 Sanger-Katz, M. "What Did Bernie Sanders Learn in His Weekend in Canada?" *New York Times*. November 2, 2017.

96 Fierlbeck, K. *Health Care in Canada: A Citizen's Guide to Policy and Politics*. University of Toronto Press; 2011, p. 12.

97 CHA 2018 report. Canada. Health Canada. Canada Health Act, Annual Report. Health Canada = Santé Canada; 1993. https://www.canada.ca/en/health-canada/services/publications/health-system-services/canada-health-act-annual-report-2016-2017.html "Protecting and upholding human rights and social justice are the fundamental objectives of social work and are closely linked to the values that underpin the Canada Health Act — equity, fairness and solidarity."

98 "There are a number of desirable qualities in any health care system: these include cost containment, efficiency, equity, universality, comprehensiveness, and responsiveness. The attainment of all these qualities is the ideal objective of health policy. The problem is that the more we move to secure one goal, the more we can undermine one or several others." Fierlbeck, K. *Health Care in Canada: A Citizen's Guide to Policy and Politics*. University of Toronto Press; 2011, p. 3.

99 Some scholars redefine equity as not the state of affairs, *per se*, but rather as the right of access to all the goods and services of society. But they still imply that there is "equal access," which leads back to it being a state of affairs. More commonly, people who promote the concept see equity to mean the "fair and equitable provision, implementation, and impact of services, programs, and policies." https://www.igi-global.com/dictionary/support-for-and-behavioral-responses-to-tolls/27342

100 "The legislated single-payer monopoly on the provision of medical and hospital services and consequent infringement on the personal and professional liberty were now justified on egalitarian grounds … Legislated equality in health care (with only a few quietly permitted loopholes, such as special VIP care for Members of Parliament) was the Canadian way, the very essence of the country's values, part of the Canadian identity. If you did not agree with these proposi-

tions, the inference would be that your Canadianism was suspect." Michael Bliss in Gratzer, D. *Better Medicine: Reforming Canadian Health Care*. ECW Press; 2002, pp. 40-41.

[101] Regarding "accomplishing objectives to reduce waiting times": "Questions can be asked about the relationship of that success to the growing role of for-profit clinics in the delivery of diagnostic and surgical procedures. The issue is not the priority given to reducing waiting times but the priority given to that objective in the absence of any agreement on the methodologies that should (and should not) be used to accomplish it." ... "On the particular issue of waiting times, a national initiative to reduce waiting times should be accompanied by a clear decision on privatization, I think everyone, including those who believe in the benefits of privatized delivery, should want it done to prevent or halt privatization by stealth." William Lahey in Fierlbeck, K., Lahey, W. *Health Care Federalism in Canada: Critical Junctures and Critical Perspectives*. McGill-Queen's University Press; 2013, p. 95.

[102] Scruton notes this is a common tactic. Long after he should have known better, Sartre urged people to "judge communism by its intentions and not by its actions." Scruton, R. *Fools, Frauds and Firebrands: Thinkers of the New Left*. Bloomsbury Continuum; 2019, p. 94. And Thomas Sowell writes: "As Hannah Arendt has pointed out, transforming questions of fact into questions of intent has been the great achievement of the twentieth-century totalitarians." Sowell, T. *The Vision of the Anointed: Self-Congratulation as a Basis for Social Policy*. Basic Books; 1995, p. 244.

[103] Where "equity" means an equal outcome, and "equality" means an equal starting point.

[104] Parfit, D. "Equality or Priority?" In *The Lindley Lecture, The University of Kansas*. Department of Philosophy, University of Kansas; 1991. Accessed August 4, 2020. https://www.stafforini.com/docs/Parfit%20-%20Equality%20or%20priority.pdf

[105] A Bob Evans coinage.

[106] Lecours, A., Marchildon, G.P., Olfert, M.R., Béland, D., Mou, H. *Fiscal Federalism and Equalization Policy in Canada: Political and Economic Dimensions*. University of Toronto Press; 2017, p. 1.

[107] Marchildon, G.P. *Making Medicare: New Perspectives on the History of Medicare*

in Canada. Institute of Public Administration of Canada; 2012, p. 6.

[108] "It is not entirely clear … why there is apparently more support for redistributing income through subsidized medical care than for simply redistributing income directly and letting individuals decide how they want to spend their money." Fuchs, V.R. *Who Shall Live? Health, Economics, and Social Choice*. Basic Books; 1974, p.131.

[109] Including me, until a few years ago.

[110] Evans, R.G., Barer, M.L., Stoddart, G.L., McGrail, K., McLeod, C.B. *An Undisciplined Economist: Robert G. Evans on Health Economics, Health Care Policy, and Population Health*. McGill-Queen's University Press; 2016, p. 209. And a few pages later, Evans writes that he believes the whole debate is about distributional issues: "the conflicts are in fact about very little else." Ibid., p. 215.

[111] The late Christie Blatchford, journalist, once complained about low-quality care and poor hospital service, in an article for the *National Post*, "I Won't Be Defined by Mediocre Medicare" (November 30, 2002).This sparked Michael Rachlis, public health expert, to write: "Blatchford is shooting at the wrong target. We tend to think of medicare as a government system, but it is still really more of an insurance program or, as University of Toronto dean of medicine Dr. David Naylor describes it, 'public payment for private practice.' The quality problems Blatchford describes are not a result of government involvement with health insurance." Rachlis, M. *Prescription for Excellence: How Innovation Is Saving Canada's Health Care System*. Harper Perennial Canada; 2005, p. 55.

[112] Martin, D. *Better Now: Six Big Ideas to Improve Health Care for All Canadians*. Penguin Random House; 2017, p. 19. See also: "Health care in Canada is government-funded but almost exclusively privately provided …" Reynolds, J.L. *Prognosis: The Current State and Shaky Future of Canada's Health System*. Penguin Canada; 2008, p. 99.

[113] "Most of our publicly financed health services — those paid for with tax dollars — are still privately delivered. This is a really important point, often misunderstood. As a doctor, I'm paid with public dollars, but I'm not an employee of the government … The minister of health is not my boss. Because I'm paid as an independent contractor for my services, the minister can't mandate that I work evening hours, for example, or correspond with my patient by email.

He or she can't fire me, because like nearly all Canadian physicians, I'm not a government employee. If they want me to practise medicine differently, policy makers in the Ministry of Health could entice me to do so by paying a premium for any patient seen after five p.m., or conversely, by cutting the rates for daytime consultation." Martin, D. *Better Now: Six Big Ideas to Improve Health Care for All Canadians.* Penguin Random House; 2017, p. 20.

[114] Ibid., p. 21.

[115] Crowley, B.L. "Why Health Care's Broken and How to Fix It." March 2014, Commentary, Macdonald-Laurier Institute.

[116] Ibid.

[117] "When people talk about Canada having a 'government monopoly' over health care services, they misunderstand our system. In fact, nearly all of our health care is privately delivered, and, as I mentioned earlier, a full 30 percent of our health care services are privately financed. Those who use words like 'monopoly' are really objecting to the fact that each province and territory has only one payer for doctors and hospitals and Canadians can't buy their way to the front of the line." Martin, D. *Better Now: Six Big Ideas to Improve Health Care for All Canadians.* Penguin Random House; 2017, pp. 21-22. In passing, notice how the "30 percent ... privately financed" comes up, as we discussed in the last chapter. Also notice how "monopoly" gets tied to "buy their way to the front of the line."

[118] "Totality" refers to the philosopher Lukacs's favourite use of the concept, as he sought to understand Marx's "total" vision. Not to be confused with dictatorial totalitarianism. Scruton, R. *Fools, Frauds and Firebrands: Thinkers of the New Left.* Bloomsbury Continuum; 2019, p. 124. Furthermore, a single purchaser is called a monopsony, not a monopoly. But this is about more than a quibble over terms.

[119] "As originally implemented, Medicare was a passive payment system that did not change the way in which existing hospitals and physicians actually worked. It was 'health insurance' rather than a 'health system.'" Marchildon, G.P., *Making Medicare: New Perspectives on the History of Medicare in Canada.* Institute of Public Administration of Canada; 2012, p. 11.

[120] As Herbert Marcuse said: "It is not the ownership alone that matters, but the control of the productive forces which is decisive." Marcuse, H., Magee, B. Her-

bert Marcuse interview with Bryan Magee (1977). YouTube. Published 1977. Accessed August 4, 2020. https://www.youtube.com/watch?v=0KqC1lTAJx4 (YouTube quote starts at 21:00 ff):

[121] Socializing an industry is like Sauron's Ring of power. It is government's ring of power. The ring will always seek to do the will of its master, government. If we use it in a desire to do good, through it, we will do evil. (Phil Whatley's insight, in conversation.)

[122] A full description of this in terms of healthcare requires a separate book. See also von Mises, L. *Socialism: An Economic and Sociological Analysis.* 2nd ed. 2012. Martino Publishing; 1932. Or anything by Friedman, Hayek, or Sowell.

[123] "State Socialism and planned economies, which want to maintain private property in name and in law, but in fact, because they subordinate the power of disposing to State orders, want to socialize property, are socialist systems in the full sense." Ibid., p. 276.

[124] In Britain, most doctors are salaried employees of the state. Those who say Canada's system is just single-payer health care insist that anything less than salaried employment, like Britain, is not socialized medicine. Therefore, Canada does not have socialized medicine. But even Britain allows private hospitals, clinics, and doctors to work as independent contractors. Patients can access private care, if wait times grow too long in the public system. And many, if not most, British doctors earn part of their income, at some point in their careers, without working as salaried employees of the state.

[125] "Private care refers to the agent who pays for the services, rather than the services being offered. If the payer is public, the services should be considered public; if the payer is the individual or a personal insurance program, the services should be considered private. Since primary care carried out by a physician is paid from the public purse, it is false to label this as part of the private sector. This artificial label for primary care has led to the undesirable outcome of creating some reluctance to fund it from the public purse since it is associated with private enterprise." Levine, D. *Health Care and Politics: An Insider's View on Managing and Sustaining Health Care in Canada.* Véhicule Press; 2015, p. 185.

[126] "The authority, not the consumers, directs production." "Some labels of the capitalistic market economy are retained, but they signify here something entirely dif-

ferent from what they mean in the market economy." von Mises, L. *Socialism: An Economic and Sociological Analysis.* 2nd ed. 2012. Martino Publishing; 1932, p. 529.

[127] Personal communication with a colleague.

[128] "To make good on its new political promise, the State had to hand itself the legal power to supervise and to ration; that is, a State right to rupture the professional private relationship between physician and patient, to police the work of hospitals, to examine, proscribe, and dictate available services, to examine patient records without any knowledge of patients, and so on." Dr. William Gairdner, retired English professor, writes a 45-page critique of medicare in a chapter titled, "Medical Mediocrity: An Autopsy on the Canadian 'Health Care' System." In Gairdner, W.D. *The Trouble with Canada ... Still! A Citizen Speaks Out.* BPS Books; 2011, pp. 284-329.

[129] Quote starts at 33:20 YouTube. Tuohy, C. "Dynamic of Health Policy Change in the UK, the US, the Netherlands, and Canada." YouTube. Published 2014. Accessed August 4, 2020. https://www.youtube.com/watch?time_continue=2&v=76RrHopbvlY&feature=emb_logo

[130] Fierlbeck, K. *Health Care in Canada: A Citizen's Guide to Policy and Politics.* University of Toronto Press; 2011, pp. 82-83.

[131] Blishen, B.R. *Doctors in Canada: The Changing World of Medical Practice.* Published in association with Statistics Canada by University of Toronto Press; 1991, p. 143.

[132] Ibid., p. 136.

[133] Boychuk in Marchildon, G.P. *Making Medicare: New Perspectives on the History of Medicare in Canada.* Institute of Public Administration of Canada; 2012, p. 114.

[134] Ibid., p. 115. Michael Rachlis, author and public health doctor, notes: "Sometimes governments use the concept of prevention simply as an excuse to slash health care budgets as part of an overall strategy of government cutbacks." Referencing the Lalonde report, he says: "It claimed that health care was not as important a determinant of health as other social factors, factors that should get more policy attention." Rachlis, M. *Prescription for Excellence: How Innovation Is Saving Canada's Health Care System.* Harper Perennial Canada; 2005, p. 176.

Chapter Four

[135] "Sudbury Patient Kept in Hospital Bathroom for 13 Days, MPP Says." CBC News. Published 2018. Accessed August 4, 2020. https://www.cbc.ca/news/canada/sudbury/sudbury-hospital-bathroom-patient-1.4545554

[136] "'Limited System-wide Capacity' to Blame for Cancelling Londoner's Bypass Four Times, Hospital Says." *London Free Press*. Published 2018. Accessed August 4, 2020. https://lfpress.com/2018/02/22/limited-system-wide-capacity-to-blame-for-cancelling-londoners-bypass-four-times-hospital-says

[137] Duffy, A. "Young Hockey Player Faces Long, Painful Wait for Hip Surgery at CHEO." *Ottawa Citizen*. Published 2017. Accessed August 4, 2020. https://ottawacitizen.com/news/local-news/young-hockey-player-faces-long-painful-wait-for-hip-surgery-at-cheo

[138] "'Her Dying Wish.' Ontario Parents Want Speedier Stem Cell Transplants After Daughter's Death." CBC Radio News. Published 2016. Accessed August 4, 2020. https://www.cbc.ca/radio/asithappens/as-it-happens-thursday-edition-1.3568451/her-dying-wish-ontario-parents-want-speedier-stem-cell-transplants-after-daughter-s-death-1.3568464

[139] Boyle, T. "Surge in Patients Forces Ontario Hospitals to Put Beds in 'Unconventional Spaces.'" Toronto Star. Published 2017. Accessed August 4, 2020. https://www.thestar.com/news/canada/2017/04/16/surge-in-patients-forces-ontario-hospitals-to-put-beds-in-unconventional-spaces.html

[140] Sher, J. "Wait Times for Knee- and Hip-replacement Surgery at Southwestern Ontario Hospitals Are Among the Longest in the Province." *Toronto Sun*. Published 2017. Accessed August 4, 2020. https://torontosun.com/2017/10/02/wait-times-for-knee--and-hip-replacement-surgery-at-southwestern-ontario-hospitals-are-among-the-longest-in-the-province/wcm/249fc7cb-fd45-4054-955a-876a4953a621

[141] Blackwell, T. "Untrained and Unemployed: Medical Schools Churning Out Doctors Who Can't Find Residencies and Full-time Positions." *National Post*. Published 2015. Accessed August 4, 2020. https://nationalpost.com/health/untrained-and-unemployed-medical-schools-churning-out-doctors-who-cant-find-residencies-and-full-time-positions

[142] Barua, B., Jacques, D. *The Private Cost of Public Queues for Medically Necessary Care, 2019.* Fraser Institute; 2019. Accessed August 4, 2020. https://www.fraserinstitute.org/studies/private-cost-of-public-queues-for-medically-necessary-care-2019?utm_source=Email&utm_campaign=Private-Cost-of-Public-Queues-2019&utm_medium=Dev_email&utm_content=Learn_More&utm_term=700

[143] Barua, B. "There Are Huge Economic Costs — Along with Health Costs — for Long Wait Times in Canada." CBC News. Published 2019. Accessed August 4, 2020. https://www.cbc.ca/news/opinion/economic-costs-waiting-1.5131406

[144] Chaoulli v. Quebec (Attorney General) — SCC Cases (Lexum). Presented at the: 2005. Accessed August 4, 2020. https://scc-csc.lexum.com/scc-csc/scc-csc/en/item/2237/index.do 5

[145] http://waittimes.cihi.ca/

[146] After two national reviews called for it (Romanow and Kirby).

[147] Colleen Flood in Leatt, P., Mapa, J. *Government Relations in the Health Care Industry.* Praeger; 2003, p. 49.

[148] Senator Mike Kirby said: "So that in a sense the way the system is currently structured, the only person who suffers when they're on a waiting list is the patient. The provincial government doesn't suffer in fact they actually save money with it, the regional health authorities, the hospital CEO's, the doctors don't suffer and so there's not really a union incentive to improve the system. The only person who suffers is the patient — who's the only person in fact who can't do anything about the situation. So the incentive that currently exists in the system for dealing with waiting times are all perverse in the sense that they put all the pressure on the one group of people called patients who can't do anything about it." "Famous Quotes About Canadian Health Care." Charter Health. Accessed August 5, 2020. https://www.charterhealth.ca/quotes/

[149] Fuchs, V.R. *Who Shall Live? Health, Economics, and Social Choice.* Basic Books; 1974, p. 71.

[150] "When Toronto Declared War on Snow and Called in the Army." CBC Archives. CBC News. Published 2019. Accessed August 5, 2020. https://www.cbc.ca/archives/when-toronto-declared-war-on-snow-and-called-in-the-army-1.4950600

[151] Vibert, J. "'Best Care' Impossible in Stressed Emergency." *Chronicle Herald.* Published 2019. Accessed August 5, 2020.

[152] Mulligan, C. "'I Thought We Were in a Third-World Country': Ontario Emergency Room Wait Times Spike." CityNews Toronto. Published 2019. Accessed August 5, 2020. https://toronto.citynews.ca/2019/01/03/i-thought-we-were-in-a-third-world-country-ontario-emergency-room-wait-times-spike/

[153] Dunn, T. "Bleeding Internally, 'Screaming in Pain,' Brampton Woman Spent 5 Days in Hospital Hallway." CBC News. Published 2017. Accessed August 5, 2020. https://www.cbc.ca/news/canada/toronto/brampton-woman-hospital-hallway-1.4070379

[154] "Patrick Brown, Brampton Council Declare Health Care Emergency." CBC News. Published 2020. Accessed August 5, 2020. https://www.cbc.ca/news/canada/toronto/brampton-health-emergency-declaration-1.5436518

[155] Annable, K. "Winnipeg Patient 'Furious' After Waiting Months for Heart Procedure." CBC News. Published 2019. Accessed August 5, 2020. https://www.cbc.ca/news/canada/manitoba/heart-wait-boniface-health-1.5242869

[156] Crabb, J. "Elderly Man in Need of Biopsy Spent 60 Hours in ER Waiting for Hospital Bed: Daughter." CTV News. Published 2019. Accessed August 5, 2020. https://winnipeg.ctvnews.ca/elderly-man-has-biopsy-after-family-speaks-out-about-months-long-wait-1.4245482

[157] Brown, L. "'This Is Not Good Medicine. This Is Cruelty': Fredericton Doctors Speak Out on Ailing ER." CTV News. Published 2019. Accessed August 5, 2020. https://atlantic.ctvnews.ca/this-is-not-good-medicine-this-is-cruelty-fredericton-doctors-speak-out-on-ailing-er-1.4424319

[158] Osman, L. "'People Are Dying': Life and Death at Level Zero." CBC News. Published 2019. Accessed August 5, 2020. https://www.cbc.ca/news/canada/ottawa/level-zero-paramedic-1.5316802

[159] Laucius, J. "Offload Delay: Ottawa Paramedics Had No One Free to Transport Patients for 7.5 Hours in June." *Ottawa Sun.* Published 2019. Accessed August 5, 2020. https://ottawasun.com/news/local-news/offload-delay-ottawa-paramedics-had-no-one-free-to-transport-patients-for-7-5-hours-in-june/wcm/eb4aab42-90e0-4a9f-9e14-7c275b7f8be2

[160] Zadorsky, J. "LHSC Planning to Close 49 Beds at Two Locations to Deal with

Deficit." *CTV News*. Published 2019. Accessed August 5, 2020. https://london.ctvnews.ca/mobile/lhsc-planning-to-close-49-beds-at-two-locations-to-deal-with-deficit-1.4622163

[161] Weldon, T. "New Brunswick Is Losing Its Only Pediatric Ophthalmologist." CBC News. Published 2019. Accessed August 5, 2020. https://www.cbc.ca/news/canada/new-brunswick/pediatric-ophthalmologist-eye-doctor-specialist-vacancy-1.5296646?cmp=rss

[162] Hennig, C. "Surgery Wait Lists in B.C. Grow Larger Than Population of Some Cities, Report Says." CBC News. Published 2019. Accessed August 5, 2020. https://www.cbc.ca/news/canada/british-columbia/bc-anesthesiologists-society-surgery-wait-list-1.4978867

[163] Tutton, M. "Critics of Canadian Health System Discover a Potent Tool: Social Media." Globalnews.ca. Published 2019. Accessed August 5, 2020. https://globalnews.ca/news/5222657/social-media-health-care/

[164] @stewartmedicine. #CanadaWaits. Twitter. https://twitter.com/stewartmedicine/status/1081367633809698816?s=12

[165] Fraser, L. "Nova Scotians Are Waiting More Than Eight Years for Weight-loss Surgery." CBC News. Published 2019. Accessed August 5, 2020. https://www.cbc.ca/news/canada/nova-scotia/weight-loss-surgery-wait-list-1.5173642

[166] "39 Cancer Patients Died While Still on Wait-list for Halifax Gastroenterologist: Study." *Chronicle Herald*. Published 2019. Accessed August 5, 2020. https://www.thechronicleherald.ca/news/local/39-cancer-patients-died-while-still-on-wait-list-for-gastroenterologist-study-304737/

[167] MacDonald, M. "Facing Four-year Wait for Hip Surgery, Young New Brunswick Woman Headed to Court." CTV News. Published 2019. Accessed August 5, 2020. https://www.ctvnews.ca/mobile/health/facing-four-year-wait-for-hip-surgery-young-new-brunswick-woman-headed-to-court-1.4359525

[168] Dunham, J. "Longer Waits for Hip, Knee Replacements, Cataract Surgeries: CIHI." CTV News. Published 2019. Accessed August 5, 2020. https://www.ctvnews.ca/health/canadians-waiting-longer-for-hip-knee-replacements-and-cataract-surgeries-cihi-1.4355589

[169] "Wait Times for Priority Procedures in Canada." Canadian Institute for Health Information. Published 2020. Accessed August 5, 2020. https://www.cihi.ca/en/

wait-times-for-priority-procedures-in-canada

170 Dearing, R. "'We're Not Just Numbers Here': Patients Complain Specialist Wait Times Too Long." CBC News. Published 2018. Accessed August 5, 2020. https://www.cbc.ca/news/canada/newfoundland-labrador/wait-times-newfoundland-labrador-1.4666800

171 Lee-Shanok, P. "Daily Bed Census May Not Capture Full Extent of Hallway Health Care." CBC News. Published 2019. Accessed August 5, 2020. https://www.cbc.ca/news/canada/toronto/daily-bed-census-doesn-t-show-full-extent-of-hall-medicine-problem-1.5003586

172 Picard, A. "'Tis the Season for Hospital Overcrowding—But the Flu Isn't to Blame." *Globe and Mail*. Published 2019. Accessed August 5, 2020. https://www.theglobeandmail.com/opinion/article-tis-the-season-for-hospital-overcrowding-but-the-flu-isnt-to-blame/

173 Schnurr, J. "Ottawa Woman with MS Back Home Today After PSW Shortage Keeps Her in Hospital for More Than a Year." CTV News. Published 2019. Accessed August 5, 2020. https://ottawa.ctvnews.ca/ottawa-woman-with-ms-back-home-today-after-psw-shortage-keeps-her-in-hospital-for-more-than-a-year-1.4239661

174 Rachlis, M. *Prescription for Excellence: How Innovation Is Saving Canada's Health Care System*. Harper Perennial Canada; 2005, p. 256.

175 "Bypass Surgery—Wait Times." Canadian Institute for Health Information. Published 2019. Accessed August 5, 2020. http://waittimes.cihi.ca/procedure/bypass?show=5090#year

176 "It is technically correct that each extra day confers some extra risk of the cancer's spreading, but the danger is very low. Some studies show no decrease in survival if breast cancer patients wait three to six months for surgery, while others show that these delays worsen survival by about 2.5 per cent per year. It looks like a few weeks' wait has negligible risk." Rachlis, M. *Prescription for Excellence: How Innovation Is Saving Canada's Health Care System*. Harper Perennial Canada; 2005, p. 257.

177 Furlong, D.J. *Medicare Myths*. Dream Catcher; 2004, p. 14.

178 Pat and Hugh Armstrong, in Gratzer, D. *Code Blue: Reviving Canada's Health Care System*. ECW Press; 1999, p. 27.

[179] Martin, D. *Better Now: Six Big Ideas to Improve Health Care for All Canadians.* Penguin Random House; 2017, p. 31.

[180] Whatley, S. *No More Lethal Waits: 10 Steps to Transform Canada's Emergency Departments.* BPS books; 2016.

[181] Reid, T.R. *The Healing of America: A Global Quest for Better, Cheaper, and Fairer Health Care.* Penguin Press; 2009, p. 129.

[182] Princeton economist Uwe Reinhardt, who grew up in Canada: "Canadians don't mind the waiting list so much … so long as the rich Canadians and the poor Canadians have to wait about the same amount of time." Ibid.

[183] CNN Editorial Research. "September 11 Fast Facts." CNN. Published 2019. Accessed August 5, 2020. https://www.cnn.com/2013/07/27/us/september-11-anniversary-fast-facts/index.html

[184] Barua, B., Esmail, N., Jackson, T. *The Effect of Wait Times on Mortality in Canada. 2014.* Accessed August 5, 2020. https://www.fraserinstitute.org/sites/default/files/effect-of-wait-times-on-mortality-in-canada.pdf

[185] The CT showed minor changes consistent with a possible sprain. Regular patients do not get CT scans for sprains, in Canada.

[186] MacLeod, A. "For-Profit Clinic Lawsuit May Transform Health Care." The Tyee. Published online 2014. Accessed August 5, 2020. https://thetyee.ca/News/2014/04/17/Clinic-Lawsuit-May-Transform-Canada-Health-Care/

[187] Square brackets in original quote. Anglin, H. "Government Has Created Healthcare Wait Lists." Toronto Sun. Published 2016. Accessed August 5, 2020. https://torontosun.com/2016/11/13/government-has-created-healthcare-wait-lists/wcm/f919d8d3-16ac-48f6-b305-5f3f632700c2

[188] "But it's important to recognize that long waits are not an inherent feature of all universal health care systems — many countries in Europe and elsewhere with strong universal systems don't experience these problems. What's different in Canada, doctors and hospitals have a high degree of autonomy, and don't always participate in efforts to reduce waits. At times they have opposed attempts to have other professionals care for patients or to shift resources into needy communities." In Martin, D. "Why It's So Hard to Reform Canadian Health Care." *New York Times.* Published 2018. Accessed August 5, 2020. https://www.nytimes.com/2018/03/23/opinion/canada-health-reform.html See also *Lan-*

cet, 2018: "The high degree of physician autonomy in Canada does little to encourage doctors to join organised programmes to reduce wait times." Martin, D, Miller, A.P., Quesnel-Vallée, A, Caron, N.R., Vissandjée, B, Marchildon, G.P. "Canada's Universal Health-care System: Achieving Its Potential." *Lancet*. 2018;391(10131):1718-1735. doi:10.1016/S0140-6736(18)30181-8

[189] Some authors suggest that waiting lists have "little to do with the health care system and much to do with greedy physicians: doctors, they explain, deliberately keep patients waiting for treatment in order to blackmail government into increasing health care funding." Gratzer, D. *Code Blue: Reviving Canada's Health Care System*. ECW Press; 1999, p. 28.

[190] Allemani, C., Weir, H., Carreira, H., et al. "Cancer Survival: The Start of Global Surveillance." A study of individual data for 25,676,887 patients from 279 population-based registries in 67 countries (CONCORD-2). CDC. *Lancet*. 2015;385(9972):977-1010. External Lancet 2015;385(9972):977–1010

[191] Picard, A. "Doug Ford Needs to Rein in Ontario's Bureaucratic Health-care Mess." Globe and Mail. Published 2018. Accessed August 5, 2020. https://www.theglobeandmail.com/opinion/article-doug-ford-needs-to-rein-in-ontarios-bureaucratic-health-care-mess/

[192] Brennan, R.J. "Closing Hospital Beds Not the Answer to Reforming Health Care, Critics Say." *Toronto Star*. Published 2013. Accessed August 5, 2020. https://www.thestar.com/news/canada/2013/02/26/closing_hospital_beds_not_the_answer_to_reforming_health_care_critics_say.html

[193] Butler, Colin. "With Nothing Left to Cut, Report Warns Ontario Healthcare Could Face an Ugly Future." *CBCNews*. December 2019. https://www.cbc.ca/news/canada/london/ontario-hospitals-efficiency-healthcare-reform-1.5406753

[194] Lister, M. "Canadian Healthcare Needs to Be Leaner." *National Post*. Published 2011. Accessed August 5, 2020. https://nationalpost.com/opinion/matthew-lister-canadian-healthcare-needs-to-be-leaner

[195] Dr. Paul Conte, physician leader and family doctor, writes: "Healthcare bureaucracy is a vortex that keeps getting bigger … The bigger the bureaucracy gets, the more layers it has and the number of well meaning 'projects' increases. That these projects have the unintended consequences of creating more rules for accessing insured care and making the lives of the professionals delivering the

care more miserable seems to be ignored. It is funny that those who decry the bureaucracy of the HMO's and health insurance companies in the USA are unaware that Ontario's one and only HMO is following in lock step with what goes on down south. We hear that there is only so much money for health care. The problem is the ever increasing pie going to over-regulation and micromanagement of providing that care is shrinking the pie that is going to the actual provision of care." (2015-07-03 10:20:07):

[196] Paikin, S. "Fifty Billion Dollars — Too Much for Bureaucracy, Not Enough for Health Care?" TVO. Published 2014. Accessed August 5, 2020. https://www.tvo.org/article/steve-paikin-fifty-billion-dollars-too-much-for-bureaucracy-not-enough-for-health-care

[197] "Alberta Healthcare Needs Fewer Bureaucrats" (www.edmontonsun.com/2015/03/18/alberta-health-care-needs-fewer-bureaucrats-not-more-cash-infusions). In the US: "Too Many Rules by Unaccountable Bureaucrats," "Are Government Bureaucracies Too Big?" (www.argusleader.com/story/news/politics/2015/05/20/rounds-many-rules-unaccountable-bureaucrats/27667759/). We hear the same thing in the UK: "Too Many Bureaucrats in the Kitchen," "Death by Bureaucracy" (spectator.org/blog/59922/too-many-bureaucrats-kitchen); "NHS Bureaucracy up 50%" (www.telegraph.co.uk/news/health/news/6890335/Spending-on-NHS-bureaucracy-up-50-per-cent.html). At one time, Britain had "... five health administrators for *each* hospital bed." In Gairdner, W.D. *The Trouble with Canada ... Still! A Citizen Speaks Out.* BPS Books; 2011, pp. 284-329.

[198] Savoie, D.J. *What Is Government Good At? A Canadian Answer.* McGill-Queen's University Press; 2015, p. 166.

[199] "This is how government operates: it is excellent at launching new bureaucratic units but largely incapable of doing away with them, even though they have outlived their purpose." Savoie, D.J. *Democracy in Canada: The Disintegration of Our Institutions.* McGill-Queen's University Press; 2019, p. 229.

[200] Savoie, D.J. *What Is Government Good At? A Canadian Answer.* McGill-Queen's University Press; 2015, p. 196. Peter Schuck notes the same thing in his writing about American government: "It is almost impossible to fire, demote, or suspend civil service employees." Schuck, P.H. *Why Government Fails So Often:*

And How It Can Do Better. Princeton University Press; 2015, p. 322.

[201] Savoie, D.J. *What Is Government Good At? A Canadian Answer*. McGill-Queen's University Press; 2015, p. 137.

[202] Macdonald, N. "Free and Timely Health Care for All Is Fiction." CBC News. Published November 3, 2016. www.cbc.ca/news/politics/health-care-baby-boomers-macdonald-1.3833563

[203] "Many public systems use GPs as 'gate keepers', so that only the most demanding cases get seen by specialist." Fierlbeck, K. *Health Care in Canada: A Citizen's Guide to Policy and Politics*. University of Toronto Press; 2011, p. 33 .

[204] "Rationing of care is necessary to control costs. Our system meets acute-care needs rapidly and efficiently. Rationing of care is mainly in the primary-care sector, for both diagnosis and follow-up care." Levine. D. *Health Care and Politics: An Insider's View on Managing and Sustaining Health Care in Canada*. Véhicule Press; 2015, p. 279.

[205] "At the health care table, all expect to sit, and the dilemma is how to obtain the necessary restrictions on consumption." Brown, M.C. *Caring for Profit: Economic Dimensions of Canada's Health Industry*. Fraser Institute; 1987, p. 165.

[206] Powell, E.J. *A New Look at Medicine and Politics*. Pitman; 1966. Accessed August 5, 2020. https://www.sochealth.co.uk/national-health-service/healthcare-generally/history-of-healthcare/a-new-look-at-medicine-and-politics/

[207] "Although the NHS has greatly increased both the potential and actual demand for health care, in practice it has been forced to ration supply by means which in their own way are almost as ruthless (but generally held to be more acceptable) as the ability to pay." Cooper, M.H. *Rationing in Health Care*. John Wiley; 1975, p. 109.

[208] "The principle that the end justifies the means is in individualist ethics regarded as the denial of all morals. In collectivist ethics it becomes necessarily the supreme rule; there is literally nothing which the consistent collectivist must not be prepared to do if it serves 'the good of the whole,' because the 'good of the whole' is to him the only criterion of what ought to be done. The *raison d'état*, in which collectivist ethics has found its most explicit formulation, knows no other limit than that set by expediency — the suitability of the particular act for the end in view. And what the *raison d'état* affirms with respect to the relations

between different countries applies equally to the relations between different individuals within the collectivist state. There can be no limit to what its citizen must be prepared to do, no act which his conscience must prevent him from committing, if it is necessary for an end which the community has set itself or which his superiors order him to achieve." Hayek, F.A., Caldwell, B. *The Road to Serfdom: Text and Documents*. University of Chicago Press; 2007, pp. 166-67.

209 "It takes some pondering to realize that in a socialized medical system patients always count as an *expense*, or cost to 'the system', and physicians under socialism represent 'a huge cost-generating entity' ... This is why a hospital that has a limited public budget will be eager to skimp on or delay services, and will kick you out of your bed as soon as possible; but a private hospital is happy to have you feeling better before you go home — 'Stay another day!'" Gairdner, W.D. *The Trouble with Canada ... Still! A Citizen Speaks Out*. BPS Books; 2011, pp. 284-329.

210 Adhopia, V. "Canadian Health Care's 'One Issue per Visit' Problem." CBC News. Published 2019. Accessed August 5, 2020. https://www.cbc.ca/news/health/second-opinion-one-problem-visit-1.5061506

211 "The worst kind of rationing is that which is unacknowledged; for it is the essence of a good rationing system to be intelligible and consciously accepted. This is not possible where its very existence has to be repudiated." Powell, E.J. *A New Look at Medicine and Politics*. Pitman; 1966. Accessed August 5, 2020. https://www.sochealth.co.uk/national-health-service/healthcare-generally/history-of-healthcare/a-new-look-at-medicine-and-politics/

212 Benner, A. "Grimsby Teen Has Endured a Life of Pain; OHIP Denies Funding for Treatment of Rare Syndrome." StCatharinesStandard.ca. *St. Catharines Standard*. Published 2019. Accessed August 5, 2020. https://www.stcatharinesstandard.ca/life/health-wellness/2019/04/08/grimsby-teen-has-endured-a-life-of-pain-ohip-denies-funding-for-treatment-of-rare-syndrome.html

213 Grech, R. "Robin's Family Overwhelmed by Support." *Daily Press* (Timmins). Published 2019. Accessed August 5, 2020. https://www.timminspress.com/news/local-news/robins-family-overwhelmed-by-support

214 C.D. v Ontario (Health Insurance Plan), 2019 CanLII 293 (ON HSARB). Published online 2019. Accessed August 5, 2020.

215 Brown, J. "Health Minister's Office Watching 'Critical Shortages of Cancer Drugs.'" Zoomer Radio AM740. Published 2019. Accessed August 5, 2020. http://www.zoomerradio.ca/news/latest-news/health-ministers-office-watching-critical-shortages-cancer-drugs/ and flu shots: https://www.cbc.ca/news/health/flu-vaccine-empty-1.5010215?cmp=rss

216 "Canada's Newly Certified Medical Specialists Struggle to Find Work." Royal College of Physicians and Surgeons of Canada. Published 2019. Accessed August 5, 2020. https://www.newswire.ca/news-releases/canada-s-newly-certified-medical-specialists-struggle-to-find-work-826961509.html

217 Grant quotes Danielle Fréchette, executive director of the Royal College's office of research, health policy and advocacy, and one of the authors of the new employment study: "The challenge is accessing the practice resources … Those who are already in practice are challenged to find operating-room time. Those who want to practice can't get their foot in the door." Grant goes on to note that the Canadian Orthopedic Association (COA) "found that of 478 graduates over six years, 159 are currently seeking full-time jobs. Another 74 have found full-time work outside of Canada, most often in the United States." Grant, K. "Nearly One in Five New Specialist Doctors Can't Find a Job After Certification, Survey Shows." *Globe and Mail*. May 1, 2019.

218 "Canada's Newly Certified Medical Specialists Struggle to Find Work." Royal College of Physicians and Surgeons of Canada. Published 2019. Accessed August 5, 2020. https://www.newswire.ca/news-releases/canada-s-newly-certified-medical-specialists-struggle-to-find-work-826961509.html

219 For example: "Thousands in Britain Left to Go Blind Due to Eye Surgery Rationing: Report." Europe News; Top Stories. *The Straits Times*. Published 2019. Accessed August 5, 2020. https://www.straitstimes.com/world/europe/thousands-in-britain-left-to-go-blind-due-to-eye-surgery-rationing-report

220 "Although the argument as to whether or not rationing is inevitable has largely been settled, there is far less of a consensus over how, and by whom, this should be carried out." Williams, I., Dickinson, H., Robinson, S. *Rationing in Health Care: The Theory and Practice of Priority Setting*. Policy Press; 2012, p. vii.

221 "Canada's Current Health Care System Is Not Sustainable; Action Needed to Maintain the System's Survival." Canadian Institute of Actuaries. Published

2013. Accessed August 5, 2020. https://www.newswire.ca/news-releases/can-
adas-current-health-care-system-is-not-sustainable-action-needed-to-main-
tain-the-systems-survival-512957101.html

[222] One physician reviewer noted how he never worries about getting sued, for not
ordering a test, by self-pay patients such as those in the Mennonite community.

[223] Paradoxically, abandoning the obsession with system citizenship ends up refo-
cusing providers on patient interests and, at least in acute care, it is the first step
to creating a more efficient emergency department. Costs per case go down,
patients' length of stay plummets, and adverse outcomes decrease. EDs function
best when they focus on patient interests and ignore fiscal/system peer pressure
at the front line. See Whatley, S. *No More Lethal Waits: 10 Steps to Transform
Canada's Emergency Departments.* BPS Books; 2016.

[224] Duic, M. Blog, shawnwhatley.com

[225] "Rationing is inevitable in the provision of health care services. Scarce resources
have to be allocated, in effective and equitable ways." Mintzberg, H. *Managing
the Myths of Health Care: Bridging the Separations Between Care, Cure, Control,
and Community.* Berrett-Koehler; 2017, p. 226.

[226] Decter, M. *Healing Medicare: Managing Health System Change the Canadian
Way.* McGilligan Books; 1994, p. 40.

[227] "The state becomes the sole provider, replacing 'demand' with 'need,' which is
for the state to determine, since it cannot be trusted to individuals." Vertesi, L.
*Broken Promises: Why Canadian Medicare Is in Trouble and What Can Be Done
to Save It.* Epic Press; 2003, p. 206.

[228] "Because patients (or GPs) do not bear direct responsibility for costs when in-
curred, there is little direct economic incentive to limit demand; and because
those making allocation decisions at the highest level do not know exactly what
is needed in every treatment area at each point in time, it is difficult to determine exactly what expenditure levels should be, and how to allocate them."
Fierlbeck, K. *Health Care in Canada: A Citizen's Guide to Policy and Politics.*
University of Toronto Press; 2011, p. 10.

[229] Savoie, D.J. *Democracy in Canada: The Disintegration of Our Institutions.*
McGill-Queen's University Press; 2019, p. 7.

[230] Le Grand, J. *Motivation, Agency, and Public Policy: Of Knights and Knaves,*

Pawns and Queens. Oxford University Press; 2004. Also: "Citizens deprived of autonomous choice are infantilized to an extent, as their capacity for reasoned deliberation and initiative atrophies." Schuck, P.H. *Why Government Fails So Often: And How It Can Do Better.* Princeton University Press; 2015, p. 100.

[231] Le Grand, J. *Motivation, Agency, and Public Policy: Of Knights and Knaves, Pawns and Queens.* Oxford University Press; 2004, p. 15. See also Dalrymple, T. *Life at the Bottom: The Worldview That Makes the Underclass.* Ivan R. Dee; 2003.

[232] The age was 43 in 2012.

[233] Savoie, D.J. *Democracy in Canada: The Disintegration of Our Institutions.* McGill-Queen's University Press; 2019, p. 7.

[234] Which, too often, is not the case in Canada.

[235] Again, Canada performs quite well on specific acute care issues, if advocates have been successful at lobbying for funding.

[236] "In 1900 there were five times as many physicians as there were faculty members of colleges and universities. Only in the early 1950s did the number of college teachers catch up with the number of physicians. Now [in 1974] the ratio is more than two to one the other way." Fuchs, V.R. *Who Shall Live? Health, Economics, and Social Choice.* Basic Books; 1974, p. 63.

Chapter Five

[237] Gratzer, D. *Better Medicine: Reforming Canadian Health Care.* ECW Press; 2002, p. 54.

[238] Martin, D. *Better Now: Six Big Ideas to Improve Health Care for All Canadians.* Penguin Random House; 2017, p. 22.

[239] Alter, D., Basinski, A., Naylor, C. "A Survey of Provider Experiences and Perceptions of Preferential Access to Cardiovascular Care in Ontario, Canada." *Annals of Internal Medicine.* 1998;129(7):567-572. Accessed August 5, 2020. https://www.ices.on.ca/Publications/Journal-Articles/1998/January/A-survey-of-provider-experiences-and-perceptions-of-preferential-access-to-cardiovascular-care

[240] Commitment to the Future of Medicare Act, 2004, S.O. 2004, c. 5. Ontario Government. Published 2004. Accessed August 5, 2020. https://www.ontario.ca/laws/statute/04c05?_ga=2.99950234.505321768.1596754440-

1132676204.1538760930

[241] When a small plane crashes, "If the pilot is … a prominent government official, it is likely that publicly owned resources will be utilized far more readily than if the pilot were unknown and poor." Fuchs, V.R. *Who Shall Live? Health, Economics, and Social Choice.* Basic Books; 1974, p. 25.

[242] Slatz, A. "Two-tier Ontario Health Care System Revealed." *The Post Millennial.* Published 2019. Accessed August 5, 2020. https://thepostmillennial.com/exclusive-two-tier-ontario-health-care-system-revealed/

[243] McCarthy, B. "Do Wealthy Canadians Donate to Hospitals to Get Better Treatment?" *Politifact.* Published 2019. Accessed August 5, 2020. https://www.politifact.com/factchecks/2019/aug/19/mark-cuban/do-wealthy-canadians-donate-hospitals-get-better-t/

[244] Recall the case of the RN who was fined for criticizing her family member's care on FaceBook. Hill, A. "Nurse Fined $26,000 for Complaining About Grandfather's Health Care on Facebook." *Daily Press* (Timmins). Published 2017. Accessed August 5, 2020. https://www.timminspress.com/2017/04/08/nurse-fined-26000-for-complaining-about-grandfathers-health-care-on-facebook/wcm/c45ab76d-967e-4f77-a91e-e9f1bbc9a666

[245] Through Altum Health_(the special tier, mentioned earlier, that government created to fast-track injured workers). Note: Altum used to post their wait times for injured workers. It seems that their website has been updated to remove those details over the last few years since attention was drawn to this fast-track service. http://www.altumhealth.com/work-related-injury-programs Accessed August 5, 2020. https://www.altumhealth.com/services/third-party/wsib/

[246] Barua, B, Jacques, D. *The Private Cost of Public Queues for Medically Necessary Care, 2019.* Fraser Institute; 2019. Accessed August 4, 2020. https://www.fraserinstitute.org/studies/private-cost-of-public-queues-for-medically-necessary-care-2019?utm_source=Email&utm_campaign=Private-Cost-of-Public-Queues-2019&utm_medium=Dev_email&utm_content=Learn_More&utm_term=700

[247] Day, B. "In Government We Trust." *BC Medical Journal.* 2010;52(4):170. Accessed August 5, 2020. https://bcmj.org/editorials/government-we-trust

[248] Ibid.

[249] Day, B. "30 Years of Health-care Dysfunction." *National Post*. https://nationalpost.com/opinion/brian-day-30-years-of-health-care-dysfunction. Published April 1, 2014. Accessed August 5, 2020.

[250] Over 214,000 people left Canada for medical reasons in 2017. The Fraser Institute surveyed physicians and reported that 63,459 Canadians left Canada specifically for care in 2016. Ren, F., Labrie, Y. "Leaving Canada for Medical Care, 2017." Fraser Institute; 2017. Accessed August 5, 2020. https://www.fraserinstitute.org/studies/leaving-canada-for-medical-care-2017

[251] NASH — North American Specialty Hospital — Global Healthcare Connections. Accessed August 5, 2020. https://globalhealthcareconnections.com/north-american-specialty-hospital

[252] These centres cater to "Canadians who are unable to get timely care in their own country." Goodman, J.C. *Priceless: Curing the Healthcare Crisis*. Independent Institute; 2012, p. 18.

[253] Robbins, J. "Patients Take Flight: Albertans Look Elsewhere to Avoid Surgery Wait Times." *Calgary Herald*. June 29, 2019.

[254] Ibid.

[255] Thea Vakil, then BC Government spokesperson and Associate Deputy Minister of Health, from "Famous Quotes About Canadian Health Care." Charter Health. Accessed August 5, 2020. https://www.charterhealth.ca/quotes/

[256] Katz, S.J., Cardiff, K., Pascali, M., Barer, M.L., Evans, R.G. "Phantoms in the Snow: Canadians' Use of Health Care Services in the United States." *Health Affairs*. 2002;21(3):19-31. doi:10.1377/hlthaff.21.3.19

[257] "Debates over health policy furnish a number of examples of these 'zombies' — ideas that, on logic or evidence, are intellectually dead — that can never be laid to rest because they are useful to some powerful interests. The phantom hordes of Canadian medical refugees are likely to remain among them." For a whole list of zombie ideas, see Martin, D. *Better Now: Six Big Ideas to Improve Health Care for All Canadians*. Penguin Random House; 2017.

[258] "How Many Hospitals Are in the US?" Definitive Healthcare. Published 2019. Accessed August 5, 2020. https://blog.definitivehc.com/how-many-hospitals-are-in-the-us

[259] "Diagnostic Imaging Centers in the US — Number of Businesses." IBIS World.

Accessed August 5, 2020. https://www.ibisworld.com/industry-statistics/num-ber-of-businesses/diagnostic-imaging-centers-united-states

[260] "U.S. Physicians — Statistics & Facts." Statista. Published 2019. Accessed August 5, 2020. https://www.statista.com/topics/1244/physicians/

[261] Reid, T.R. *The Healing of America: A Global Quest for Better, Cheaper, and Fairer Health Care.* Penguin Press; 2009, p. 139.

[262] Ibid., pp. 139-40. Said, no doubt, for the author's benefit. After almost thirty years in medicine, I have never heard a Canadian physician, ever, say such a thing.

[263] Ibid., p. 138.

[264] Ibid., p. 228.

[265] Breton, M., Wong, S., Smithman, M., et al. "Centralized Waiting Lists for Unattached Patients in Primary Care: Learning from an Intervention Implemented in Seven Canadian Provinces." *Healthcare Policy | Politiques de Santé.* 2018;13(4):65-82. doi:10.12927/hcpol.2018.25493

[266] Decter, M., Grosso, F. *Navigating Canada's Health Care: A User Guide to Getting the Care You Need.* Penguin Canada; 2006.

[267] Ibid., p. xiii.

[268] Ibid., p. 83.

[269] Goodman, J.C., Musgrave, G.L., Herrick, D.M. National Center for Policy Analysis (US). *Lives at Risk: Single-Payer National Health Insurance Around the World.* Rowman & Littlefield; 2004, p. 31.

[270] Martin, D., Miller, A.P., Quesnel-Vallée, A., Caron, N.R., Vissandjée, B., Marchildon, G.P. "Canada's Universal Health-care System: Achieving Its Potential." *Lancet.* 2018;391(10131):1718-1735. doi:10.1016/S0140-6736(18)30181-8

[271] Glauser, W. "Medical Trainees Warn Practice Permits Will Drive Away Doctors." *Canadian Medical Association journal = journal de l'Association medicale canadienne.* 2019;191(49):E1365-E1366. doi:10.1503/cmaj.1095835

[272] "The supply and distribution of health resources generally is inversely related to medical need and is so prevalent that it has been granted the status of a health care law — the Inverse Need Law (Hart 1971)." Battistella, R.M. *Health Care Turning Point: Why Single Payer Won't Work.* MIT Press; 2012, p. 82. For the Inverse Care Law, see Tudor, H.J. "The Inverse Care Law." *Lancet.* 1971;297(7696):405-412. doi:10.1016/S0140-6736(71)92410-X_

Chapter Six

[273] "Implementation must pass though *multiple decision points* (most of which may effectively be *veto* points), a number that increases as the implementation process unfolds." Schuck, P.H. *Why Government Fails So Often: And How It Can Do Better.* Princeton University Press; 2015, p. 236.

[274] "The forte of the Canadian system since the early 1970s has been its ability to contain total costs." Brown, M.C. *Caring for Profit: Economic Dimensions of Canada's Health Industry.* Fraser Institute; 1987, p. 160.

[275] Decter, M. *Healing Medicare: Managing Health System Change the Canadian Way.* McGilligan Books; 1994, p. 39. Decter compares higher number of MRI in the US versus Canada and actually celebrates the fact of "higher efficiency" in Canada.

[276] Goodman, J.C., Musgrave, G.L., Herrick, D.M. National Center for Policy Analysis (US). *Lives at Risk: Single-Payer National Health Insurance around the World.* Rowman & Littlefield; 2004, p. 79.

[277] Fierlbeck, K. *Health Care in Canada: A Citizen's Guide to Policy and Politics.* University of Toronto Press; 2011, p. 3.

[278] Goodman, J.C., Musgrave, G.L., Herrick, D.M, National Center for Policy Analysis (US). *Lives at Risk: Single-Payer National Health Insurance Around the World.* Rowman & Littlefield; 2004, p. 85.

[279] **(a)** Steven Lewis, author, health policy consultant, and long-time medicare advocate. "Healthcare Spending Overshoots a Threat to Sustainability." C.D. Howe Institute. With respect to Canada's efficiency and our reputation world wide, Lewis writes: "Chris Ham from the University of Birmingham, an astute international healthcare system observer, tells a revealing story. As the architects of the UK's National Health System (NHS) transformation charted their course at the beginning of this century, they looked, Ham recounts, elsewhere for inspiration and cautionary tales. The worst possible outcome, they concluded, would be to increase spending from 6% to 10% of GDP and end up looking like Canada." Baker et al. *High-performing Healthcare Systems, 2008.* Longwoods. **(b)** Docs who worked before medicare used to say: "If you think that medical

care is expensive now, wait until it is free." Furlong, D.J. *Medicare Myths.* Dream Catcher; 2004, p. 85.

[280] "There are two reasons why Canada has chosen the single-payer model of health insurance. The first is equity, or fairness. With only one payer, the queue for treatment is ordered on the basis of need, not ability to pay... The second reason we have a single-payer system for doctors and hospitals in Canada — a reason that doesn't get enough attention in my view — is that these systems are much less administratively expensive than the alternatives ... Canada's elegantly simple single-payer system spends less than 2 percent on insurance overhead for the public plans found in each province and territory." Martin, D, *Better Now: Six Big Ideas to Improve Health Care for All Canadians.* Penguin Random House; 2017, p. 18. See also *Lancet* review, 2018: "Another benefit is cost containment: within Canadian publicly funded insurance plans, administrative overhead is extremely low—less than 2%—because of the simplicity of the single-payer scheme." https://www.thelancet.com/journals/lancet/article/PIIS0140-6736(18)30181-8/fulltext

[281] Blumberg, M. "How Much Should a Canadian Charity Spend on Overhead Such as Fundraising and Administration?" *Canadian Charity Law.* Published 2008. Accessed August 5, 2020. https://www.canadiancharitylaw.ca/blog/how_much_should_canadian_charity_spend_on_overhead/

[282] "America's health insurance industry spends roughly 20 cents of every dollar for nonmedical costs: paperwork, reviewing claims, marketing, profits, and so on ... Canada's universal insurance system, run by government bureaucrats, spend 6 percent on administration" Reid, T.R. *The Healing of America: A Global Quest for Better, Cheaper, and Fairer Health Care.* Penguin Press; 2009, p. 229.

[283] Himmelstein, D.U., Campbell T., Woolhandler, S. "Health Care Administrative Costs in the United States and Canada, 2017." *Annals of Internal Medicine.* 2020;172(2):134. doi:10.7326/M19-2818

[284] "Top 100 Rated Charities." Charity Intelligence Canada. Published 2019. Accessed August 5, 2020. https://www.charityintelligence.ca/top-100-rated-charities

[285] "The Canadian system, also called Medicare, guarantees coverage to every resident north of the U.S. border." Kelly, C. "What Medicare for All Really Looks Like." *The American Prospect.* Published online January 2020.

[286] Church, E. "Auditor-General Tells Ontario to Take a 'Hard Look' at Home Care Services." *Globe and Mail.* 2015. https://www.theglobeandmail.com/news/national/auditor-general-tells-ontario-to-take-hard-look-at-home-care-services/article26495778/

[287] Decter, M. *Healing Medicare: Managing Health System Change the Canadian Way.* McGilligan Books; 1994, p. 177.

[288] "The true costs also include the *private costs* that private compliance with the programs requires. These costs may vastly exceed the public outlays, yet they do not appear on any public budget and thus are unlikely to be fully considered by [government] officials — unless officials are somehow forced to do so." Schuck, P.H. *Why Government Fails So Often: And How It Can Do Better.* Princeton University Press; 2015, p. 151.

[289] Roy, A. "The Myth of Medicare's 'Low Administrative Costs.'" *Forbes.* Published 2011. Accessed August 6, 2020. https://www.forbes.com/sites/theapothecary/2011/06/30/the-myth-of-medicares-low-administrative-costs/#680b3375140d

[290] Galles, G.M. "6 Questions for Those Claiming Medicare for All Will Lower Administrative Costs." Foundation for Economic Education. Published 2019. Accessed August 6, 2020. https://fee.org/articles/6-questions-for-those-claiming-medicare-for-all-will-lower-administrative-costs/

[291] Book, R.A. "Medicare Administrative Costs Are Higher, Not Lower, Than for Private Insurance." The Heritage Foundation. Published 2009. Accessed August 6, 2020. https://www.heritage.org/health-care-reform/report/medicare-administrative-costs-are-higher-not-lower-private-insurance

[292] Serna, L., Johnson, A. "The Medicare Advantage Program: Status Report." Medpac; 2019. Accessed August 6, 2020. http://medpac.gov/docs/default-source/default-document-library/ma-dec19.pdf?sfvrsn=0

[293] Blaze, C.K. "Money-losing Tim Hortons in St. John's, Newfoundland Hospital a 'Cautionary Tale': Critics.". *National Post.* Published 2012. Accessed August 6, 2020. https://nationalpost.com/news/canada/money-losing-tim-hortons-in-st-johns-hospital-a-cautionary-tale-critics

[294] "Public tax-based systems such as those of Britain and Sweden have historically been strong in cost containment and equity and weaker in efficiency and

responsiveness." Fierlbeck, K. *Health Care in Canada: A Citizen's Guide to Policy and Politics.* University of Toronto Press; 2011, p. 241.

[295] "Government agencies are notorious not only for wild spending binges at the end of every budget year (in order to justify more funding) and for over-staffing (a great way to spend money year after year), but for *promoting* incompetent government employees to another agency or division in a different location because of the near impossibility of firing them." DiLorenzo, T.J. *The Problem with Socialism.* Regnery Publishing; 2016, p. 50.

[296] We ended up spending close to half a million dollars on the system and never used it. During the trial phase, we could not justify the expense of lost badges. For some reason, they kept ending up in the laundry attached to nurses' scrubs.

[297] As an aside, we had to fight hard to make sure PNs held a new role, not one currently held by any single unionized employee. Once unionized, the PNs would be restricted to much lower wages, as dictated by the union, seniority rules, without any emphasis on reward for performance.

[298] Leung, A.K., et al. "Impact of Physician Navigators on Productivity Indicators in the ED." *Emergency Medicine Journal.* 2018 Jan; 35(1):5-11. doi:10.1136/emermed-2017-206809. Epub 2017 Aug 8. Note: We initially called them patient navigators. But the unions argued that they move patients, ergo, the PNs were a union position. Furthermore, the name confused people with other descriptions of PN in the literature. So we retitled them as physician navigators and published our findings using this moniker.

[299] Our physician group received a final notice from our site admin. The Ministry of Health had dictated that every physician must complete a survey. If not, we could risk losing our funding for our electronic medical record (EMR). The survey had close to one hundred questions and took two hours to read carefully and answer accurately. It could be completed only by a physician. Over 11,000 Ontario physicians who use EMRs, had to invest two hours. 11,000 docs x 2 hours each = 22,000 hours, spent on one survey instead of on patient care. 22,000 hours divided by 50 hours per work week, for 46 weeks per year = 9.6 years of clinical care from one physician in a busy practice. Given average gross physician billings, this one survey carried an unreported cost of $3.252 million: 9.6 years x $340,000 (average gross billings). This represents only one survey of

only one sub-group of doctors. We did not mention all the surveys that nurses and other providers must complete.

[300] "Health Spending." Canadian Institute for Health Information. Published 2019. Accessed January 8, 2019. https://www.cihi.ca/en/health-spending

[301] Palacios, M., Barua, B. *The Price of Public Health Care Insurance, 2019.* Fraser Institute. Accessed August 6, 2020. https://www.fraserinstitute.org/studies/price-of-public-health-care-insurance-2019-edition

[302] Goodman, J.C., Musgrave, G.L., Herrick, D.M. National Center for Policy Analysis (US). *Lives at Risk: Single-Payer National Health Insurance Around the World.* Rowman & Littlefield; 2004, p. 1.

[303] Mackie, R. "Ontario to Re-introduce Health-care Premiums." *Globe and Mail.* Published 2004. Accessed August 6, 2020. https://www.theglobeandmail.com/news/national/ontario-to-re-introduce-health-care-premiums/article1136845/

[304] "The Fiscal Burden of Provincial Government Health Spending Across Canada: 2017." 2017 Health System Metrics Report. *Canadian Health Policy Journal.* Accessed August 6, 2020. https://www.canadianhealthpolicy.com/products/the-fiscal-burden-of-provincial-government-health-spending-across-canada.html

[305] "Unfortunately, we were a victim of our own success. The health care system grew and evolved at such a tremendous rate that, combined with the unforeseeable global recession of the early 1970s, it threatened to push our country into bankruptcy. In order to save our health care system — and our country — we were obliged to shift our shared-cost program into a block-funding program in 1977." Fierlbeck, K. *Health Care in Canada: A Citizen's Guide to Policy and Politics.* University of Toronto Press; 2011, p. 45.

[306] "As long as the health-care system is publicly organized and financed, especially the way that Canada has chosen to structure medicare, it will be governed by public-sector norms, which means ultimate political control, a high degree of unionization, very strong 'path dependence,' large and not very nimble bureaucracies, a high value on process over outcomes and an inherent tendency to expand." Simpson, J. *Chronic Condition: Why Canada's Health-care System Needs to Be Dragged into the 21st Century.* Allen Lane; 2012, p. 214.

[307] Finkelstein, A., Arrow, K.J., Gruber, J., Newhouse, J.P., Stiglitz, J.E. *Moral Hazard in Health Insurance.* Columbia University Press; 2014.

308 Coyne, A. "Ontario Tinkers with Health Care, and Still Nobody Knows What Anything Costs." *National Post*. Published 2019. Accessed August 6, 2020. https://nationalpost.com/opinion/andrew-coyne-ontario-tinkers-with-health-care-and-still-nobody-knows-what-anything-costs

309 A Ponzi scheme is unethical in itself. However, while it is necessary for keeping socialized medicine going, it is not a prerequisite for socialized medicine. Some people understandably view borrowing from unborn taxpayers as part of the moral case against the welfare state. However, I do not think it is unique to socialized medicine *per se*.

310 Butler, C. "With Nothing Left to Cut, Report Warns Ontario Healthcare Could Face an Ugly Future." CBC News. Published 2019. Accessed August 5, 2020. https://www.cbc.ca/news/canada/london/ontario-hospitals-efficiency-health-care-reform-1.5406753

311 "[In] a bureaucratic system ... *increase in expenditure* will be matched by *fall in production* ... Such systems will act rather like 'black holes,' in the economic universe, simultaneously sucking in resources, and shrinking in terms of 'emitted' production." Friedman, M. "Gammon's 'Black Holes'; Collected Works of Milton Friedman." *Newsweek*. Published online November 1977:84. Accessed August 6, 2020. https://miltonfriedman.hoover.org/objects/58137/gammons-black-holes

312 Birch, S. "Reining in Ballooning Medical Costs." TheSpec.com. *Hamilton Spectator*. Published 2014. Accessed August 6, 2020. https://www.thespec.com/opinion/columnists/2014/04/10/reining-in-ballooning-medical-costs.html

313 McSmith, A. "The Birth of the NHS." *The Independent*. Published 2008. Accessed August 6, 2020. https://www.independent.co.uk/life-style/health-and-families/features/the-birth-of-the-nhs-856091.html

314 Quote starts at 10:20, Friedman, M. "Milton Friedman on Medical Care" (full lecture). YouTube. Published 1978. Accessed August 6, 2020. https://www.youtube.com/watch?v=ss5PxPlnmFk

315 Quoted by Seeman in Gratzer, D. *Better Medicine: Reforming Canadian Health Care*. ECW Press; 2002, p. 86.

316 A favourite line that Glen Tecker, governance and management consultant, uses in his lectures.

[317] In a free enterprise system: "The worker himself is therefore concerned that his productivity should be as great as possible," because he is paid in proportion to the value of the product of his labour. von Mises, L. *Socialism: An Economic and Sociological Analysis*. 2nd ed. 2012. Martino Publishing; 1932, p. 173.

[318] Belluz, J. "Does How We Pay Health-care Workers Affect How They Treat Us?" *Maclean's*. Published online June 2012. https://www.macleans.ca/society/health/does-how-we-pay-health-care-workers-affect-how-they-treat-us/See also Gosden, T., Forland. F., Kristiansen, I., et al. "Capitation, Salary, Fee-for-Service and Mixed Systems of Payment: Effects on the Behaviour of Primary Care Physicians." *Cochrane Database of Systematic Reviews*. Published online July 24, 2000. doi:10.1002/14651858.CD002215

[319] Lewis, S., Sullivan, T. "Deal with Doctors." *Policy Options*. 2013;(June). https://www.researchgate.net/publication/258021560_Deal_with_doctors

[320] Robinson, J.C. "Theory and Practice in the Design of Physician Payment Incentives." *The Milbank Quarterly*. 2001;79(2):149-177, III. doi:10.1111/1468-0009.00202

[321] Mark Britnell, health consultant, writes about his work around the world as a health consultant with KPMG. "An increasing number of organizations now see enhancing value for patients—in other words, concentrating on what matters to them—as a fundamental goal. Putting patient value at the heart of the system is the first step to unlocking higher quality, lower costs and better productivity." Britnell, M. *In Search of the Perfect Health System*. 1st ed. Red Globe Press; 2015, p. 180.

Chapter Seven

[322] "We have identified that a lack of alignment between payers, providers, patients, professionals, policy-makers, politicians, the public and the press is a serious drag on innovation and progress." Ibid., p. 163.

[323] Taylor, M.G. *Health Insurance and Canadian Public Policy: The Seven Decisions That Created the Canadian Health Insurance System and Their Outcomes*. McGill-Queen's University Press; 2009, p. 421.

[324] Although extra-billing supplied only 1.3% of total billing, as we saw earlier.

[325] Douglas T. "S.O.S. Medicare Conference—Ottawa 1979." YouTube.

Published 1979. Accessed August 6, 2020. https://www.youtube.com/watch?v=V1A0vrz36Sc

[326] In his speech, Douglas talked about preventive medicine and group practice. Preventive medicine was popular in the 1970s and 80s, the latest fad that promised to decrease pressure on public finances. The prevention-as-a-path-to-savings fad passed long ago. Although prevention is a good thing, it does not save money. It might even cost more. Group practice remains a popular push, even though small practices easily outperform the efficiency of large, bureaucratic clinics (e.g., Family Health Teams). If he were giving the speech today, Douglas might talk about "integration of care," or "evidence-based care," or "the triple aim," without changing the focus of his message. "Phase number two" was about redesign, "alter[ing] our delivery system." It was about applying the control we mentioned in the last chapter though central planning.

[327] The legislation, if the services were above a prescribed maximum during a specific time period, "also granted the government broad regulatory powers" to control spending, as well as the number of physicians and where they practiced. Tuohy, C.H. *Accidental Logics: The Dynamics of Change in the Health Care Arena in the United States, Britain, and Canada.* Oxford University Press; 1999, p. 280 footnote 19.

[328] "Re-engineering the supply side of health services is underway," and "managing the demand for health services is the next key challenge." Decter, M. *Healing Medicare: Managing Health System Change the Canadian Way.* McGilligan Books; 1994, p. 10.

[329] Gratzer, D. *Code Blue: Reviving Canada's Health Care System.* ECW Press; 1999, p. 150.

[330] "To continue to afford the latest technology, we need better assessment and better planning." Decter, M. *Healing Medicare: Managing Health System Change the Canadian Way.* McGilligan Books; 1994, p. 38.

[331] Evans, R.G. *Strained Mercy: The Economics of Canadian Health Care.* Butterworths; 1984, p. 329.

[332] "Governments are shifting from an insurance role to a more directive managerial role. In a number of instances, governments in Canada are acting unilaterally, through legislation or policy to accomplish change. This new role is much

more intrusive than governments have played in the past … hard choices will need to be made." Decter, M. *Healing Medicare: Managing Health System Change the Canadian Way*. McGilligan Books; 1994, p. 168.

[333] "We closed tens of thousands of hospital beds … we did that with very little real insight into the impacts." Decter, M. "Does Money Buy Change?" You-Tube. Published 2012. Accessed August 6, 2020. https://www.youtube.com/watch?v=u0WyX4GEapg

[334] "Its justification for such intervention can be found in overwhelming public support for the Medicare program." Evans, R.G. *Strained Mercy: The Economics of Canadian Health Care*. Butterworths; 1984, p. 329.

[335] Martin D. *Better Now: Six Big Ideas to Improve Health Care for All Canadians*. Penguin Random House; 2017, pp. 75-76.

[336] Personal conversation with a self-described Red Tory.

[337] Berlinski, C. *"There Is No Alternative": Why Margaret Thatcher Matters*. Basic Books; 2008, p. 283.

[338] "Contrary to a rather widespread popular misconception, there is no necessary social virtue in 'planning.'" Burnham, J. *The Managerial Revolution: What Is Happening in the World*. Greenwood Press; 1941, p. 137.

[339] "What those who call themselves planners advocate is not the substitution of planned action for letting things go. It is the substitution of the planner's own plan for the plans of his fellow-man." von Mises, L. *Socialism: An Economic and Sociological Analysis*. 2nd ed. 2012. Martino Publishing; 1932, p. 538. See also: "When people wish to plan for humanity, they cannot allow human life to take its natural course, since that is a course inimical to comprehensive planning." Scruton, R. *A Political Philosophy: Arguments for Conservatism*. Bloomsbury; 2006, p. 173.

[340] Scruton, R. *Fools, Frauds and Firebrands: Thinkers of the New Left*. Bloomsbury Continuum; 2019, p. 12.

[341] Taylor, M.G. *Health Insurance and Canadian Public Policy: The Seven Decisions That Created the Canadian Health Insurance System and Their Outcomes*. McGill-Queen's University Press; 2009, p. 2.

[342] Roosevelt also liked the phrase "freedom from want." Röpke writes: "This easy-going slogan means, in fact, throwing into one and the same kettle real freedom

and false freedom, liberty in the highest ethical sense along with a pseudofreedom that means only the absence of something tiresome which limits perfect happiness." Meyer, F.S. *What Is Conservatism? — A New Edition of the Classic by 12 Leading Conservatives.* Intercollegiate Studies Institute; (1946) 2015, p. 105.

³⁴³ "[Liberalism] came to be regarded as a 'negative' creed because it could offer to particular individuals little more than a share in the common progress ... Because of the success already achieved, man became increasingly unwilling to tolerate the evils still with him which now appeared both unbearable and unnecessary." Hayek, F.A., Caldwell, B. *The Road to Serfdom: Text and Documents.* University of Chicago Press; 2007, p. 72.

³⁴⁴ "Centralized government planning would 'introduce order in the economic field,' as opposed to the supposed 'chaos' of capitalism." DiLorenzo, T.J. *The Problem with Socialism.* Regnery Publishing; 2016, p. 71.

³⁴⁵ "Private activity was inherently suspect and ... society had to be planned and regulated on a national basis." Olsen, H. *The Working Class Republican: Ronald Reagan and the Return of Blue-Collar Conservatism.* Broadside Books; 2017, p. 147.

³⁴⁶ "The modern state does not comprehend how anyone can be guided by something other than itself. In its eyes pluralism is treason." Weaver, R.M. *Ideas Have Consequences.* University of Chicago Press; 1948, p. 125.

³⁴⁷ "Keynesianism took for granted the notion that government policy-makers could be all-knowing. Going even further, it made the extraordinary assumption that those who shape policy will always act in the broader public interest." Harper, S. *Right Here, Right Now: Politics and Leadership in the Age of Disruption.* Signal; 2018, p. 24.

³⁴⁸ "Do politicians and bureaucrats not have their own unique self-interests and imperfections? Will a politician really put the best economic outcome ahead of an electoral objective? Will a bureaucrat always prioritize the management of economic cycles ahead of padding his or her own budget? These were plainly obvious questions that Keynesians failed to ask and refused to answer." Ibid.

³⁴⁹ Ibid., p. 29.

³⁵⁰ Evans, R.G., Barer, M.L, Stoddart, G.L., McGrail, K., McLeod, C.B. *An Undisciplined Economist: Robert G. Evans on Health Economics, Health Care Policy, and*

Population Health. McGill-Queen's University Press; 2016, p. 101.

351 "New doctors still graduate into a culture where it's common to view account-ability to society for our own practice as optional at best and inappropriate in-terference at worst." Martin, D. *Better Now: Six Big Ideas to Improve Health Care for All Canadians*. Penguin Random House; 2017, p. 230.

352 Ibid., p. 229.

353 "How needs are defined and recognized, and especially how and how exten-sively they are responded to, are highly variable both within and between health care systems ..." Evans, R.G., Barer, M.L., Stoddart, G.L., McGrail, K., McLeod, C.B. *An Undisciplined Economist: Robert G. Evans on Health Economics, Health Care Policy, and Population Health*. McGill-Queen's University Press; 2016, p. 112. Also: "The pervasive cultural belief has been that, as independent practi-tioners, doctors are best able [to] provide patients with the individualized care they need ..." Martin, D. *Better Now: Six Big Ideas to Improve Health Care for All Canadians*. Penguin Random House; 2017, pp. 220, 228.

354 Kirk. R. *The Conservative Mind: From Burke to Eliot*. 7th ed. Regnery Publish-ing; 2001, p. 124.

355 Evans, R.G., Barer, M.L., Stoddart, G.L., McGrail, K., McLeod, C.B. *An Undisci-plined Economist: Robert G. Evans on Health Economics, Health Care Policy, and Population Health*. McGill-Queen's University Press; 2016, p. 101.

356 Ibid., p. 112.

357 Ibid., p. 113.

358 "Private medicine is not the threat to public health care in Canada. It is govern-ment mismanagement, and insistence on economic models that do not work, that are the real threats. It is the breaking of the medicare promise itself that threatened medicare, not the existence of an alternative. The extent to which private medicine actually spreads is simply an indicator that our public system is failing, as people are forced to resort to paying for services that were promised to them and they thought were guaranteed." Vertesi, L. *Broken Promises: Why Canadian Medicare Is in Trouble and What Can Be Done to Save It*. Epic Press; 2003, p. 292.

359 "Closer to the truth is that the complications arise when the comprehensible components of health care are combined into the administrative 'systems,'

whether public or private. In other words, the problem is not in the activities themselves so much as in how we bring them together: something is terribly wrong with how we organize and administer health care." Mintzberg, H. *Managing the Myths of Health Care: Bridging the Separations Between Care, Cure, Control, and Community.* Berrett-Koehler Publishers; 2017, p. 147.

[360] And when wait times are long or care seems inadequate, it's a natural reaction to think that more resources are the solution. Too long to see a doctor? Add more doctors! Too long to get a scan? Add more machines! Those measures don't solve the problem — because the problems lie in the design of the system itself." Martin, D. *Better Now: Six Big Ideas to Improve Health Care for All Canadians.* Penguin Random House; 2017, p. 152. And: "Reorganize care and make better decisions — ensuring that only those who really would benefit from a scan are on the list and centralizing access to the available resources so that the queue is organized." Ibid., p. 153.

[361] "The more we control to correct, the deeper into dysfunction we get." Mintzberg, H. *Managing the Myths of Health Care: Bridging the Separations between Care, Cure, Control, and Community.* Berrett-Koehler Publishers; 2017, p. 214.

[362] Schuck, P.H. *Why Government Fails So Often: And How It Can Do Better.* Princeton University Press; 2015, p. 167.

[363] Scott, J.C. *Seeing Like a State: How Certain Schemes to Improve the Human Condition Have Failed.* Yale University Press; 1998, p. 343.

[364] Evans, R.G., Barer, M.L., Stoddart, G.L., McGrail, K., McLeod, C.B. *An Undisciplined Economist: Robert G. Evans on Health Economics, Health Care Policy, and Population Health.* McGill-Queen's University Press; 2016, p. 80 footnote 38.

[365] "When we discover that certain ideas about man, history and society seem, to those who believe them, to be either self-evident or so manifestly correct that opposing them is a mark of stupidity or malice, then we may be fairly sure that we are dealing with an *ideology* or *ideological thinking.*" Burnham, J. *Suicide of the West: An Essay on the Meaning and Destiny of Liberalism.* Encounter Books; 1964, p. 104.

[366] Heilbroner, R.L. "After Communism." *New Yorker.* September 10, 1990:91-100 https://www.newyorker.com/magazine/1990/09/10/after-communism

[367] "It turns out, of course, that Mises was right. The Soviet system has long been

dogged by a method of pricing that produced grotesque misallocations of effort." Ibid.

[368] "And how can they possibly know how much to lower the price today so they won't have to raise it tomorrow?" Ibid.

[369] OHIP Schedule of Benefits, Venipuncture, adult: G489 $3.54.

[370] I believe the NWT may adopt the BC schedule of benefits, with minor tweaks.

[371] "As a military campaign, which central planning resembles in many ways, production is brought about by a series of commands from the top, not by the independent decisions of regimental commanders, company captains, and platoon sergeants. This means that the economy 'works' because — and only to the extent that — the quantity, quality, size, weight, and selling price of every nut, bolt, hinge, beam, tractor, and hydro-electric turbine have been previously determined." Heilbroner, R.L. "After Communism." *New Yorker*. September 10, 1990:91-100. https://www.newyorker.com/magazine/1990/09/10/after-communism

[372] See Levine, re: "the resistance of civil servants to accept any proposal differing from what they had previously determined." Levine, D. *Health Care and Politics: An Insider's View on Managing and Sustaining Health Care in Canada*. Véhicule Press; 2015, p. 181. And, of course, this is exactly why the CMA fought against socialized medicine in the 1950s when it still cared about such things. The CMA warned about "enforced subservience to either the false god of paternalism or to the equally dangerous one of bureaucratic power." Naylor, C.D. *Private Practice, Public Payment: Canadian Medicine and the Politics of Health Insurance, 1911-1966*. McGill-Queen's University Press; 1986, p. 159.

[373] "The most difficult step was to establish 'success indicators' — desired performance targets — for enterprises. For many years, targets were given in physical terms ..." Heilbroner, R.L. "After Communism." *New Yorker*. September 10, 1990:91-100. https://www.newyorker.com/magazine/1990/09/10/after-communism

[374] This example was previously published in *Healthy Debate*. "When quality trumps service, patients lose out." *Healthy Debate*, February 24, 2014. https://healthydebate.ca/opinions/when-quality-trumps-service-patients-lose-out

[375] "Moving to Patient-based Funding Will Improve Care." Ministry of Health Ontario. Published 2012. Accessed August 6, 2020. https://news.ontario.ca/mohltc/en/2012/03/moving-to-patient-based-funding-will-improve-care.html

[376] "Are Hospital Funding Mechanisms in Canada Designed to Provide Efficient Care?" 2010. Accessed August 6, 2020. https://pdfs.semanticscholar.org/64f3/36f662937 b2853a41c5ff775428f4247c570.pdf

[377] Patient-based funding promised to "breathe new life into hospitals" (www. theglobeandmail.com/life/health-and-fitness/patient-based-funding-breathes-new-life-into-hospitals/article554728/) and move hospitals "into the 21st century" (www.theglobeandmail.com/globe-debate/ontario-hospitals-time-to-move-into-the-21st-century/article12707248/). Some described it as a "financial ray of sunshine" (cgmh.on.ca/?p=822). Health System Funding Reform (HSFR) promised a new era in healthcare.

[378] Laupacis, A., Petch, J. "Will More Finance Reform Improve Quality in Ontario's Hospitals?" *Healthy Debate*. Published 2013. Accessed August 6, 2020. http://healthydebate.ca/2013/03/topic/quality/will-more-finance-reform-improve-quality-in-ontarios-hospitals

[379] Furlong, D.J. *Medicare Myths*. Dream Catcher; 2004, p. 113. Marsh, a British surgeon, describes the NHS experience, which is identical to Canada in this respect. "The greater part of the notes … consist of nursing charts recording the patient's passing of bodily fluids on previous admissions and are no longer of any interest or importance." Marsh, H. *Do No Harm: Stories of Life, Death, and Brain Surgery*. Picador; 2016, p. 264.

[380] "Where Is Most of the Money Being Spent in 2019?" Canadian Institute for Health Information. Published 2019. Accessed August 6, 2020. https://www.cihi.ca/en/where-is-most-of-the-money-being-spent-in-2019

[381] "What Are Hospitals Spending On? Hospital Expenditures 2017-2018." Canadian Institute for Health Information. Published 2018. https://www.cihi.ca/en/what-are-hospitals-spending-on

[382] "Growing costs, in turn, lead to more regulation of hospitals and medical care, further increasing administration costs and leading to the bureaucratization that is so prominent a feature of medical care today." Friedman, M. "How to Cure Health Care." Hoover Institution. Published 2001. Accessed August 6, 2020. https://www.hoover.org/research/how-cure-health-care-0

[383] Will, G.F. *The Conservative Sensibility*. Hachette Books; 2019, p. 33.

[384] Bothwell, R. *The Penguin History of Canada*. Penguin; 2006, p. 419.

[385] "This 'managerial liberalism' celebrates the role of intellectuals and other policy elites in rationalizing society from above, wielding the federal government and the 'science' of public administration, meaning bureaucracy. This liberalism promises that government's mastery of economic management will end business cycles, thereby guaranteeing a steady flow of revenues for building more than a merely good society, but a Great Society." Will, G.F. *The Conservative Sensibility*. Hachette Books; 2019, p. 33. See also Donald Savoie: "The thinking or the hope was that government managers would focus on performance and outcomes rather than on processes and procedures." It creates a "relentless tide of change masquerading as improvement." Savoie, D.J. *What Is Government Good At? A Canadian Answer*. McGill-Queen's University Press; 2015, p. 114.

[386] "The size and unwieldiness of the modern welfare state had raised concerns about responsiveness of those providing services to those for whom such services were designed." Fierlbeck, K. *Health Care in Canada: A Citizen's Guide to Policy and Politics*. University of Toronto Press; 2011, p. 76.

[387] "This resulted in a greater tendency to micromanage governance from the top." Ibid., p. 79.

[388] *Life* magazine listed it as one of the top 100 books between 1924 and 1944. Goodreads. www.goodreads.com/list/show/127821.100_Outstanding_Books_1924_1944

[389] "What is occurring in this transition is a drive for social dominance, for power and privilege, for the position of ruling class, by the social group or class of the *managers*." Burnham, J. *The Managerial Revolution: What Is Happening in the World*. Greenwood Press; 1941, p. 71. Note: Max Weber, a staunch socialist, wrote about bureaucracy in the 1920s. His famous "iron cage" came from a translation of his 1920 book *The Protestant Ethic and the Spirit of Capitalism*. So Weber deserves the first description of the bureaucratic mindset. Weber, M., Parsons, T. (translator). *The Protestant Ethic and the Spirit of Capitalism*. Vigeo Press; 2017; 1904.

[390] Klikauer, T. "What Is Managerialism?" *Critical Sociology*. 2015;41(7-8):1103-1119.

[391] "Indeed it was Hegel, ideologist of 'bourgeois society', who identified the civil servants as its true upper class." Scruton, R. *Fools, Frauds and Firebrands: Thinkers of the New Left*. Bloomsbury Continuum; 2019, p. 158.

[392] "Managerial society is a class society, a society in which there are the powerful and the weak, the privileged and the oppressed, the rulers and the ruled." Burnham, J. *The Managerial Revolution: What Is Happening in the World.* Greenwood Press; 1941, p. 138.

[393] "Sovereignty has shifted from parliament to the administrative bureaus." Ibid., p. 147.

[394] "The nominal rulers — presidents and kings and congressmen and deputies and general and admirals — are not the actual rulers." Ibid., p. 155.

[395] "The managers will strengthen and consolidate their social position, and will establish society on a strong basis that will guarantee their rule, whoever may be the figures who stand in the political limelight." Ibid., p. 160.

[396] Burnham was in transition when he wrote his book. He had spent years in active support of the Soviet revolutionary Leon Trotsky. But he broke with Trotsky after Stalin invaded Poland and neighbouring countries in late 1939. Burnham and others formed their own Workers Party. It was only in May 1940 that Burnham finally broke with Marxism and all its various sects. He had left the Left but still had a very clear sense of the thinking involved. And he had not (yet) become a fan of free enterprise. As such, his book offers a dispassionate observation of a politics that he still, in many ways, supported.

[397] "In truth, the [medical profession] has in large measure lost confidence in its own ideologies." Burnham, J. *The Managerial Revolution: What Is Happening in the World.* Greenwood Press; 1941, p. 36.

[398] Martin, D. *Better Now: Six Big Ideas to Improve Health Care for All Canadians.* Penguin Random House; 2017, p. 230.

[399] "They naturally tend to identify the welfare of mankind as a whole with their own interests and the salvation of mankind with their assuming control of society." Burnham, J. *The Managerial Revolution: What Is Happening in the World.* Greenwood Press; 1941, p. 193.

[400] Which leads these kinds of people to avoid managerialized industries. "Entrepreneurs avoid the health care industry because the government has usurped and constrained so many business functions." Herzlinger, R.E. *Who Killed Health Care? America's $2 Trillion Medical Problem — and the Consumer-driven Cure.* McGraw Hill; 2007, p. 212.

[401] Burnham, J. *The Managerial Revolution: What Is Happening in the World*. Greenwood Press; 1941, p. 197.

[402] Ibid., p. 215.

[403] Ibid., p. 281.

[404] "Ownership *means* control; if there is no control, then there is no ownership … If ownership and control are in reality separated, then ownership has changed hands to the 'control,' and the separated ownership is a meaningless fiction." Ibid., pp. 92-93.

[405] The owner "controls access to those instruments [of the business] and controls preferential treatment in the distribution of their products." Ibid., p. 93.

[406] However, this idea has been challenged and may be changing. A human rights tribunal ruled in 2019 that estheticians do not have to work, against their will, on the male genitals of transgender people.

[407] Managerialism creates a continual push for government to invade the economy. Burnham, J. *The Managerial Revolution: What Is Happening in the World*. Greenwood Press; 1941, p. 106. It moves in the name of fairness and equality. "There is not a trace of a [sic] magic in the structure of state ownership which could in some mysterious and necessary way eliminate class rule and domination."Ibid., p.122. "Government is moving always more widely into the economy." Ibid., p. 106.

[408] "Through the state, [managers] will control access to the instruments of production. Through the state, they will control the distribution of the products of those instruments so that they themselves receive the privileged share." Ibid., p. 123.

[409] "There is nothing arbitrary about the extension of the state into the economy. It is not the result of a plot or conspiracy." Ibid., p. 129. George Orwell took Burnham to task. He thought Burnham too dispassionate, verging on admiration. Writing years later, he criticized Burnham for not singling out fascism for particular rebuke, even in 1940. However, it seems Burnham did not support any ruling class, anywhere.

[410] Ibid., p. 151.

[411] "Managerial crises will, it would seem, be technical and political in character: they will result from breakdowns in bureaucratized administration when faced with, say, the complicated problems of sudden shifts to war or peace or abrupt

technological changes; or from mass movements of dissatisfaction and revolt which, with the state and economy fused, would be automatically at once political and economic in character and effect." Ibid., p. 132.

412 "Propaganda that weakens confidence in the basic ideas and slogans supporting [medical] institutions, and popularizing ideas and slogans suited for the transition to the managerial structure." Ibid., p. 259.

413 "The traditional zones of power in the health care organizations shift from the internal clinical groupings of physicians, department heads, nurses and other professionals to the external zones of power: the media and the Ministry of Health." Levine, D. *Health Care and Politics: An Insider's View on Managing and Sustaining Health Care in Canada.* Véhicule Press; 2015, p. 248.

414 Ibid., p. 248.

415 Evans, R.G., Barer, M.L., Stoddart, G.L., McGrail, K., McLeod, C.B. *An Undisciplined Economist: Robert G. Evans on Health Economics, Health Care Policy, and Population Health.* McGill-Queen's University Press; 2016, p. 181.

416 Decter, M. *Healing Medicare: Managing Health System Change the Canadian Way.* McGilligan Books; 1994, p. 31.

417 Bliss in Gratzer, D. *Better Medicine: Reforming Canadian Health Care.* ECW Press; 2002, p. 41.

418 "As soon as the state takes upon itself the task of planning the whole economic life ... As the coercive power of the state will alone decide who is to have what, the only power worth having will be a share in the exercise of this directing power. There will be no economic or social questions that would not be political questions in the sense that their solution will depend exclusively on who wields the coercive power, on whose are the views that will prevail on all occasions." Hayek, F.A., Caldwell, B. *The Road to Serfdom: Text and Documents.* University of Chicago Press; 2007, p. 138.

419 "In Canada, for example, such dinosaur-like icons as Air Canada, Canadian National Railways, and Petro-Canada — all of which had been repeatedly trumpeted as example of Canadian distinctiveness and excellence — were privatized." Bliss in Gratzer, D. *Better Medicine: Reforming Canadian Health Care.* ECW Press; 2002, p. 41.

420 Davis, K., Stremikis, K., Squires, D., Schoen, C. *Mirror, Mirror on the Wall, 2014*

Update: How the U.S. Health Care Systems Compares Internationally; 2014. See also Schneider, E.C., Sarnak, D.O., Squires, D., Shah, A., Doty, M. *Mirror, Mirror 2017: International Comparison Reflects Flaws and Opportunities for Better U.S. Health Care*; 2017.

Chapter Eight

[421] Not his real name.

[422] It reflects the "analytic intellect favoured by the Enlightenment ... the analytic faculty or method that collects, classifies, experiments, takes to pieces, reassembles, defines, deduces, and establishes probabilities ..." Berlin, I. *The Proper Study of Mankind: An Anthology of Essays*. 2nd ed., 2013. Vintage; Random House; 1997, p. 261.

[423] "The rationalist who desires to subject everything to human reason is thus faced with a real dilemma. The use of reason aims at control and predictability. But the process of the advance of reason rests on freedom and the unpredictability of human action. Those who extol the powers of human reason usually see only one side of that interaction of human thought and conduct in which reason is at the same time used and shaped. They do not see that, for advance to take place, the social process from which the growth of reason emerges much remain free from its control." Hayek, F.A., Hamowy, R. *The Constitution of Liberty: The Definitive Edition*. University of Chicago Press; 2011, p. 89.

[424] "I shall reconsider human knowledge by starting from the fact that *we can know more than we can tell*." Polanyi, M. *The Tacit Dimension*. Doubleday; 1966, p. 4. Italics in original.

[425] Oakeshott, M. *Rationalism in Politics and Other Essays*. Liberty Fund; 1991, p. 16.

[426] Ibid., p. 37.

[427] Ibid., pp. 8-9. Note that some bits in medicine — many, in fact — have been painful nonsense, and patients feel relief when we abandon them (bloodletting, leeches, trephination, etc.). However, it is not easy to determine which bits should stay in and which should be thrown out.

[428] Compare logical positivism.

[429] Ibid., p. 37.

[430] Ibid., pp. 8-9.

[431] Bosworth in Nisbet, R., Douthat, R. *The Quest for Community: A Study in the Ethics of Order and Freedom.* 2019 ed. ISI Books; 1953, p. 279.

[432] Bosworth in ibid., p. 281.

[433] Both Oakeshott and Nisbet use the phrase "sovereignty of technique" at different times without referencing each other. Compare Nisbet, R., Douthat, R. *The Quest for Community: A Study in the Ethics of Order and Freedom.* 2019 ed. ISI Books; 1953, p. 199.

[434] See also Reeves, R. "To William Beveridge's Five Giant Evils We Must Add a Sixth — Loneliness." *New Statesman.* Also: https://www.theguardian.com/society/2017/oct/10/beveridge-five-evils-welfare-state

[435] Oakeshott, M. *Rationalism in Politics and Other Essays.* Liberty Fund; 1991, p. 11.

[436] Marsh L., Moscovitch, A. *Report on Social Security for Canada: New Edition.* McGill-Queen's University Press; 2018.

[437] Martin, D., Miller, A.P., Quesnel-Vallée, A., Caron, N.R., Vissandjée, B., Marchildon, G.P. "Canada's Universal Health-care System: Achieving Its Potential. *Lancet.* 2018;391(10131):1718-1735. doi:10.1016/S0140-6736(18)30181-8

[438] Oakeshott, M. *Rationalism in Politics and Other Essays.* Liberty Fund; 1991, p. 26.

[439] Ibid., pp. 26-27.

[440] "Entrepreneurship is the launching of surprises." Gilder, G.F. *Wealth and Poverty: A New Edition for the Twenty-first Century.* Regnery Publishing; 2012, p. xxxi.

[441] "This is a symptom of the triumph of technique which we have seen to be the root of modern Rationalism; for what the book contains is only what it is possible to put into a book — rules of a technique." Oakeshott, M. *Rationalism in Politics and Other Essays.* Liberty Fund; 1991, p. 27.

[442] Zimmerman, B, Lindberg, C., Plsek, P. *Edgeware: Lessons from Complexity Science for Health Care Leaders.* VHA; 1998.

[443] Oakeshott, M. *Rationalism in Politics and Other Essays.* Liberty Fund; 1991, p. 28.

[444] "All the Rationalist can do when left to himself is to replace one rationalist project in which he has failed by another in which he hopes to succeed." Ibid., p. 37.

[445] "Socialism assumes that we already have most of the knowledge we need to accomplish our national goals." Gilder, G.F. *Wealth and Poverty: A New Edition for the Twenty-first Century.* Regnery Publishing; 2012, p. 47.

446 "Search and you shall find: give and you will be given until; supply creates its own demand … The socialist economy proceeds from a rational definition of needs or demands to a prescription of planned supplies. In a socialist economy, one does not supply until the demands have already been determined and specified. Rationality rules …" Ibid., pp. 47-48.

447 Thaler, R.H., Sunstein, C.R. *Nudge: Improving Decisions About Health, Wealth, and Happiness.* Yale University Press; 2008.

448 "Categorization, commodification, and calculation can certainly render the administration of health care easier, and less expensive — for example, in figuring out how to remunerate the providers. That is why government and insurers alike have been promoting these three Cs for years. But what effect does this have on the quality of services? But does the fact that so many powerful forces in health care — governments, insurers, managers, economists, doctors — line up behind categorization, commodification, and calculation make it some sort of administrative panacea? Not at all: these three Cs need to be recognized for how they hinder as well as help the practices of health care." Mintzberg, H. *Managing the Myths of Health Care: Bridging the Separations Between Care, Cure, Control, and Community.* Berrett-Koehler Publishers; 2017, p. 52.

449 "You have to wonder if analysts will soon outnumber clinicians in health care. But the direct costs of their efforts are not the only costs. How about the costs of the distractions to the clinicians — for example, by having to record so much data — plus the costs of the political battles that ensue over who is measuring what, how, where, when, and for whom." Ibid., pp. 72-73.

450 Britnell, M. *In Search of the Perfect Health System.* 1st ed. Red Globe Press; 2015, p. 175. 5.

451 Rona Ambrose, then federal Minister of Health, spoke to several hundred doctors at CMA annual meeting in August 2014. From my notes, she said: "Facts must guide public policy. We know medicine is an art and a science, but we need science to guide public policy." She called it "informed public policy."

452 "But too often evidence is seen as motherhood, or at least truth, as is science. Who can possibly be against evidence? Me, for one. At least when the use of evidence becomes obsessive — a club to beat up on experience." Mintzberg, H. *Managing the Myths of Health Care: Bridging the Separations Between Care,*

Cure, Control, and Community. Berrett-Koehler Publishers; 2017, p. 131.

[453] "Evidence has to be put in its place — namely, were it can aid judgement, not replace it." Ibid., p. 65.

[454] "It is judgement that lies at the heart of diagnosis, of therapy, and of all that is gathered under the umbrella of what clinicians call case management. Inherent in the nature of clinic decision making is the realization that, perforce, it must always be accomplished in the face of incomplete and largely ambiguous information. The process is one of sifting, weighing, and judging and will ever be thus. Disease never reveals all of itself; the path toward healing may appear visible, but it is always poorly lit and subject to changes in direction." Nuland, S.B. *The Uncertain Art: Thoughts on a Life in Medicine.* Random House; 2008, p. xv.

[455] "Simplification, abstraction, and standardization … are necessary for state officials' observations." Scott, J.C. *Seeing Like a State: How Certain Schemes to Improve the Human Condition Have Failed.* Yale University Press; 1998, p. 81.

[456] Ibid., p. 82.

[457] Ibid., p. 22.

[458] "[Medicine] is the totality of this unique combination which constitutes the clinical moment and the clinical encounter, without which authentic medicine does not exist. No simplistic neo-Cartesian reduction of medicine to sciences of mind, arithmetically added to science of the body and tied together with a ribbon of moral science, is adequate to explain this synthesis. Nor is this merely biology. Neither plants nor animals — granted they become ill as well as humans — can enter into a relationship with the healer in which the patient participates as subject and object simultaneously." Pellegrino, E.D., Thomasma, D.C. *A Philosophical Basis of Medical Practice: Toward a Philosophy and Ethic of the Healing Professions.* Oxford University Press; 1981, p. xxx.

[459] "At a minimum, socialism has what economists would categorize as an 'incentive problem'; a 'knowledge problem'; and an 'economic calculation problem.'" DiLorenzo, T.J., in *The Problem with Socialism*, quoted in Rothbard, M.N. "The End of Socialism and the Calculation Debate Revisited." *Review of Austrian Economics.* 1991;5(2):51-76. Accessed August 6, 2020. https://mises.org/library/end-socialism-and-calculation-debate-revisited-0.

[460] Hayek, F.A. "The Use of Knowledge in Society." *American Economic Review.*

1945; XXXV (No. 4):519-530. Accessed August 6, 2020. https://www.jstor.org/stable/1809376?seq=1

[461] "Any attempt by a single agency to steer and economy constitutes a case of the blind leading the sighted." Lavoie, D., Coyne, C. (ed.) *National Economic Planning: What Is Left?* Mercatus Center, George Mason University; 1985, p. 4.

[462] "It goes without saying that much of the dignity of statesmanship is lost in the current deference towards the 'expert opinion', the 'advisory body', the 'commission of inquiry', the complex of established civil servants whose expert knowledge can never amount to wisdom, and who are themselves in need of the guidance which no mere body of facts or statistics could provide." Scruton, R. *The Meaning of Conservatism.* St. Augustine's Press; 2002, p. 177.

[463] Attributed to Sir Josiah Stamp, 1928, cited in Mintzberg, H. *Managing the Myths of Health Care: Bridging the Separations Between Care, Cure, Control, and Community.* Berrett-Koehler Publishers; 2017, p. 67.

[464] "The minister and the Ministry of Health see health care institutions and the system in which they function as a mechanistic bureaucracy and it is this vision that has led to the reform in Quebec. But a professional bureaucracy cannot be centrally run and therein lies the error in the vision of Bill 10 and the present reform." Levine, D. *Health Care and Politics: An Insider's View on Managing and Sustaining Health Care in Canada.* Véhicule Press; 2015, p. 245.

[465] Ibid., p. 245.

[466] Mintzberg, H. *Managing the Myths of Health Care: Bridging the Separations Between Care, Cure, Control, and Community.* Berrett-Koehler Publishers; 2017, p. 152.

[467] "If you want to understand the professional organization, simply take every characteristic of the machine organization and turn it upside down: you won't be far off." Ibid., p. 156.

[468] "Most everywhere, the essential problem in health care may lie in forcing detached administrative solutions on to practices that require informed and nuanced judgments." Ibid., p. 165. Or as an American author puts it: "Only recently has medical care been recast in our society as if it took place in a factory, with doctors and nurses as shift workers, labouring on an assembly line of the ill. The new people in charge, many with degrees in management economics,

believe that care should be configured as a commodity, its contents reduced to equations, all of its dimensions measured and priced, all patient choices formulated as retail purchases. Their experience of illness is being stripped of its symbolism and meaning, emptied of feeling and conflict. The new era rightly embraces science but wrongly relinquishes the soul." Jerome Groopman in Mintzberg, ibid., p. 156.

[469] Wilson, J.Q. *Bureaucracy: What Government Agencies Do and Why They Do It.* 2nd ed. Basic Books; 1991.

[470] "A school administrator cannot watch a teacher teach (except through classroom visits that momentarily may change the teacher's behaviour) and cannot tell how much students have learned (except by standardized tests that do not clearly differentiate between what the teacher has imparted and what the student has acquired otherwise)." Ibid., p. 168.

[471] "They can try to recruit the best people (without having much knowledge about what the 'best person' looks like), they can try to create an atmosphere that is conducive to good work (without being certain what 'good work' is) and they can step in when complaints are heard or crises erupt (without knowing whether a complaint is justified or a crisis symptomatic or atypical)." Ibid., p. 168.

[472] "In procedural organizations the general bureaucratic tendency to manage on the basis of process rather than outcome is much magnified because processes can be observed and outcomes cannot. Since the work of operators must be watched, it is watched all the time. Managers use many forms of continuous surveillance to ensure conformity to correct procedures, ranging from direct observation to periodic statistical reports." Ibid., p. 174.

[473] "In coping organizations, effective management is almost impossible." Ibid., p. 175. "Of course some work can be observed some of the time and some examples of results achieved do occasionally come into view ... A police sergeant periodically sees a patrol officer working the street ... Commending those employees whose good conduct happens to come to light also sends a message, but since citizens have more incentive to complain of the abuses they have suffered than to praise the virtues they have seen there tends to be more punishment than commendations issued by coping managers." Ibid.

[474] Ibid.

[475] "External control of an organization, whether by private owners or public authorities, tends to centralize and formalize, namely bureaucratize, its structure … all of which can weaken the professionals' natural engagement with their work — their sense of calling." Mintzberg, H. *Managing the Myths of Health Care: Bridging the Separations Between Care, Cure, Control, and Community.* Berrett-Koehler Publishers; 2017, p. 110.

[476] Schuck, P.H. *Why Government Fails So Often: And How It Can Do Better.* Princeton University Press; 2015, p. 324.

Chapter Nine

[477] I am grateful to Professor Bruce Pardy for sharing this reference.

[478] Cross, P. "Ontario's Staggering 380,000 Regulations Are Warping the Way Business Runs." *Financial Post. National Post.* Published 2016.

[479] Silverglate, H.A. *Three Felonies a Day: How the Feds Target the Innocent.* Encounter Books; 2011.

[480] And in other areas of life also: "Never before has the government concerned itself so minutely with the detailed interactions of daily life." Schuck, P.H. *Why Government Fails So Often: And How It Can Do Better.* Princeton University Press; 2015, p. 277.

[481] Nisbet, R., Douthat, R. *The Quest for Community: A Study in the Ethics of Order and Freedom.* 2019 ed. ISI Books; 1953, p. 174.

[482] Pardy, B. *Ecolawgic: The Logic of Ecosystems and the Rule of Law.* 5th Forum Press; 2015.

[483] Ibid., p. 2.

[484] Ibid., p. 7.

[485] Ibid., p. 8.

[486] "Regulation is an effort to replace knowledge with power. The government cannot be sure what complex corporations like AIG are doing. It does not know how to make AIG better at what it does, how to improve its efficiency and effectiveness as a global insurance company. So it imposes an array of rules that have the effect of distracting the company from its corporate purposes and toward government purposes, making AIG less like an entrepreneurial corporation and

more like a government bureaucracy. The rules from outside AIG attempt to substitute for the actual knowledge residing within the company about its operations and markets." Gilder, G.F. *Wealth and Poverty: A New Edition for the Twenty-first Century*. Regnery Publishing; 2012, p. xxxvi.

[487] See section on rationalism in politics (chapter eight).

[488] Gilder, G.F. *Wealth and Poverty: A New Edition for the Twenty-first Century*. Regnery Publishing; 2012, p. xxvii.

[489] Bardach, E, Kagan R. *Going by the Book: The Problem of Regulatory Unreasonableness*. Transaction. Routledge; 2002, back flap.

[490] Ibid., pp. xii, 300.

[491] Hayek, F.A., Hamowy, R. *The Constitution of Liberty: The Definitive Edition*. University of Chicago Press; 2011, p. 216.

[492] This example comes from Gairdner, W.D. Celebrating the West. *Civil Conversations*. Published online July 2020.

[493] Oved, M.C. "Bill Would Require Doctor Cautions, Complaints to Be Public." *Toronto Star*. Published 2014.

[494] Bardach, E., Kagan, R. *Going by the Book: The Problem of Regulatory Unreasonableness*. Transaction. Routledge; 2002, p. x.

[495] Bardach E, Kagan R. *Going by the Book: The Problem of Regulatory Unreasonableness*. Transaction. Routledge; 2002.

[496] Ibid., p. 197.

[497] The Patient Safety and Quality Improvement group from Duke University says: *"This 'shame and blame' approach leads to hiding rather than reporting of errors, and thus is the antithesis of a culture of safety. Recent efforts have tried to change this — to encourage people to report problems rather than hide them, so they can be addressed."* The World Health Organization, writing on safety cultures, notes that blame and shame does not work. It does not improve safety. The Canadian Patient Safety Institute says the same thing. For one of dozens of academic articles suggesting better alternatives to blame and shame, see onlinelibrary.wiley.com/doi/10.1111/j.1475-6773.2008.00918.x/full

[498] Bill 29, Medicine Amendment Act, 2014. https://www.ola.org/en/legislative-business/bills/parliament-41/session-1/bill-29. This private member's bill passed first reading in October 2014 but never made it to committee. Regardless, the CPSO

appears to have implemented everything the bill called for and more.

[499] Bardach, E., Kagan, R. *Going by the Book: The Problem of Regulatory Unreasonableness*. Transaction. Routledge; 2002, p. xii.

[500] Ibid., p. xxxii.

[501] A few years ago, a colleague of mine, an in-house legal counsel, added up all the statutes that regulate medical practice in Ontario, going back to 1907. Each statute can have many provisions. Statutes spawn even more regulations, but he ignored all these to make a simple point. He graphed his findings:

[502] Isaiah Berlin discussed this in his essay "Two Concepts of Liberty." He called this positive freedom, which includes an understanding that there is one best way to live. If so: "We recognize that it is possible, and at times justifiable, to coerce men in the name of some goal (let us say, justice or public health) which they would, if they were more enlightened, themselves pursue, but do not, because they are blind or ignorant or corrupt." Berlin, I. *The Proper Study of Mankind: An Anthology of Essays* (Vintage Classics). 2nd ed., 2013. Vintage; Random House; 1997, p. 204.

[503] Scott Kapoor comment on blog: shawnwhatley.com (2013-09-21 00:30:53).

[504] Phil Whatley comment on blog: shawnwhatley.com (2013-09-23 12:17:10).

[505] Britnell, M. *In Search of the Perfect Health System*. 1st ed. Red Globe Press; 2015, p. 171.

[506] Price, G. "Healthcare Is Turning into an Industry Focused on Compliance, Regulation Rather Than Patient Care." *Forbes*. November 5, 2013. http://www.forbes.com/sites/physiciansfoundation/2013/11/05/healthcare-is-turing-into-an-industry-focused-on-compliance-regulation-rather-than-patient-care/

[507] Franz, J. "The Effects of Health Care Over-Regulation." *Del Mar Times*. August 31, 2016. http://www.delmartimes.net/news/2014/jun/26/the-effects-of-health-care-over-regulation/

[508] Holly, M. "How Government Regulations Made Healthcare So Expensive." *Mises Wire*. May 19, 2017. https://mises.org/wire/how-government-regulations-made-healthcare-so-expensive

[509] Bardach, E., Kagan, R. *Going by the Book: The Problem of Regulatory Unreasonableness*. Transaction. Routledge; 2002, p. xxxii.

[510] Schuck, P.H. *Why Government Fails So Often: And How It Can Do Better*. Princ-

eton University Press; 2015, pp. 279-80.

511 "What stops other well-educated, highly skilled and supremely well-motivated people in teams making health and care higher quality, better integrated, less fragmented and ultimately more sustainable? Ironically, the short answer is the organizations in which they work and the pressures, incentives and regulatory circumstances in which they operate." Britnell, M. *In Search of the Perfect Health System*. 1st ed. Red Globe Press; 2015, p. 166.

512 Fuchs, V.R. *Who Shall Live?Health, Economics, and Social Choice*. Basic Books; 1974, p. 103.

513 Powell, E.J. *A New Look at Medicine and Politics*. Pitman; 1966. Accessed August 5, 2020. https://www.sochealth.co.uk/national-health-service/healthcare-generally/history-of-healthcare/a-new-look-at-medicine-and-politics/

514 http://www.tbs-sct.gc.ca/rtrap-parfa/index-eng.asp

515 http://actionplan.gc.ca/en/initiative/reducing-red-tape

516 Harper, S. *Right Here, Right Now: Politics and Leadership in the Age of Disruption*. Signal; 2018, p. 96.

517 The Hon. Warren K. Winkler, Q.C. Conciliator's Report. December 11, 2014. http://www.health.gov.on.ca/en/news/bulletin/2015/docs/hb_20150115.pdf

518 This same line of thinking applies to clinical guidelines, which too often carry the force of law themselves. "Guidelines: often conflict, are written for the average patient, are often created by parties who are interested in the outcomes (ie drug companies), studies exclude huge swaths of the population by design; tough to make a truly randomized trial; based on assumption that similar patients should be treated in a similar way ... that is, guidelines assume similar response to treatment, not individuality." Goodman, J.C. *Priceless: Curing the Healthcare Crisis*. Independent Institute; 2012, pp. 57-59.

519 "We cannot legislate for the unknown consequences of consequences of consequences [sic]." Berlin, I. *The Proper Study of Mankind: An Anthology of Essays* (Vintage Classics). 2nd ed., 2013. Vintage; Random House; 1997, p. 12.

520 Fuchs, V.R. *Who Shall Live? Health, Economics, and Social Choice*. Basic Books; 1974, p. 142.

521 Bardach, E., Kagan, R. *Going by the Book: The Problem of Regulatory Unreasonableness*. Transaction. Routledge; 2002, p. xxi.

[522] Ibid., p. xi.

[523] Berlin, I. *The Proper Study of Mankind: An Anthology of Essays* (Vintage Classics). 2nd ed., 2013. Vintage; Random House; 1997, p. 16.

[524] Bardach, E., Kagan, R. *Going by the Book: The Problem of Regulatory Unreasonableness*. Transaction. Routledge; 2002, p. xxix.

[525] Ibid., p. 185. And the authors note that the criticism of risking life and limb will always outweigh financial concerns. Ibid., p. 198.

[526] Ibid., p. 195.

[527] Ibid., p. 196.

[528] Ibid., p. xxxii.

[529] For example, Dr. Hsu.

[530] With this, the registrar of the College of Physicians and Surgeons of Ontario (CPSO) wrapped up his final note in *From the Registrar's Desk*, April 3, 2017, after several decades of holding official positions. Dr. Rocco Gerace joined the Disciplines Committee in 1995, served as president in 2000-2001, and held the registrar's position from 2002 to 2018. https://www.cpso.on.ca/News/News-Articles/Registrar-Dr-Rocco-Gerace-Stepping-Down

[531] http://www.prisonexp.org/ Note: Some have criticized the study design, suggesting it was open to bias.

[532] For a list of other prerequisites, see Pardy, B. *Ecolawgic: The Logic of Ecosystems and the Rule of Law*. 5th Forum Press; 2015, pp. 40-48. See also Locke and Montesquieu.

[533] Blishen, B.R. *Doctors in Canada: The Changing World of Medical Practice*. Published in association with Statistics Canada by University of Toronto Press; 1991, p. 6.

[534] "Men are qualified for civil liberty, in exact proportion to their disposition to put moral chains upon their appetites; in proportion as their love of justice is above their rapacity; in proportion as their soundness and sobriety of understanding is above their vanity and presumption; in proportion as they are more predisposed to listen to the counsel of the wise and good, in preference to the flattery of knaves." Burke, quoted in Hayek, F.A., Hamowy, R. *The Constitution of Liberty: The Definitive Edition*. University of Chicago Press; 2011, p. 123 footnote 38.

Chapter Ten

[535] Boal, P. "Ottawa Man Finds Out in a Letter He Is Dumped by His Doctor." CTV News. November 10, 2017. ottawa.ctvnews.ca/ottawa-man-finds-out-in-letter-he-is-dumped-by-his-doctor-1.3672828

[536] Note: I received permission from her to blog about it, and the following content draws on information previously posted in the blog. And to be clear, I have no idea what Dr. Bartlett thinks about socialized medicine either way.

[537] The internal, intangible requirements for excellence include a sense of ownership. In a discussion about high-performing businesses and the need for a sense of ownership, Gilder writes: "Leibenstein's data show, observation suggest, and long history confirms, the spirit factor is best elicited by ownership." Gilder, G.F. *Wealth and Poverty: A New Edition for the Twenty-first Century.* Regnery Publishing; 2012, pp. 44-46. Mayer and Jensen write about "owners versus renters" and about "hardwiring flow: "High performers feel they 'own' their piece of the organization and hold themselves deeply responsible for not only their performance but that of the entire team." On the other hand: "Renters are just 'hanging out' at work, often seeming to have 'retired on the job.' They occupy space and drain resources, but contribute little to the organization's purpose." *Hardwiring Flow: Systems and Processes for Seamless Patient Care,* Fire Started Publishing; 2009, p. 101.

[538] Kamruzzaman, M.D. "Extrinsic and Intrinsic Motivation on Work Engagement in the Hospitality Industry: Test of Motivation Crowding Theory [Summary]." *Virginia Tech.* 2020-02-13. https://vtechworks.lib.vt.edu/handle/10919/96884

[539] Fischer, C., et al. "The Influence of Intrinsic Motivation and Synergistic Extrinsic Motivators on Creativity and Innovation." *Frontiers in Psychology.* February 4, 2019. https://doi.org/10.3389/fpsyg.2019.00137 https://www.frontiersin.org/articles/10.3389/fpsyg.2019.00137/full

[540] Carleton, K. "How to Motivate and Retain Knowledge Workers in Organizations: A Review of the Literature." *International Journal of Management.*28: 2. June 2011, pp. 459-68.

[541] Or even worse, employees become passionless labour, hating their jobs but chained to their position with gold handcuffs.

[542] Adam Smith in *The Theory of Moral Sentiments* (1759) offers a book-length treatment about human motivations and how they go far beyond just *homo economicus*. Consider his opening paragraph: "How selfish soever man may be supposed, there are evidently some principles in his nature, which interest him in the fortune of others, and render their happiness necessary to him, though he derives nothing from it except the pleasure of seeing it. Of this kind is pity or compassion, the emotion which we feel for the misery of others, when we either see it, or are made to conceive it in a very lively manner. That we often derive sorrow from the sorrow of others, is a matter of fact too obvious to require any instances to prove it; for this sentiment, like all the other original passions of human nature, is by no means confined to the virtuous and humane, though they perhaps may feel it with the most exquisite sensibility. The greatest ruffian, the most hardened violator of the laws of society, is not altogether without it."

[543] The only example offered often and loudly is that Canadian physicians only have to submit one bill, while American docs submit many.

[544] Herzer, K.R., Pronovost, P.J. "Physician Motivation: Listening to What Pay for Performance Programs and Quality Improvement Collaboratives Are Telling Us." *The Joint Commission Journal on Quality and Patient Safety*. 2015 Nov; 41(11): 522-28.

[545] "Systems awareness and systems design are important for health professionals, but are not enough. They are enabling mechanisms only. It is the ethical dimension of individuals that is essential to a system's success. Ultimately, the secret of quality is love." Donabedian, A. "A Founder of Quality Assessment Encounters a Troubled System Firsthand." Interview by Mullan, F. *Health Affairs* (Millwood). 2001;20(1):137–141. Accessed September 30, 2015. http://content.healthaffairs.org/content/20/1/137.full.html

[546] Abraham Maslow described his hierarchy of needs in 1943. He argued that humans have a spectrum of needs starting with basic needs and progressing to higher, intangible needs: physiologic, safety, social belonging, esteem, self-actualization, self-transcendence. Government involvement can have a positive or negative impact at the lowest, most basic levels. At higher levels, government loses its ability for positive influence, but its ability to harm remains. Dohlman L., et al. "Global Brain Drain: How Can the Maslow Theory of Motivation Improve

Our Understanding of Physician Migration?" *International Journal of Environmental Research and Public Health*. 2019, 16(7), 1182. https://doi.org/10.3390/ijerph16071182

547 Dermot Quinn, from the introduction of Röpke, W. *A Humane Economy: The Social Framework of the Free Market*. ISI Books, 1999 ed. (originally published 1958), p. xi. Further, Berlin writes: "The French *philosophes* and their English followers tell us that men seek only to obtain pleasure and avoid pain, but this is absurd. Men seek to live, create, love, hate, eat, drink, worship, sacrifice, understand, and they seek this because they cannot help it." Berlin, I. *The Proper Study of Mankind: An Anthology of Essays* (Vintage Classics). 2nd ed., 2013. Vintage; Random House; 1997, p. 253.

548 Evans, R.G., Barer, M.L., Stoddart, G.L, McGrail, K., McLeod, C.B. *An Undisciplined Economist: Robert G. Evans on Health Economics, Health Care Policy, and Population Health*. McGill-Queen's University Press; 2016, p. 273.

549 Scruton, R. *A Political Philosophy: Arguments for Conservatism*. Bloomsbury; 2006, p. 39. Scruton goes on: "What is needed is a non-egoistic motive that can be elicited in ordinary members of society, and relied upon to serve the longterm [social] goal. Burke proposed 'the hereditary principle', as protecting important institutions from pillage or decay, and believed that people have a natural tendency to accept the limits that this principle places on their desires. Hegel argued for priority of non-contractual obligations, of the kind that sustain the family, and believed that similar obligations could be recuperated and exercised at the political level. In a similar vein, de Maistre gave a central place to piety, as a motive that puts divinely ordained traditions and constitutions above the temptations of self-interest."

550 "We move on an intermediate plane. It is not the summit of heroes and saints, of simon-pure altruism, selfless dedication, and contemplative calm, but neither is it the lowlands of open or concealed struggle in which force and cunning determine the victor and the vanquished." Röpke, W. *A Humane Economy: The Social Framework of the Free Market*. ISI Books, 1999 ed. (originally published 1958), p. 116.

551 Marsh, H. *Do No Harm: Stories of Life, Death, and Brain Surgery*. Reprint ed. Picador; 2016, p. 31.

[552] In 1966, the CMA set up a special committee on collective bargaining. In its report, the committee noted that "henceforth in Canada the economic position of doctors in the community will be largely determined by the results of meetings between representatives of the doctors and representatives of the public and/or government …" Naylor, C.D. *Private Practice, Public Payment: Canadian Medicine and the Politics of Health Insurance, 1911-1966.* McGill-Queen's University Press; 1986, p. 241.

[553] Ontology and remuneration are two different things.

[554] Whatley, S.D. "Borrowed Philosophy: Bedside Physicalism and the Need for a *Sui Generis* Metaphysic of Medicine." *Journal of Evaluation in Clinical Practice.* 20:6. July 5, 2014. https://doi.org/10.1111/jep.12214

[555] "The belief that wealth consists not in ideas, attitudes, moral codes and mental discipline, but in definable and static things that can be seized and redistributed, is the materialist superstition." Gilder, G.F. *Wealth and Poverty: A New Edition for the Twenty-first Century.* Regnery Publishing; 2012, p. xxxix.

[556] Röpke, W. *A Humane Economy: The Social Framework of the Free Market.* ISI Books, 1999 ed. (originally published 1958), p. 106. Those on the left use the "commodification of health care" to bolster the need to remove any vestige of prices, performance, or any other accoutrement of market-based, neoliberal, or neoconservative thinking. This works well with the managerialism we discussed earlier, but not so well for patients. Paradoxically, the economic materialists are also the ones who bemoan the commodification of medical care. They apply the materialist's acid of economic reductionism and then complain that there is nothing left but talk about productivity and efficiency. "The focus on outcomes and objectives can, however, reinforce the idea, already prevalent, that Canadians care about the productivity and efficiency of their health care system, not the means deployed to achieve productivity or efficiency. It can in other words reinforce the commodification of health care, as styles of health care governance that rely on soft law have been said to do in Europe." Fierlbeck, K, Lahey, W. *Health Care Federalism in Canada: Critical Junctures and Critical Perspectives.* McGill-Queen's University Press; 2013, p. 94.

[557] "[Medicare] is an economic model with the sophistication of a giant soup kitchen, with one group of people deciding what will be in the soup and how

much to give, and another group in the line-up waiting for their turn." "It should be clear by now that adding more layers to our current health system will not help, just as adding more cooks would not help change the dependency on the soup kitchen." Vertesi, L. *Broken Promises: Why Canadian Medicare Is in Trouble and What Can Be Done to Save It.* Epic Press; 2003, p. 207.

[558] "The means of production of entrepreneurs are not land, labour or capital but minds and hearts. Capitalism is a system that begins not with taking but with giving to others." Gilder, G.F. *Wealth and Poverty: A New Edition for the Twenty-first Century.* Regnery Publishing; 2012, p. xi.

[559] "The heart of the capitalist approach to economics is neither private property, nor markets, nor profits (all these the third world has), but rather invention." Novak, M. *The Spirit of Democratic Capitalism.* Madison Books; 1990, p. 419. And Kirk: "The principal producer of wealth is not Labour, but *Ability*." Kirk, R. *The Conservative Mind: From Burke to Eliot.* 7th ed. Regnery Publishing; 2001, p. 404.

[560] "Cultures in which individuals are not taught how to cooperate, compromise, and discipline themselves to practical communal tasks can make neither democratic politics nor market economies work." Novak, M. *The Spirit of Democratic Capitalism.* Madison Books; 1990, p. 134.

[561] "Were the impulse of capitalism solely materialistic, the system would have long since fallen into narcissism, hedonism, and death." Ibid., p. 437.

[562] "Cultures in which individuals are not taught how to cooperate, compromise, and discipline themselves to practical communal tasks can make neither democratic politics nor market economies work." Ibid., p. 134.

[563] George Gilder called this the "materialist superstition": "The belief that wealth consists not in ideas, attitudes, moral codes and mental disciplines, but in definable and static things that can be seized and redistributed, is the materialist superstition. It stultified the works of Marx and other prophets of violence and envy. It betrays every person who seeks to redistribute wealth by coercion. It balks every socialist revolutionary who imagines that by seizing the so-called means of production he can capture the crucial capital of an economy." Gilder, G.F. *Wealth and Poverty: A New Edition for the Twenty-first Century.* Regnery Publishing; 2012, p. xxxix.

564 Novak, M. *The Spirit of Democratic Capitalism*. Madison Books; 1990, p. 434. See also: "Nonetheless, powerful vested interests and intellectual transitions are quite opposed to granting any moral standing to the capitalist part of democratic capitalism. Many are prepared to admire democracy (the protection of individual rights and the checks and balances achieved by the democratic republic), and many are prepared to admire pluralism. Many fewer are willing to notice the moral qualities inherent in capitalism." Ibid., p. 434.

565 "… A revolution in the direction of democracy and capitalism must have moral depth, or it cannot long endure." Ibid., p. 438.

566 "Only a pile of statistical ashes, a dry and sterile residue of numbers, from which to reconstruct the edifice of economic activity." Gilder, G.F. *Wealth and Poverty: A New Edition for the Twenty-first Century*. Regnery Publishing; 2012, p. 45.

567 "Under capitalism, wealth is less a stock of goods than a flow of ideas and information, the defining characteristic of which is surprise." Ibid., p. xxxiii.

568 Gilder G.F. *Wealth and Poverty: A New Edition for the Twenty-first Century*. Regnery Publishing; 2012.

569 Ibid., p. xiv.

570 "[Medicine] is a system that begins not with taking but with giving to others." Ibid., p. xi.

571 Ibid., p. 31.

572 For example, Bob Evans writes: "…the health care systems of the world have settled this long ago. *Of course*, capacity generates use, that is why capacity control — hospital beds, physicians supply — is always among the first steps taken in strategies for cost control." But he offers no reference. "… an overwhelming majority of the economists, as well as the physicians, that he [Fuchs] surveyed agree that *doctors can and do shift the demand curve for their own services*, and are more likely to do so when demand is low. Yet an overwhelming majority of the formal analyses … suppress this reality" (pp. 63-64). Again, no references. "… two-thirds of both health economists and physicians believed that such shifting occurs …" (p. 64). Evans, R.G., Barer, M.L., Stoddart, G.L., McGrail, K., McLeod, C.B. *An Undisciplined Economist: Robert G. Evans on Health Economics, Health Care Policy, and Population Health*. McGill-Queen's University Press; 2016.

[573] Gilder, G.F. *Wealth and Poverty: A New Edition for the Twenty-first Century.* Regnery Publishing; 2012, p. 33.

[574] Ibid., p. 39.

[575] Ibid., pp. 44-46.

[576] Ibid., p. 48.

[577] Montgomery, K. *How Doctors Think: Clinical Judgement and the Practice of Medicine,* 1st ed. Oxford University Press; 2005, pp. 4-5.

[578] "With its invariable replicability and law-like precision, this view of science is a matter of simple logic with readily deduced details and rule-governed consequences." Ibid., pp. 4-5.

[579] Ibid.

[580] Ibid., p. 9.

[581] Ibid., p. 33.

[582] Michael Polanyi, a philosopher of science who trained first in medicine, offers a long passage on what a surgeon must know to perform surgery deep inside someone's abdomen. Polanyi, M. *Personal Knowledge: Towards a Post-critical Philosophy.* University of Chicago Press; 1958. 1974 ed., p. 89.

[583] Marshall McLuhan.

[584] "In discussing traditions, we are not discussing arbitrary rules and conventions. We are discussing *answers* that have been discovered to enduring *questions.* These answers are tacit, shared, embodied in social practices and inarticulate expectations." Scruton, R. *How to Be a Conservative.* Bloomsbury Continuum; 2015, p. 21.

[585] The loss of a larger understanding of all that is included in medicine is also an issue for Western society as a whole. "In large part, the present crisis of liberal thought in the West comes, I believe, from the increasing loss of correspondence between the basic liberal values and the prejudgments and social contexts upon which the historic success of liberalism has been predicated." Nisbet, R., Douthat, R. *The Quest for Community: A Study in the Ethics of Order and Freedom.* 2019 ed. ISI Books; 1953, p. 201.

[586] "A scholar's parrot may talk Greek ..." from "As the Ruin Falls," a poem by C.S. Lewis. Thanks to P. Whatley for this reference.

[587] Oakeshott, M. *Rationalism in Politics and Other Essays.* Liberty Fund; 1991, p. 12.

[588] Ibid., p. 15.

[589] Ibid., p. 16.

[590] Whatley, S.D. "Borrowed Philosophy: Bedside Physicalism and the Need for a *Sui Generis* Metaphysic of Medicine." *Journal of Evaluation in Clinical Practice.* 20:6. July 5, 2014. https://doi.org/10.1111/jep.12214

[591] "Zombies." *Stanford Encyclopedia of Philosophy.* March 2019. plato.stanford.edu/entries/zombies/

[592] en.wikipedia.org/wiki/Sexual_Sterilization_Act_of_Alberta

[593] "Alberta Apologizes for Forced Sterilization." CBC News. November 09, 1999. www.cbc.ca/news/canada/alberta-apologizes-for-forced-sterilization-1.169579

[594] "Alberta's Sex Sterilizations Re-examined." CBC News. October 23, 2010. www.cbc.ca/news/canada/edmonton/alberta-s-sex-sterilizations-re-examined-1.871749

[595] en.wikipedia.org/wiki/Clarence_B._Farrar

[596] Dabu Nonato, S. "Female Genital Mutilation a 'Human Rights Violation': Canadian Gynaecologists." *National Post.* February 21, 2012. news.nationalpost.com/2012/02/21/female-genital-mutilation-a-human-rights-violation-canadian-gynaecologists/

[597] Perron, L., et al. "Female Genital Cutting." *Journal of Obstetrics and Gynaecology Canada.* November 2013; Nov; 35(11):1028-1045. www.ncbi.nlm.nih.gov/pubmed/24246404

[598] Kielburger, C., Kielburger, M. "Female Genital Mutilation Is a Canadian Issue Too." *HuffPost.* 03/06/2013 www.huffingtonpost.ca/craig-and-marc-kielburger/female-genital-mutilation_b_2813119.html

[599] Slate. "Gender Selection Has Become a Multimillion-dollar Industry." *HuffPost.* 09/17/2012. www.huffingtonpost.com/2012/09/17/gender-selection-_n_1889991.html

[600] Clarke, S. Sex Selection & Abortion: Canada. Library of Congress Law. June 2009. www.loc.gov/law/help/sex-selection/canada.php

[601] Sawa, T., Burns, P. "A. Fetal Gender Testing Offered at Private Clinics – Raises Fears That Gender Selection Happening in Canada." CBC News. June 12, 2012. www.cbc.ca/news/canada/fetal-gender-testing-offered-at-private-clinics-1.1183673 And Mickleburgh, R. "Media Scolded for Promoting Gender Se-

lection Facility."*Globe and Mail.* April 23, 2012.m.theglobeandmail.com/news/british-columbia/media-scolded-for-promoting-gender-selection-facility/article4102049/?service=mobile And CTVNews.ca Staff. "U.S. Clinic Offers Sex Selection Service to Indo-Canadians." April 18, 2012. www.ctvnews.ca/u-s-clinic-offers-sex-selection-service-to-indo-canadians-1.798147

[602] Schouten, M. "Doctors Should Be Allowed to Opt Out of Providing Birth-control Pills or Abortions." *National Post.* July 9, 2014. news.nationalpost.com/2014/07/09/mike-schouten-doctors-should-be-allowed-to-opt-out-of-providing-birth-control-pills-or-abortions/

[603] "Thoughts become words; words become actions; actions habits; habits character; and character destiny." Paraphrased from Ghandi, Lao Tzu, Margaret Thatcher, and others.

[604] "In others, good behaviour is simply discouraged or not rewarded. And in still others, formal and informal institutions serve to support and reward honesty, thrift, self-reliance, and independence of mind. That is why some writers have even spoken of 'statecraft as soul craft.'" Crowley, B.L. *Fearful Symmetry: The Fall and Rise of Canada's Founding Values.* Key Porter Books; 2010, p. 311. And see Will, G.F. *Statecraft as Soulcraft: What Government Does.* Touchstone; 1983. See also, Scruton: "It is not the economic system of a nation that determines its character but its political institutions." Scruton, R. *Fools, Frauds and Firebrands: Thinkers of the New Left.* Bloomsbury Continuum; 2019, p. 49.

[605] Robin F. Badgley and Samuel Wolfe in Naylor, C.D. *Canadian Health Care and the State: A Century of Evolution.* McGill-Queen's University Press; 1992, p. 220. Bob Bell, former deputy minister of health in Ontario, blames doctors for wait times: "Why would any referring doctor leave their patient on a one-year wait-list for total hip or total knee when much shorter times are evident in [the] vast majority [of Ontario] hospitals?" Dr. Bob Bell on Twitter, March 16, 2019. https://twitter.com/drbobbell/status/1107006465481408512?s=12 One health policy consultant complains: "It is more lucrative to practice bad medicine than good medicine, particularly in family practice." ("Healthcare Spending Overshoots a Threat to Sustainability," for the C.D. Howe Institute, p. 268, https://www.cdhowe.org/public-policy-research/healthcare-spending-overshoots-threat-sustainability) Government sends mixed signals on quality versus vol-

ume, and other "professionals are woefully underused." Doctors refuse to play along with government planning. "Lured by every imaginable form of incentive, family doctors still largely will not go to or stay in rural and remote Canada" (p. 269). Lewis goes on to criticize. "The guilds are powerful and it is instructive to observe how medicine has managed to change the focus to physicians' assistants (i.e., a hierarchical, doctor-controlled approach) from an expanded nurse practitioner model (i.e., collaborative and egalitarian approach)." No surprise that Lewis does not mention that PAs existed long before NPs. He just needs PAs long enough to use in a sentence to pummel physicians.

[606] "Bending the Healthcare Cost Curve." TVO. *The Agenda with Steve Paikin*. April 27, 2010. https://www.youtube.com/watch?v=8Rrio2UyUz4 ~48:45 start.

[607] Martin, D. *Better Now: Six Big Ideas to Improve Health Care for All Canadians*. Penguin Random House; 2017, p. 93.

[608] However, many medications start out designed to treat one condition and turn out to have happy side effects which add more value than the original label promised, e.g., Viagra.

[609] ~29:35 start, same video, Bending the Healthcare Cost Curve

[610] Decter, M. *Healing Medicare: Managing Health System Change the Canadian Way*. McGilligan Books; 1994, p. 37.

[611] Ibid., p. 171.

[612] Ibid., p. 109.

[613] Blishen, B.R. *Doctors in Canada: The Changing World of Medical Practice*. Published in association with Statistics Canada by University of Toronto Press; 1991, p. 131. Note: Having one or two representative physicians in government is no guarantee of government being properly informed; for example, the Wynne Liberal government.

[614] Taylor, M.G. *Health Insurance and Canadian Public Policy: The Seven Decisions That Created the Canadian Health Insurance System and Their Outcomes*. McGill-Queen's University Press; 2009, p. 491.

Chapter Eleven

[615] Credit to Philip Whatley: The government ring of power will always seek to do the will of government.

[616] M. Lister in a lecture given to OMA.

[617] Lecture given to the Physician Leadership Development Program, 2012.

[618] The process may have even been updated in the few years since his lecture, but the general approach still stands.

[619] "Centralized decision-making, under the supervision of elected officials, is moreover impaired by the fact that politicians seldom have comprehensive knowledge of the issues; their role is to represent the constituents on a myriad of topics as well as face the innumerable demands of campaigning." Battistella, R.M. *Health Care Turning Point: Why Single Payer Won't Work.* MIT Press; 2012, p. 87.

[620] Bill Gairdner calls the modern approach to the welfare state "libertarian socialism." See Gairdner, W.D. *The Great Divide: Why Liberals and Conservatives Will Never, Ever Agree.* Encounter Books, 2015.

[621] Aster, H., Axworthy, T. (eds.) *Searching for the New Liberalism: Perspectives, Policies, Prospects.* Mosaic Press; 2003. Searching for the New Liberalism: Essays in Renewal_www.amazon.ca/gp/product/0889627975/ref=as_li_ss_tl?ie=UTF8&camp=15121&creative=390961&creativeASIN=0889627975&linkCode=as2&tag=shawnwhatleym-20

[622] John Roberts in ibid., p. 19.

[623] Graham T. Allison, quoted in Taylor, M.G. *Health Insurance and Canadian Public Policy: The Seven Decisions That Created the Canadian Health Insurance System and Their Outcomes.* McGill-Queen's University Press; 2009, p. 496.

[624] Savoie, D.J. *What Is Government Good At? A Canadian Answer.* McGill-Queen's University Press; 2015, p. 10.

[625] Ibid., p. 11.

[626] Schuck, P.H. *Why Government Fails So Often: And How It Can Do Better.* Princeton University Press; 2015, p. 20.

[627] Ibid., p. 26. And also: "Whereas markets severely punish irrationality, politics does not; indeed, it magnifies it" (p. 156).

[628] Savoie, D.J. *What Is Government Good At? A Canadian Answer.* McGill-Queen's University Press; 2015, p. 14.

[629] Refers to sociologist Peter Rossi's Brass Law of Evaluation. Schuck, P.H. *Why Government Fails So Often: And How It Can Do Better.* Princeton University Press; 2015, p. 21.

[630] Ibid., p. 51.

[631] Ibid., p. 73.

[632] "As with most large and complex organizations, public administration does not deal well with individual initiatives, creativity, entrepreneurship or original thinking. It does not adjust rapidly to new situations." Levine, D. *Health Care and Politics: An Insider's View on Managing and Sustaining Health Care in Canada.* Véhicule Press; 2015, p. 208.

[633] Ibid., p. 212.

[634] Ibid., p. 219.

[635] Schuck quoting John Donahue. Ibid., p. 326.

[636] "Far from being epiphenomenal, [bureaucracy] independently shapes those policies by virtue of its own structural, endemic features." Ibid., p. 307.

[637] "The public policy world brims with interesting, provocative, often plausible ideas for improving social welfare." Ibid., p. 229.

[638] Italics in original. Ibid., p. 150.

[639] Ibid.

[640] Italics in original. Ibid., p. 365.

[641] "These findings are essential to sound policy making where what is being targeted is individual behaviour. It is easier to alter people's incentives than to change their values or character … What seems to work in a pilot project run by true believers often fails when it is routinized and bureaucratized in the less rarefied real world." Ibid., p. 367.

[642] Ibid., p. 380.

[643] Ibid., p. 372.

[644] "Bureaucrats … mistake their interests for those of the people they purport to serve." Olsen, H. *The Working Class Republican: Ronald Reagan and the Return of Blue-Collar Conservatism.* Broadside Books; 2017, p. 83.

[645] "… as with all monopolies, the convenience of administrators and employees comes before the needs of the customers, because customers will always be there. They have no choice." DiLorenzo, T.J. *The Problem with Socialism.* Regn-

ery Publishing; 2016, p. 174.

[646] "By explaining everything, the self-interest hypothesis would explain nothing." Schuck, P.H. *Why Government Fails So Often: And How It Can Do Better.* Princeton University Press; 2015, p. 132.

[647] Ibid., p. 131.

[648] Ibid., p. 132.

[649] Ibid., p. 133.

[650] "Political actors design policy-making institutions and processes to advance their self interest." Ibid., p. 135.

[651] "Successful politicians garner credit for popular programs and policies while simultaneously diffusing their responsibility among underlings and opponents for whatever goes bad and concealing mistakes and embarrassments. They deploy 'trial balloons' to reduce the risk of innovation and they never knowingly allow opponents to define themselves, the issues or monopolize attention. They usually avoid flat, forthright statements and commitments about uncertain futures and unabashedly steal popular issues and proposals whenever possible. They trust few and pick their enemies with care, for competing politicians are highly valuable targets. And they always honor the self-interests of those to whom they appeal but cloak those same interests in the language of the national interest, social needs, and entitlements." Simmons, R.T. *Beyond Politics: The Roots of Government Failure.* Independent Institute; 2011, p. 66.

[652] Ibid., p. 80.

[653] "We must not be insensitive to the role bureaucrats play in shaping the demand for their own services nor in their power to influence the cost conditions under which they produce their services." Ibid., p. 76.

[654] Ibid.

[655] Ibid.

[656] "Such oversight is a two-edged sword for it also entails red tape, public hearings, appeal procedures, and tedious legalities." Ibid., p. 77.

[657] "Indeed, in government, the *worse* a government agency performs, the *more* money it can claim from a legislature, city council, or county commission." DiLorenzo, T.J. *The Problem with Socialism.* Regnery Publishing; 2016, p. 45.

[658] Simmons, R.T. *Beyond Politics: The Roots of Government Failure.* Independent

Institute; 2011, p. 78.

[659] Ibid., p. 78.

[660] Ibid., p. 88.

[661] Ibid., p. 86.

[662] Macdonald, N. "Canada's Health Care System Is Hopelessly Sclerotic. We Need to Wake Up." CBC News. June 12, 2019. https://www.cbc.ca/news/opinion/health-care-1.5170948

[663] "Once a huge spending program is in place, vested interest constituencies form around every part of it." Goodman, J.C., Musgrave, G.L., Herrick, D.M, National Center for Policy Analysis (US). *Lives at Risk: Single-Payer National Health Insurance around the World.* Rowman & Littlefield; 2004, p. 108.

[664] "The Pareto-superior condition is never possible in politics; public policies invariably make some citizens better off at the expense of other citizens who are made worse off." Schuck, P.H. *Why Government Fails So Often: And How It Can Do Better.* Princeton University Press; 2015; p. 156.

[665] "Did Trudeau's health minister, Monique Bégin, descend from Mount Sinai Hospital with five pillars carved in stone? If not, why can't we change the CHA instead of running from pillar to post, for instance alternating payment per procedure and block funding like Soviet planners setting nail quotas by number and getting pins, then by weight and getting one big spike. Since nobody has new ideas, here's an old one: socialism doesn't work. We make healthcare the way the U.S.S.R. made cars, wonder why we get Ladas, and say they're the best in the world as the door falls off. But without market forces you cannot allocate resources efficiently. Not 'might not.' Not 'oh oh markets are mean.' Cannot. We've been spinning our rusty wheels on this one for decades. No to markets, no to cuts, no to private insurance, yes to the same old system that has always failed but will suddenly work if we're sufficiently obtuse and smug. Code beige. Run in circles. Again." Robson, J. "The Health-Care Crisis in Canada Is That Nothing Ever Changes." *National Post.* May 7, 2019. https://nationalpost.com/opinion/john-robson-the-health-care-crisis-in-canada-is-that-nothing-ever-changes

[666] Herzlinger, R.E. *Who Killed Health Care? America's $2 Trillion Medical Problem — and the Consumer-driven Cure.* McGraw Hill; 2007, p. 225.

[667] Schuck, P.H. *Why Government Fails So Often: And How It Can Do Better.* Princ-

eton University Press; 2015, p. 51.

668 Röpke, W. *A Humane Economy: The Social Framework of the Free Market.* ISI Books, 1999 ed. (originally published 1958), p. 142.

669 It reminds me of a joke from the days of the IRA: A group of young men shove a pedestrian up against a wall, in Northern Ireland. "Are you protestant or catholic?" they ask. "I'm neither," the man says. "I'm an atheist." The punks stop to think. "Well, all right then. Are you a Protestant atheist or a Catholic atheist?"

670 www.unifor.org/en/about-unifor

671 "Workers to Surround Clinic on Day 121 of Thunder Bay Strike." Notice on Unifor.org. www.unifor.org/en/whats-new/press-room/workers-surround-clinic-day-121-thunder-bay-strike

672 www.unifor.org/en/whats-new/press-room/workers-surround-clinic-day-121-thunder-bay-strike

673 www.unifor.org/sites/default/files/attachments/unifor_financial_statement_2014.pdf

674 pahealthcentre.com/physicians.html

675 Reminiscent of James Burnham's prediction in 1941 that managers will decide "who shall be denied access to a factory or a mine or a large farm." Burnham, J. *The Managerial Revolution: What Is Happening in the World.* Greenwood Press Publishers; 1941, p. 159.

676 Prokopchuk, M., Jung, C. "Defying Injunction 'a Gamble' Labour Law Expert Says as Thunder Bay Clinic Dispute Back in Court." CBC News. August 10, 2018. www.cbc.ca/news/canada/thunder-bay/michael-lynk-port-arthur-clinic-strike-1.4779886

677 Marchildon, G.P, *Making Medicare: New Perspectives on the History of Medicare in Canada.* Institute of Public Administration of Canada; 2012, p. 15.

678 The Labour Relations Act outlaws doctor unions. But medical associations act as pseudo unions, powerful stakeholders. They fight to protect their own interests, often before the interests of their members. Association leaders can fall for an easy deal with government to enhance their own standing in the system.

679 Regarding wage costs in hospitals: "In 1961, 68.7% of total hospital spending ... By 1988, ... 76.3%." Decter, M. *Healing Medicare: Managing Health System Change the Canadian Way.* McGilligan Books; 1994, p. 91.

[680] Ibid., p. 102.

[681] Simpson, J. *Chronic Condition: Why Canada's Health-care System Needs to Be Dragged into the 21st Century*. Allen Lane; 2012, p. 41.

[682] "Public sector unions also need to ask themselves whether their approach harks back to an irrelevant era and whether they have become part of what ails government operations." Savoie, D.J. *What Is Government Good At? A Canadian Answer*. McGill-Queen's University Press; 2015, p. 255.

Conclusion

[683] Martin, D., Miller, A.P., Quesnel-Vallée, A., Caron. N.R., Vissandjée, B., Marchildon, G.P. "Canada's Universal Health-care System: Achieving Its Potential." *Lancet*. 2018;391(10131):1718-1735. doi:10.1016/S0140-6736(18)30181-8

[684] Quoted in Will, G.F. *Statecraft as Soulcraft: What Government Does*. Touchstone; 1983, p. 16.

[685] "The good Saxon word, freedom; freedom in every sense of the term, freedom of speech, freedom of action, freedom in religious and civil life and last but not least, freedom in commercial life." Sir Wilfrid Laurier, 1896, from Crowley, B.L., Clemens, J., Veldhuis, N. *The Canadian Century: Moving out of America's Shadow*. Key Porter Books; 2010, p. xxx.

[686] "We must show that liberty is not merely one particular value but that it is the source and condition of most moral values." Hayek, F.A., Hamowy, R. *The Constitution of Liberty: The Definitive Edition*. University of Chicago Press; 2011, p. 52.

[687] "And the more thoroughly we understand our own political tradition, the more readily its whole resources are available to us, the less likely we shall be to embrace the illusions which wait the ignorant and unwary." Oakeshott, M., in Kirk, R. *The Conservative Mind: From Burke to Eliot*. 7th ed. Regnery Publishing; 2001, p. 474.

[688] Naylor, C.D. *Private Practice, Public Payment: Canadian Medicine and the Politics of Health Insurance, 1911-1966*. McGill-Queen's University Press; 1986, p. 60.

[689] Tucker, R.C. (ed.). *The Marx-Engels Reader, 2nd ed*. W.W. Norton; 1978, p. 477.

690 I have written elsewhere about fiscal transfer payments and the possibility

of trading GST for the CHT payments. But this cannot come before understanding all the things in the book so far. See Whatley, S.D. "The Most Responsible Politician: Who's the MRP for Health Care in Canada?" August 2019. Accessed August 3, 2020. https://macdonaldlaurier.ca/files/pdf/MLI_MostResponsible_Whatley_FWeb.pdf

691 Recall Oakeshott quoted earlier: "All the Rationalist can do when left to himself is to replace one rationalist project in which he has failed by another in which he hopes to succeed." Oakeshott, M. *Rationalism in Politics and Other Essays.* Liberty Fund; 1991, p. 37.

692 Sowell, T. *Basic Economics: A Common Sense Guide to the Economy, 5th ed.* Basic Books; 2014.

693 *Basic* care is not as simple as it sounds. *Basic,* for doctors, means whatever the experts in a particular specialty have defined as the standard of care for that field, based on the latest research. But standards change over time. New treatments, with better outcomes, create new standards; new baselines for acceptable care. This process is easy when new treatments are less expensive and carry fewer side effects. But new often means expensive. Who gets to decide whether a really expensive new treatment is worth the benefit it offers? Furthermore, a huge and unending burden of chronic disease has no end to what could be spent on personal help, treatments, accommodations to living conditions, research, and so on. However, this debate applies more to other countries, such as the US. *Basic* in Canada too often means substandard elsewhere. When we say Canadians need more care, it means what most people in the industry would support as necessary care.

694 And it misses an important fact: "The most basic part, often obscured in public discussions, is that the public must pay for care under any system of finance." Fuchs, V.R. *Who Shall Live? Health, Economics, and Social Choice.* Basic Books; 1974, p. 127. No matter how we pay for care, and who gets to control how payments are made, all the funding for care will come from the public. The choice of funding approach will make a difference for the highest and lowest paid, but "the average family will have to pay the same share under any system." Ibid., p. 128.

695 Compare Buber's I-Thou vs. I-It.

696 In reference to medical savings accounts, Janice Stein writes: "We could shop for

health care wherever we like." Stein, J.G. *The Cult of Efficiency*. House of Anansi Press; 2002, p. 110.

[697] "We ought to prefer [freedom] even if it were less advantageous from a material point of view. Freedom is such a precious good that we ought to be ready to sacrifice everything for it, possibly even prosperity and abundance, should we be compelled to do so by the necessities of economic freedom. Then we can point out that, luckily for us, an economic system based on liberty — without which liberty itself cannot exist — is at the same time infinitely more productive than a system of controlled economy." Meyer, F.S. *What Is Conservatism? — A New Edition of the Classic by 12 Leading Conservatives*. Intercollegiate Studies Institute; (1946) 2015, p. 99.

[698] "To respect humanity is to raise the human subject above the world of objects, into a realm of responsible choice." Ends vs. means; subjects vs. objects; value vs. price; virtue vs. vice ... or the human may "fall into the world of mere things, so as to become a thing himself." Scruton, R. *Fools, Frauds and Firebrands: Thinkers of the New Left*. Bloomsbury Continuum; 2019, p. 279.

[699] Also as healthism: the pursuit of good health as a medicalized end in itself. See Skrabanek, P. *The Death of Humane Medicine and the Rise of Coercive Healthism*. Social Affairs Unit; 1994. Thanks to Dr. DiStefano for this.

[700] Le Fanu, J. *The Rise and Fall of Modern Medicine*. Basic Books; 1999.

[701] Boozary, A., Laupacis, A. "The Mirage of Universality: Canada's Failure to Act on Social Policy and Health Care." *CMAJ*. 2020;192(5):E105-E106. doi:10.1503/CMAJ.200085 And D. Martin, et al., in *Lancet* February 2018, re: "Profound health inequities ..." in Canada. Martin, D., Miller, A.P., Quesnel-Vallée, A., Caron, N.R., Vissandjée, B., Marchildon, G.P. "Canada's Universal Healthcare System: Achieving Its Potential." *Lancet*. 2018;391(10131):1718-1735. doi:10.1016/S0140-6736(18)30181-8

[702] As others have said, we could find useful ways to keep spending more on care, until we invest our whole GDP into medical services and things related to health in general." Goodman, J.C., Musgrave, G.L., Herrick, D.M., National Center for Policy Analysis (US). *Lives at Risk: Single-Payer National Health Insurance Around the World*. Rowman & Littlefield; 2004, p. 1.

[703] "Economically ignorant moralism is as objectionable as morally callous econo-

mism." Röpke, W. *A Humane Economy: The Social Framework of the Free Market.* ISI Books; 1999 ed. (originally published 1958), p. 104.

[704] Christopher Coyne, in Lavoie, D., Coyne, C. (ed.). *National Economic Planning: What Is Left?* Mercatus Center, George Mason University; 1985, p. ix.

[705] Nuland, S.B. *The Uncertain Art: Thoughts on a Life in Medicine.* Random House; 2008.

[706] "They talk as if they were indifferent to all questions of social philosophy and as if it were beneath their dignity as scientists to have an opinion on nonmaterial values, or at least to voice such opinions. They have become mere economic technicians — economocrats, experts in whose hands economics is becoming purely instrumental." Meyer, F.S. *What Is Conservatism? — A New Edition of the Classic by 12 Leading Conservatives.* Intercollegiate Studies Institute; (1946) 2015, p. 107.

[707] "The opponents of conservatism ... regard political issues as concerned with 'control of the means of production', and [they] set up a simple-minded dichotomy between socialism and capitalism as containing the whole of contemporary politics. For conservatives that dichotomy is naive, for it simplifies beyond recognition the principle of their outlook, which is the absolute and ineradicable need of private property. Ownership is the primary relation through which man and nature come together" (p. 92). It socializes. "Through property an object ceases to be a mere inanimate thing, and becomes instead the focus of rights and obligations" (p. 93). Scruton, R. *The Meaning of Conservatism.* St. Augustine's Press; 2002.

[708] Ouchi makes the observation that markets, bureaucracies, and clans each offer different ways to decrease the transactional costs in society. Each "mode of control" has unique normative and informational requirements. Markets require reciprocity and prices. Bureaucracies require reciprocity and legitimate authority, while relying on rules for information. Clans need reciprocity, legitimate authority, and common values and beliefs, as normative requirements. Clans' informational requirements are supplied by traditions. Clans seem to offer an organizational framework most reflective of how medicine functions in reality. In other words, markets work on reciprocity guided by prices. Two people agree to trade (reciprocity), and prices supply the information. Bureaucracies require reciprocity — there are always at least two parties involved — plus legitimate

authority. And bureaucracies rely on rules for information. Medicine, like many other social exchanges, has always used extra layers beyond markets and bureaucracies. Medicine requires common values and beliefs, in addition to reciprocity and legitimate authority. All of this forms the fabric, or normative requirements, upon which medicine functions. The information that medicine requires to make the exchange comes from traditions. As Mintzberg writes, "Community matters in health care, even if it is largely ignored in economics." Mintzberg, H. *Managing the Myths of Health Care: Bridging the Separations Between Care, Cure, Control, and Community.* Berrett-Koehler Publishers; 2017, p. 111.

[709] "The literateur and bureaucrat, both alien to an atmosphere of business activity, are filled with envy and rage when they think of fortunate speculators and successful entrepreneurs." von Mises, L. *Socialism: An Economic and Sociological Analysis.* 2nd ed. 2012. Martino Publishing; 1932, p. 205.

[710] Modified from an example used by Dinesh D'Souza.

[711] See, for example, *"The New England Journal of Medicine*: Business is Evil." In Herzlinger, R.E. *Who Killed Health Care? America's $2 Trillion Medical Problem — and the Consumer-driven Cure.* McGraw Hill; 2007, p. 139. Also, consider the following short list: *Profit* — It is distasteful to profit from another's illness. Despite the fact that everyone in healthcare earns an income, the notion of profit seems unbecoming of patient care. Business success "is portrayed as something of a Faustian bargain: businesspeople succeed by appealing to our baser instincts; they are motivated by greed and too often may bend the rules. But hey, they give us more material things, so we tolerate their less-than-moral activities." Forbes in the foreword to Gilder, G.F. *Wealth and Poverty: A New Edition for the Twenty-first Century.* Regnery Publishing; 2012, p. x. *Equality* — Many physicians believe that a nurse is a nurse is a nurse. There is no difference between workers and to say otherwise betrays prejudice, bias, or maybe a personality clash. We must not differentiate workers on performance.*Ignorance* — Many doctors believe patients make bad choices. Look at the junk people buy and unhealthy things they do. Capitalism offers patients things they should never be allowed to purchase. Patients don't always know what's best for them. *Disorder* — Capitalism thrives on economic freedom and freedom from over-regulation. But public health requires central control, statewide programs and special

powers to limit freedom for the good of all. Public health hates capitalism. Capitalistic freedom causes obesity, bad teeth and measles outbreaks. *Taste* — Free markets promote tasteless content like too much collagen and botox. Whatever sells proliferates. Healthcare should stand in a class above consumerism. *Civility* — Like lawyers chasing ambulances, advertising for patients feels unseemly and morbid. Capitalism spawns billboards. *Competition* — Competition means cutting corners on products and services. It fosters increased supply in the face of unmet demand. Complaining aside, doctors like feeling wanted and in demand. *Waste* — Capitalism promotes two people doing the same work to compete against each other. And it creates redundant product. Why make two kinds of toilet paper when one will do? *Morality* — Many doctors bristle at performance, efficiency, outcomes, and benchmarks. They believe clinical care should be judged like masterpieces in an art gallery, each one unique and valuable in its own, unhurried way. Efficiency contradicts quality. *Oppression* — Industries have no heart. They oppress the weak and the poor. They keep workers on slave wages. *Abandonment* — A "more capitalist" system would leave poor people in the dirt. Care should go first to those most in need.

[712] Other writers have worked to dispatch anti-capitalism, for example, Ludwig von Mises, in his *The Anti-Capitalist Mentality.* And still others have worked out a moral case in support of capitalism, such as Michael Novak in his *The Spirit of Democratic Capitalism*, and George Gilder in his *Wealth and Poverty.* See also works by Hayek, Nisbet, Röpke, Friedman, Sowell, Gilder, Will, and Scruton, as a start.

[713] Taylor, R. *God Bless the NHS: The Truth Behind the Current Crisis.* Faber and Faber; 2001.

[714] "Antipathy to capitalism is of legendary proportions, especially among the classes whose status is higher under aristocracies and dictatorships: aristocrats, clergy, scholars, artists, and of course government officials. Working people tend to prefer democratic capitalism which, as the Italian Marxist Antonio Gramsci pointed out, quickly raises them into the middle class." Novak, M. *The Spirit of Democratic Capitalism.* Madison Books; 1990, p. 434.

[715] The business community "ignores such questions or leaves them, with contempt, to the 'unbusinesslike' intellectuals, and these same intellectuals' distrust of the business world match and mutually exacerbate each other. If the business world

loses its contact with culture and the intellectuals resentfully keep their distance from economic matters, then the two spheres become irretrievably alienated from each other." Röpke, W. *A Humane Economy: The Social Framework of the Free Market.* ISI Books; 1999 ed. (originally published 1958), p. 115.

[716] The Labour theory of value sees no value in the entrepreneur. It "sees the entrepreneur as someone alien to the process of production, someone whose whole work consists in the appropriation of surplus value. It would be sufficient to expropriate these parasites to bring about a socialist society." von Mises, L. *Socialism: An Economic and Sociological Analysis.* 2nd ed. 2012. Martino Publishing; 1932, p. 212.

[717] "Those who plan the production and distribution of goods in a great society are trying to achieve the impossible. The plan is bound to interfere with the free relations between people, and thereby to destroy the normal and unintended effects of human freedom, economic coordination being one of them. Planning, in such circumstances, threatens to destroy the human relations on which it depends." Scruton, R. *The Meaning of Conservatism.* St. Augustine's Press; 2002, p. 41.

[718] "The utilitarian model of society as a trading-company held together solely by contractual obligations, the world of 'sophisters, economists, and calculators' who are blind and deaf to the unanalyzable relationships." Berlin, I. *The Proper Study of Mankind: An Anthology of Essays* (Vintage Classics). 2nd ed., 2013. Vintage; Random House; 1997, p. 256.

[719] Edmund Burke.

[720] On the need for professions (doctors, lawyers, teachers) to maintain a self-image, in the form of flourishing institutions and societies, within the presence of the welfare state: "The state may profit from those institutions, but it cannot wholly absorb them, without risking the hostility or the demoralization of the professional class. If it profits from these institutions it is because they have a life of their own, and it cannot be part of the pursuit of welfare to destroy that life." Scruton, R. *The Meaning of Conservatism.* St. Augustine's Press; 2002, p. 171.

[721] "When it is scientifically considered ... the doctrine of equality will be exposed as a fallacy; for equality is the death of progress. Throughout history, progress of every sort, cultural and economic, has been produced by the desire of men for

inequality. Without the possibility of inequality, a people continue on the dreary level of bare subsistence ... granted inequality, the small minority of men of ability turn barbarism into civilization. Equality benefits no one. It frustrates men of talent; and it reduces the poor to a poverty still more abject." Kirk, R. *The Conservative Mind: From Burke to Eliot*. 7th ed. Regnery Publishing; 2001, p. 403.

[722] This discussion also relates to Parfit's discussion (1991) about the levelling down we see in equalitarianism. In *The Meaning of Conservatism*, Scruton describes how the welfare state is a "social and political necessity." Scruton, R. *The Meaning of Conservatism*. St. Augustine's Press; 2002, p. 171. And for it to work, it involves a "separation of the idea of public welfare from the egalitarian crusades with which it has become entangled. The purpose of the welfare state is not to abolish the distinction between rich and poor, but to encourage people to accept it." Ibid., p. 172.

[723] On this point, naysayers apply an hermeneutics of suspicion and insist that the *only* reason doctors built the plans was to remove the need for government to socialize medicine. How is this any different from government building medicare to achieve its own ends of wealth redistribution, nation building, and so on? But this misses the point and commits a category mistake. We need citizens to find solutions to social problems so government can focus on things citizens cannot fix on their own. Citizens solving problems is categorically different from government taking control of an industry. Furthermore, doctors building insurance plans so they can provide *more* care is substantively different from government socializing medicine so it can *redistribute* and *regulate* care.

[724] Universal care works best when physicians are intimately involved with the design, function, leadership, and ownership of the model, whether it is insurance-based or otherwise. Kaiser Permanente has proven this for over eighty years, in the USA. Canadian planners love the Kaiser model, but they have a harder time accepting the fact that Kaiser succeeds, in part, because patients can choose to leave Kaiser for a different plan, if it fails to offer great service. The need for physician involvement, as a central pillar in the Kaiser approach, also seems odious to some.

[725] Naylor, C.D. *Private Practice, Public Payment: Canadian Medicine and the Politics of Health Insurance, 1911-1966*. McGill-Queen's University Press; 1986, pp. 148-50, 168, 179.

726 "One should ask, too, whether political actors *should* [italics original] be protected from the performance of components of the health care system: isn't the idea of public responsibility for health care the very point of having a public health care system?" Fierlbeck, K. *Health Care in Canada: A Citizen's Guide to Policy and Politics.* University of Toronto Press; 2011, p. 239.

727 Coyne, A. "How to Save the Conservative Party." *Walrus Magazine.* May 2017.

728 Not to mention the difficulties associated with establishing whether different patients offer an equal amount of risk based on age, burden of disease, etc. As we discussed earlier, medicine is a coping organization, like education or peace keeping. It is notoriously difficult to determine when, where, and to what extent education, peace keeping, or medical care happened. If we tie performance incentives to the volume of clinical services provided, then more patients would receive care, but patients might hate the experience. And patient satisfaction scores cannot save us either. They are also notoriously difficult to interpret and easy for organizations to game.

729 Some of those working in the narrative medicine movement have tackled this work. However, tackling research of any social institution, such as medicine, risks distraction with all the heated and popular social issues that fill social media. Given the pressure to secure grants and publications, too many academics latch onto the grievance agenda, to stand out for their wokeness. This only serves to retrench the rationalists, who see the debates as impractical: medicine is nothing but applied physiology. Physicians' general distaste for politically motivated nonsense ruins efforts at understanding medicine as a body of knowledge beyond what we can see and touch.

730 "On the supply side, we have the islands of excellent (Mayo, Intermountain Healthcare, Cleveland Clinic, etc.). On the demand side, we have a whole slew of experiments with pay-for-performance and other pilot programs designed to see whether demand-side reforms can provoke supply-side behavioural improvements. And never the twain shall meet. We cannot find a single institution providing high-quality, low-cost care that was created by any demand-side buyer of care. Not the Centers for Medicare and Medicaid Services (CMS), which runs Medicare and Medicaid. Not BlueCross. Not any employer. Not any payer, anytime, anywhere. As for the pilot programs, their performance has been

lacklustre and disappointing. What about other demand-side reforms: forcing/
inducing/coaxing providers to adopt electronic medical records, to coordinate
care, to integrate care, to manage care, to emphasize preventative care, to adopt
evidence-based medicine, and so on? The Congressional Budget Office (CBO)
has reviewed the evidence on all these reforms and concluded that the savings
will be meagre, if they materialize at all." Goodman, J.C. *Priceless: Curing the
Healthcare Crisis*. Independent Institute; 2012, p. 31.

[731] There are lots of examples of successful entrepreneurship in healthcare. There
are very few examples of successful bureaucracy. "Can you think of any market
where the buyers of a product are trying to tell the sellers how to efficiently produce it?" Ibid., p. 74.

[732] "The tug of war between conservatives and progressives can only affect the
speed, not the direction, of contemporary developments." Hayek in Meyer, F.S.
*What Is Conservatism? — A New Edition of the Classic by 12 Leading Conserva-
tives*. Intercollegiate Studies Institute; 2015, p. 111.

[733] Government could shift focus by addressing the following questions, before
starting any new program: Does it serve the public interest? Is government involvement necessary? Is this an appropriate federal or provincial role? What is
the scope of public private partnerships, for this issue? What is the scope of
any increase in efficiency? Is this effort affordable? This list, which I modified
slightly, is the result of a conversation with P. Cross.

[734] "There is a vast difference between the type of planning — whether in the large
State, industry, or the school — that seeks to enmesh the individual in a custodial
network of detailed rules for his security and society's stability, and the type of
planning that is concerned with the creation of a political and economic *context*
within which the spontaneous associations of men are the primary sources of
freedom and order." Nisbet, R., Douthat, R. *The Quest for Community: A Study
in the Ethics of Order and Freedom*. 2019 ed. ISI Books; 1953, pp. 255-56.

[735] The "political action that I propose is formulated in terms of trusteeship rather
than enterprise, of conversation rather than command, of friendship rather than
the pursuit of some common cause." Scruton, R. *Green Philosophy: How to Think
Seriously About the Planet*. Atlantic; 2012, p. 13. Scruton also references Trusteeship with Burke; conversation with Oakeshott; and friendship with Aristotle.

Every form of government holds within itself the potential for its own destruction (see Röpke quote below). Of course, this applied also to forms of governance within any organization. Democracy risks arbitrariness and demagogy. Given this, do we want governments, or government organizations, managing the medical industry? Good government requires trade-offs and an awareness of its own inherent weaknesses. Unfortunately, trade-offs are boring; they do not win elections. "Ownership ends up in plutocracy, authority in bondage and despotism, democracy in arbitrariness and demagogy. Whatever politics tendencies or currents we choose as examples, it will be found that they always sow the seed of their own destruction when they lose their sense of proportion and overstep their limits. In this field, suicide is the normal cause of death." Röpke, W.

[736] "Where ends are agreed, the only questions left are those of means, and these are not political but technical, that is to say, capable of being settled by experts or machines, like arguments between engineers or doctors. That is why those who put their faith in some immense, world-transforming phenomenon, like the final triumph of reason or the proletarian revolution, must believe that all political and moral problems can thereby be turned into technological ones. That is the meaning of Engels' famous phrase ... about replacing the government of persons by the administration of things." Berlin, I. "Two Concepts of Liberty." *Four Essays on Liberty*. Oxford University Press; 1969, pp. 118-72.

[737] In some ways, public health has been trying to usurp medicine for three thousand years. Asclepius, the Greek god of medicine, controlled all the healing arts. Asclepius had five daughters, among them: Hygieia (hygiene), Panacea (remedy), Iaso (recuperation), and Aceso (healing). Hygieia is the god of public health and is usually depicted in Greek mythology as an attendant of Asclepius.

Selected Bibliography

Baker et al. *High-performing Healthcare Systems: Delivering Quality by Design.* Longwoods; 2008.

Bardach, E., Kagan, R. *Going by the Book: The Problem of Regulatory Unreasonableness.* Transaction. Routledge; 2002.

Battistella, R.M. *Health Care Turning Point: Why Single Payer Won't Work.* MIT Press; 2012.

Blishen, B.R. *Doctors in Canada: The Changing World of Medical Practice.* Published in association with Statistics Canada by University of Toronto Press; 1991.

Britnell, M. *In Search of the Perfect Health System.* Red Globe Press; 2015.

Brown, M.C. *Caring for Profit: Economic Dimensions of Canada's Health Industry.* Fraser Institute; 1987.

Burnham, J. *The Managerial Revolution: What Is Happening in the World.* Greenwood Press; 1941.

Cooper, M.H. *Rationing in Health Care.* John Wiley; 1975.

Crowley, B.L. *Fearful Symmetry: The Fall and Rise of Canada's Founding Values.* Key Porter Books; 2010.

Crowley, B.L., Clemens, J., Veldhuis, N. *The Canadian Century: Moving out of America's Shadow*. Key Porter Books, 2010.

Decter, M. *Healing Medicare: Managing Health System Change the Canadian Way*. McGilligan Books; 1994.

Decter, M., Grosso, F. *Navigating Canada's Health Care: A User Guide to Getting the Care You Need*. Penguin Canada; 2006.

Douglas, T.C., Thomas, L.H., Higginbotham, C.H. *The Making of a Socialist: The Recollections of T.C. Douglas*. University of Alberta Press; 1984.

Evans, R.G. *Strained Mercy: The Economics of Canadian Health Care*. Butterworths; 1984.

Evans, R.G., Barer, M.L., Stoddart, G.L., McGrail, K., McLeod, C.B. *An Undisciplined Economist: Robert G. Evans on Health Economics, Health Care Policy, and Population Health*. McGill-Queen's University Press; 2016.

Fierlbeck, K. *Health Care in Canada: A Citizen's Guide to Policy and Politics*. University of Toronto Press; 2011.

Fierlbeck, K., Lahey, W. *Health Care Federalism in Canada: Critical Junctures and Critical Perspectives*. McGill-Queen's University Press; 2013.

Finkelstein, A., Arrow, K.J., Gruber, J., Newhouse, J.P., Stiglitz, J.E. *Moral Hazard in Health Insurance*. Columbia University Press; 2014.

Fuchs, V.R. *Who Shall Live? Health, Economics, and Social Choice*. Basic Books; 1974.

Furlong, D.J. *Medicare Myths*. Dream Catcher; 2004.

Gilder, G.F. *Wealth and Poverty: A New Edition for the Twenty-first Century.* Regnery Publishing; 2012, p. xxxi.

Goodman, J.C. *Priceless: Curing the Healthcare Crisis.* Independent Institute; 2012, p. xvii.

Goodman, J.C., Musgrave, G.L., Herrick, D.M. National Center for Policy Analysis (US). *Lives at Risk: Single-Payer National Health Insurance around the World.* Rowman & Littlefield; 2004.

Gratzer, D. *Better Medicine: Reforming Canadian Health Care.* ECW Press; 2002.

Gratzer, D. *Code Blue: Reviving Canada's Health Care System.* ECW Press; 1999.

Hall, Emmett, et al. *Royal Commission on Health Services, 1961 to 1964. Canada.Ca.*; 1964.

Harper, S. *Right Here, Right Now: Politics and Leadership in the Age of Disruption.* Signal; 2018.

Hayek, F.A., Caldwell B. *The Road to Serfdom: Text and Documents.* University of Chicago Press; 2007.

Hayek, F.A., Hamowy, R. *The Constitution of Liberty: The Definitive Edition.* University of Chicago Press; 2011.

Herzlinger, R.E. *Who Killed Health Care? America's $2 Trillion Medical Problem — and the Consumer-driven Cure.* McGraw Hill; 2007.

Lavoie, D., Coyne, C. (ed.) *National Economic Planning: What Is Left?* Mercatus Center, George Mason University; 1985.

Leatt, P., Mapa, J. *Government Relations in the Health Care Industry.* Praeger; 2003.

Le Fanu, J. *The Rise and Fall of Modern Medicine.* Basic Books; 1999.

Le Grand, J. *Motivation, Agency, and Public Policy: Of Knights and Knaves, Pawns and Queens.* Oxford University Press; 2004.

Levine, D. *Health Care and Politics: An Insider's View on Managing and Sustaining Health Care in Canada.* Véhicule Press; 2015.

Marchildon, G.P. *Making Medicare: New Perspectives on the History of Medicare in Canada.* Institute of Public Administration of Canada; 2012.

Marsh, H. *Do No Harm: Stories of Life, Death, and Brain Surgery.* Picador; 2016.

Marsh, L., Moscovitch, A. *Report on Social Security for Canada: New Edition.* McGill-Queen's University Press; 2018.

Martin, D. *Better Now: Six Big Ideas to Improve Health Care for All Canadians.* Penguin Random House; 2017.

Mayer T., Jensen K. *Hardwiring Flow: Systems and Processes for Seamless Patient Care.* Fire Started Publishing; 2009.

Mintzberg, H. *Managing the Myths of Health Care: Bridging the Separations Between Care, Cure, Control, and Community.* Berrett-Koehler; 2017.

Montgomery, K. *How Doctors Think: Clinical Judgement and the Practice of Medicine,* 1st ed. Oxford University Press; 2005.

Naylor, C.D. *Canadian Health Care and the State: A Century of Evolution.*

McGill-Queen's University Press; 1992.

Naylor, C.D. *Private Practice, Public Payment: Canadian Medicine and the Politics of Health Insurance, 1911-1966*. McGill-Queen's University Press; 1986.

Nisbet, R., Douthat, R. *The Quest for Community: A Study in the Ethics of Order and Freedom*. 2019 ed. ISI Books; 1953.

Novak, M. *The Spirit of Democratic Capitalism*. Madison Books; 1990.

Nuland, S.B. *The Uncertain Art: Thoughts on a Life in Medicine*. Random House; 2008.

Oakeshott, M. *Rationalism in Politics and Other Essays*. Liberty Fund; 1991.

Pardy, B. *Ecolawgic: The Logic of Ecosystems and the Rule of Law*. 5th Forum Press; 2015.

Pellegrino, E.D., Thomasma, D.C. *A Philosophical Basis of Medical Practice: Toward a Philosophy and Ethic of the Healing Professions*. Oxford University Press; 1981.

Picard, A. *The Path to Health Care Reform*. The Conference Board of Canada; 2013.

Pipes, S. Fraser Institute (Vancouver, BC), Pacific Research Institute for Public Policy. *Miracle Cure: How to Solve America's Health Care Crisis and Why Canada Isn't the Answer*. Pacific Research Institute; 2004.

Powell, E.J. *A New Look at Medicine and Politics*. Pitman; 1966.

Rachlis, M. *Prescription for Excellence: How Innovation Is Saving Canada's*

Health Care System. Harper Perennial Canada; 2005.

Reid, T.R. *The Healing of America: A Global Quest for Better, Cheaper, and Fairer Health Care*. Penguin Press; 2009.

Reynolds, J.L. *Prognosis: The Current State and Shaky Future of Canada's Health System*. Penguin Canada; 2008.

Röpke, W. *A Humane Economy: The Social Framework of the Free Market*. ISI Books, 1999 edition (originally published 1958).

Savoie, D.J. *Democracy in Canada: The Disintegration of Our Institutions*. McGill-Queen's University Press; 2019.

Schuck, P.H. *Why Government Fails So Often: And How It Can Do Better*. Princeton University Press; 2015.

Scott, J.C. *Seeing Like a State: How Certain Schemes to Improve the Human Condition Have Failed*. Yale University Press; 1998.

Scruton, R. *Fools, Frauds and Firebrands: Thinkers of the New Left*. Bloomsbury Continuum; 2019.

Scruton, R. *How to Be a Conservative*. Bloomsbury Continuum; 2015.

Scruton, R. *The Meaning of Conservatism*. St. Augustine's Press; 2002.

Scruton, R. *A Political Philosophy: Arguments for Conservatism*. Bloomsbury; 2006.

Simmons, R.T. *Beyond Politics: The Roots of Government Failure*. Independent Institute; 2011.

Simpson, J. *Chronic Condition: Why Canada's Health-care System Needs to Be Dragged into the 21st Century.* Allen Lane; 2012.

Skrabanek, P. *The Death of Humane Medicine and the Rise of Coercive Healthism.* Social Affairs Unit; 1994.

Taylor, M.G. *Health Insurance and Canadian Public Policy: The Seven Decisions That Created the Canadian Health Insurance System and Their Outcomes.* McGill-Queen's University Press; 2009.

Taylor, R. *God Bless the NHS: The Truth Behind the Current Crisis.* Faber and Faber; 2001.

Vertesi, L. *Broken Promises: Why Canadian Medicare Is in Trouble and What Can Be Done to Save It.* Epic Press; 2003.

von Mises, L. *Socialism: An Economic and Sociological Analysis.* 2nd ed. 2012. Martino Publishing; 1932.

Whatley, S. *No More Lethal Waits: 10 Steps to Transform Canada's Emergency Departments.* BPS books; 2016.

Will, G.F. *The Conservative Sensibility.* Hachette Books; 2019.

Williams, I., Dickinson, H., Robinson, S. *Rationing in Health Care: The Theory and Practice of Priority Setting.* Policy Press; 2012.

Wilson, J.Q. *Bureaucracy: What Government Agencies Do and Why They Do It.* 2nd ed. Basic Books; 1991.

Zimmerman, B, Lindberg, C., Plsek, P. *Edgeware: Lessons from Complexity Science for Health Care Leaders.* VHA; 1998.

Index